VIET SOCIALIST REPUBLICS

SOVIET NAVAL STRATEGY

SOVIET NAVAL STRATEGY

Fifty Years of Theory and Practice

by

ROBERT WARING HERRICK

COMMANDER, U.S. NAVY (RETIRED)

UNITED STATES NAVAL INSTITUTE

Annapolis, Maryland

COPYRIGHT © 1968

by

UNITED STATES NAVAL INSTITUTE

ANNAPOLIS, MARYLAND

Library of Congress Catalogue Card No. 67-26080

Printed in the United States of America

To my mother and father

Foreword ★

Two world wars, Korea, Vietnam, the Cuban missile incident, and many small incidents of lesser significance have caused the Soviets to realize the importance of sea power and the necessity for a world power to have control of the seas if it is to carry on operations across the oceans.

The Soviets are, above all, realists. They understand very well that the USSR would have many obstacles to overcome before she could control the seas or deny their use to the nations of the Free World. Geography is a handicap; and so, for centuries, Russia, and later the USSR, has tried to get control of the Baltic, the Turkish Straits, and warm-water egress to the Pacific.

An even greater obstacle is their complete lack of naval accomplishments. The Tzarist navies were ineffective. So was the Soviet Navy in World War II. No matter what the reasons were, the experiences of the Soviet Navy in combat cannot be a matter of pride to the present generation of naval personnel. Until recently, many experienced naval officers were liquidated one way or another, and it is not easy to build an experienced cadre of operating personnel under such circumstances.

The quality of their ships and armament must cause Soviet officials some concern as they compare their capabilities with those of other large navies.

The development of a Navy by a weak power, as the USSR was, is a difficult task; and as Commander Herrick has well described, the Soviets went from one concept to another in their attempts to develop a strategy and the corresponding equipment that would enable them to negate the naval power of the Western nations, and to do that within their economic means. They have developed a large, strong submarine force, including a ballistic and homing missile capability; a sizable ASW force; and a surface force with surface-to-surface and surface-to-air missiles. They have no strike carriers and a weak amphibious force suitable only for operations in the vicinity of the USSR.

This analysis of Soviet naval capabilities and the author's estimate of USSR intentions for their use are in accord with the prudent Soviet actions of the past.

What might the Soviet Navy do in a limited-war situation like Vietnam? Certainly it is obvious that United States assistance to South Vietnam is dependent entirely on the ability of the United States to operate her naval forces off Vietnam and her ability to supply both the South Vietnamese forces and our own by surface ships. The Soviet Union has tremendous submarine forces; but if she started to deploy significant numbers of submarines from her home ports to the South China Sea or the approaches thereto, that change in employment would be detected by the United States before the Soviet submarines could arrive on station. There would surely be warnings sent to Moscow; and if those warnings were ignored and one of our ships were torpedoed, the least that could happen would be a war at sea. The Soviets realize that the ultimate outcome of such a war would be annihilation of their Navy. The risk to the Soviets of such an attack provoking the United States to general war or to an attack on their naval installations would be great. The possible gains to the Soviets from such an attack by their Navy well beyond their own waters would not be comparable to the inherent risk. Still, although the Soviets are not given to adventurous actions, they are capable of nonrational actions at times, and they might convince themselves, by misreading our probable reactions, to take the risk. Highly improbable—but still conceivable.

Should the Soviets ever decide to initiate a general nuclear war, they are going to be faced with the decision as to whether or not they should deploy their ballistic missile submarines to launching positions before they start the war. If they do, it is very probable they will be detected and thereby "telegraph their punch" on their intentions to strike. If they don't, their ballistic missile submarines will not be second strike but a long delayed strike.

The Soviets will also have to decide what they think they can do to prevent our Polaris submarines from destroying a large part of the Soviet Union immediately following the initial Soviet attack. Without carriers and a very much larger ASW force (and more protection for it than they now have) they cannot prevent the Polaris submarines from launching. It is doubtful also whether they can convince themselves that any antiballistic missile system they can deploy will be sufficiently effective to prevent our warheads from reaching many of their targets. The Soviets will have doubts about how good their antiballistic missile system really is against multiple warheads coming at them from many directions all at once, along with some countermeasures they may not have anticipated. If they consider starting a general nuclear war, they have the high probability of destruction of the USSR as a consequence—that is, so long as the relative naval capabilities remain approximately what they are now.

Then why have the Soviets developed a Navy at all? To defend the waters contiguous to her shore line. To support her ground forces. To conduct short-haul amphibious operations close to territory she holds. To destroy Free World merchantmen and naval ships in the event of a "conventional war." To dominate the waters of her adjacent nation neighbors, and, thus, to intimidate them.

But probably primarily: To provide tangible support to the psychological, political, and economic warfare, at which she has demonstrated so much adeptness under the umbrella of "peaceful coexistence." As her merchant marine continues to expand rapidly, as she increases the size of her Navy and the operating skill of her sailors, as she manipulates favorable trade agreements, as she gradually extends the operating areas of her men-of-war, the Soviet Union may hope the time will come when she can gain domination of the world in spite of not having the ability to control the seas.

The Soviet Navy has a formidable task. So have the Free World navies.

Arleigh Burke

ARLEIGH BURKE
Admiral, U.S. Navy (Retired)

October 5, 1967

ix

Publisher's Preface ★

The U. S. Naval Institute was founded in 1873 for the purpose of fostering discussion of important naval issues. Soviet naval strategy—past, present, and future—obviously merits the widest and deepest possible discussion in naval circles, and the Naval Institute Board of Control is therefore most pleased to have the opportunity to present in this book Commander Robert W. Herrick's valuable contribution to this important discussion. That his conclusions—forthrightly stated—are not shared by all thinkers on naval strategy will, of course, come as no surprise to the reader, for a rather wide range of conclusions may be drawn from the record.

In discussing this book manuscript the Board of Control raised a number of questions that ultimately led to an examination of Commander Herrick's thesis that the Soviet Navy is still basically a defensive military force. For example, is the Soviet Union, in the pursuit of its interests, moving from a continental strategy to a global one? If so, what role can the Soviet Navy play? Is the Soviet Navy moving to evolve new doctrines and tactics that will broaden the military options available to Soviet strategic policy planners? The relevance of categorizing these new doctrines and tactics as either "offensive" or "defensive" was debated. It was wondered whether the lack of Soviet attack aircraft carriers is as crippling to their naval balance and capability to support Soviet interests as would be a similar gap in U. S. naval forces.

While discussion of these and other points raised in this book showed that the members of the Board of Control were not in unanimous agreement with Commander Herrick's assessment of the objectives and capabilities of the Soviet Navy, the Board of Control was unanimous in its decision to publish Commander Herrick's book as a valuable reference work, a statement of one definitive point of view, and hence a useful catalyst for further study and analysis of the manner in which Soviet naval strategy is intended to further Soviet aims. It is hoped that this book will, indeed, stimulate further research, writing, and thinking in this important area. The reader is invited to submit written comments on this book, advancing the discussion of Soviet naval strategy, to the Naval Institute's monthly journal, the U. S. Naval Institute *Proceedings*.

UNITED STATES NAVAL INSTITUTE
Annapolis, Maryland

Preface ★

The scope of this study may be seen from the series of questions which it undertakes to answer:

1. What is current Soviet naval strategy? What are the factors that have influenced its evolution and any discernible patterns of recurrence? Are there any detectable differences between strategic theory and practice?

2. What are the strengths and weaknesses of the existing Soviet capabilities for carrying out various wartime naval missions in opposition to NATO's naval forces?

3. What are the major interests of Party leaders in involving themselves in naval strategy formulation and how extensive is their involvement? What are the results for naval strategy of the USSR's having an interlocking party-government organization and a unified defense ministry?

4. What strategic role in the USSR's grand strategy is played by Soviet naval propaganda? Has the technological revolution really affected naval strategy in the manner claimed by the Soviet leaders so that aircraft carriers have been made obsolete and their role as queen of the seas taken over by submarines? What merit is to be ascribed to Soviet claims to having developed into a "mighty sea and oceanic power" with naval forces capable of carrying out any and all missions despite NATO opposition?

5. Is the general Western conception of Soviet naval strategy as at least discernibly evolving toward an offensive, high seas fleet concept correct? If not, what does the foreseeable future appear to hold for Soviet naval strategy? What advantages does such a strategy as the USSR

appears to have adopted offer? What limitations does it impose? Judged in terms of the USSR's own particular objective requirements for naval power, is the Soviet strategy an irrational one? Or is it rational when viewed in the Soviet context?

One facet of this study has been to emphasize the relationships between developments in Soviet naval strategy and those in foreign affairs. To mention but one example: The unwillingness of the United States Navy to build battleships for the Soviet Union had a crippling effect on Stalin's prewar effort to build a big navy. Additionally, there are included a number of incidents of some interest from the viewpoint of political science. One of these, for example, is the way in which Admiral Sergei Gorshkov, the Soviet Commander in Chief, was able to win *de facto* approval for the theoretically untenable tolerance of cruisers in the composition of the Navy.

Other aspects of this study of particular note for political scientists vary from the much-stressed Soviet effort to substitute propaganda for naval strength down to the necessarily brief mention of what little could be found out about Naval Commissar Zof's seeming development of a new institutional loyalty to the Navy in place of the Party once he had been given the navy post.

As a glance at the Table of Contents will confirm, the basic method employed in the first six chapters and most of Chapter VII is historical. In the remaining three chapters the methodology is that of a functional analysis of the various Soviet naval missions and capabilities.

Throughout the study, I have felt free to depart from the historical recording of developments long enough to adduce whatever amount of analysis and interpretation seemed desirable at any given juncture. In a number of cases, specifically in Chapters II through V, substantial analyses have been appended as the final section of each chapter. In this way the final chapter has been kept short.

A word is in order on such limitations placed on the findings due to the nature and extent of the data, my assumptions and approach to the subject, or the methodology employed. Taking each of these points in turn, but in reverse order, the following observations merit recording:

1. No major limitation derived from use of a basically historical method combined with a functional analysis in the final chapters. It is possible, however, that the historical approach may have contributed to an undue emphasis on the extent of the shifts involved in the changes from old school to young school strategies, particularly as to the degree of change in the theories held by the naval leaders. This possibility was suggested to me by "Former Soviet Naval Officer," who is such a knowl-

edgeable individual that it would have been remiss not to take note of it. This I have done in the footnote at the outset of Chapter IV.

2. On the score of limitations incurred in the study's findings as a result of my assumptions and approach to the subject, a number of points should be made. In the first place, I undertook the study without a preconception of the ultimate findings but even with the erroneous assumption, which hopefully publication of the study will clear up, that Soviet naval strategy had been and remained an offensive one. I had no thought that one result of the ultimate findings would be to give theoretical support to the aircraft carrier for any navy that would contest for command of the seas. Despite having been a naval officer for ten years at the time this study was undertaken, it was only through research and reflection over the subsequent ten years, particularly in the last two spent as Staff Intelligence Officer at the United States War College, that I arrived at anything approaching my present understanding of the aircraft carrier's indispensable role for a realistic nuclear age naval strategy.

3. As to the limitations placed on the findings by the nature and extent of the data, they are unquestionably very substantial indeed. The paucity of information on the subject proved a constant source of concern. Some aspects of the subject remain obscure and the interpretations given them are admitted to be no more than informed speculation. For example, until the recent appearance of Admiral Kuznetsov's memoirs, the Navy's longstanding interest in having aircraft carriers had been so concealed as to defy the best efforts to uncover convincing documentation.

Hopefully, this study will serve both as an encouragement to others to conduct research and to write in this "underdeveloped" but fascinating field and also as an initial contribution to the eventual writing of as definitive a work of Soviet naval history as the sparse information on the subject permits. Only the opening up to non-Communist researchers of the Soviet naval archives in Leningrad would make possible the writing of a definitive work. Since that event seems highly unlikely for the forseeable future, the effort to piece together and interpret the scraps of information that can be gleaned from the open literature will continue to be worthwhile.

Robert Waring Herrick

ROBERT WARING HERRICK
Commander, U. S. Navy (Retired)

Munich, Germany
7 November 1967

Acknowledgments ★

A brief essay on the research material used in this work is offered to assist others who may wish to explore this fascinating subject. To the same end, an extensive bibliography of the most useful material has been appended, irrespective of whether individual entries have been cited specifically in the text.

For the interwar period, stenographic reports of Supreme Soviet and Party congresses were of substantial assistance, but by far the best single source available was the Soviet Navy's professional journal, *Morskoi Sbornik*. The Library of Congress has nearly complete holdings of this monthly publication for the interwar period. It is now available on subscription, but the issues from 1947 through 1961, although recently requested by The Library of Congress from the Lenin Library at my suggestion, are still unavailable as indicated by inquiries in the United States, England, France, Germany, and Japan. Consequently, I have had to use the more propagandistic Soviet military press extensively for the postwar period. A saving grace in this regard has been the availability for consultation in the West of a few former Soviet naval officers, whose firsthand knowledge has kept me from several misinterpretations and has yielded a number of salient facts not otherwise available. Of similar benefit were the several visits I made to each of the four Soviet fleet areas and short cruises aboard a Northern Fleet minesweeper and a Pacific Fleet destroyer while serving as an assistant naval attaché in the Soviet Union from 1954 to 1956.

I was fortunate in being able to obtain from the National Archives of the United States the official reports on Soviet naval matters submitted by U.S. naval attachés and other non-Communist observers during the interwar period. Estimates of Soviet naval capabilities obtained from the German naval archives have been of significant value; many of these documents are listed in the bibliography of Professor John Erickson's pioneering work, *The Soviet High Command, A Military-Political History, 1918–1941.* Japanese naval and diplomatic archives, available on microfilm from The Library of Congress, yielded only a few relevant reports and nothing of actual use.

Almost no useful and reliable information could be obtained from the few books in Western languages that purport to treat of the Soviet Navy. The sketchy or uneven treatment reflects the paucity of information available outside of the USSR. Research at The Library of Congress and the British Museum Library failed to turn up a single book covering Soviet naval history that had used the available Russian-language materials in anything approaching a serious attempt to exploit them for study of the Soviet Navy. A search through the periodical literature in English and French was similarly unproductive. In fact, most books and articles in English and French were found to be based on the largely inaccurate accounts carried in the Western press.

My sincere appreciation goes to the many friends and colleagues whose constructive criticism and other significant assistance contributed to this book. I wish specifically to thank Herman Dworkin; John Erickson; Rear Admiral E. M. Eller, U.S. Navy; Fritz Ermarth; and, particularly, "Former Soviet Naval Officer" for his invaluable help. Also, W. T. R. Fox; Raymond L. Garthoff; Richard Rockingham Gill; Loren Graham; Andrew Gyorgy; Lawrence Healey; John Leggat; Captain Walter Morgan, U.S. Navy; Ralph E. Purcell; Henry L. Roberts; Theodore Ropp; and W. R. Schilling. Additionally, John S. Shearer, Samuel Smiley, C. Jay Smith, Ray Stewart, and Lawrence Whetten.

I was greatly sustained in the decade of spare-time research and writing of this book by the encouragement and support of three people whose exceptional kindness deserves special mention: Admiral Arleigh Burke, U.S. Navy (Retired), for reading the initial outline years ago and encouraging me to carry the study to completion; Gisela Weinfeld, Slavic reference librarian of The Library of Congress, for her expert and unfailing helpfulness; and Philip E. Mosely, in particular, for guiding me through the oral examination for a doctorate in international relations and through the difficult early stages of formulating and obtaining approval as a dissertation for the outline of this study, and, in general, for putting into daily practice his evident faith that extra effort to widen the intellectual horizons of the military personnel among his graduate students at the Russian Institute of Columbia University would yield worthwhile dividends in the country's interest.

Special recognition and thanks go to Mrs. Marion Bliss and Yeoman Bill Allison of the U.S. Naval War College staff for their fine assistance and perserverance in preparing the materials for my annual War College lectures on Soviet sea power in 1963 and 1964, which were eventually expanded into Chapters V through IX of this book. Similarly, I would like to express my very real gratitude to Norman Hall, the *de facto* chief administrator of the War College, for arranging and supervising the printing of the original manuscript for this study.

Additionally, sincere thanks go to Donald Brooks and Margaret Semsroth of Radio Free Europe in Munich for irreplaceable assistance in rushing the revised manuscript to completion in time to meet the schedule for defense of dissertation. A cordial salute, in passing, to Commanders Ted Fielding, Dave Hartshorne, Scotty Scoggins, and Bill McKenzie, as well as to Charles Frentzos, for their informative discussions on Soviet naval strategy and other subjects at the Markay annex to the War College.

Contents ★

Introduction ★

Among the reasons we are interested in Soviet naval strategy is the increasing attention being attracted by the whole range of political, economic, and to a lesser extent military involvements of the USSR around the world. The United States, as a world power for some decades, and as a world maritime power for many more, has long been deeply involved all over the globe—despite our traditional "isolationism." Russia, on the other hand, despite its long status as one of "the Powers" (of Europe), has traditionally been regarded as a continental land power that has only rarely, and even more rarely with success, ventured far beyond its natural land frontiers. To be sure, the Soviet Union is not the Russia of the mid-nineteenth century—but, then, neither is the United States today the same as it was a century ago.

The Soviet Union has been indelibly marked by the ideological motivations and legacy of its founders, and also by economic, technological, geostrategic, and even historical, influences which affect the application of ideological considerations. The USSR is a Communist state, but it is a state existing in the world community of states, and it has learned to coexist for half a century and to prepare for an indefinite (if not admittedly permanent) continued coexistence. Though the Soviet leaders use the slogan of "peaceful coexistence" for their own propaganda purposes, the fact of coexistence and avoidance of war represents a gradual, reluctant, but significant compromise of the ideology with reality.

The remarks preceding may seem a tangential digression, but they are intended to sketch out one of the parameters of an analysis of Soviet naval strategy. They are pertinent to a historical approach to the subject, such as is offered in this volume. This study is essentially an internal historical analysis—that is, an examination of the development of naval strategy in the Soviet Union, rather than of the development of the Soviet Union from a naval point of view. Nonetheless, it has been undertaken in the context of the author's appreciation of the general course of historical development of the Soviet state, internally and in relation to the world order.

Another major strand contributing to the evolution of naval strategy has been the pace of technological advance. Relatively slow in the 1920's and 1930's, the quickening pace of naval technology during and especially since World War II, and the parallel trend with respect to military technology in general, has had a wide and deep impact on Soviet naval strategy, as this study shows.

Given the changing geostrategic position of the Soviet Union after World War II, the Soviet Navy (and air forces) were suddenly faced with "requirements" incomparably beyond their existing capabilities. Eventually, the Soviet Strategic Rocket Forces (a separate command, unlike our assignment of these weapons to the Strategic Air Command) took over the weight of the strategic offensive-deterrent role from the weak Long Range Aviation. The Soviet Navy has, in the 1960's, acquired a modest strategic supporting role for its ballistic missile launching submarine force. But the Soviet Navy, unlike the U.S. Navy, has neither traditionally nor lately been accustomed or charged with truly "strategic" operations. It has always been primarily designed and prepared for tactical support to land armies on their maritime flanks.

Commander Herrick has had the courage to call his shots as he sees them. While not all will agree with his conclusion that Soviet naval strategy continues to be strategically defensive, anyone who is inclined to challenge this conclusion should first test his views against the data and argumentation of this study.

Throughout the course of Soviet history, the Soviet Navy and Soviet naval strategy have become increasingly professional. While standards vary in some respects, on the whole the Soviet Navy is a competent and proficient element of the armed forces. On the level of tactical operations and doctrine, the same can be said. With respect to naval thinking on the problems of war at sea at great distance from the Soviet Union itself, for reasons evident in this book, the level of achievement is much less.

In recent years, the Soviet Navy has begun to increase both the distance and the frequency of operation of naval forces. They have, through staggered rotation, developed what in effect is a modest permanent presence in the Mediterranean, without operational bases there. On a less constant basis, they have from time to time done the same thing in the North Atlantic and the Pacific. I do not believe this necessarily portends a shift away from the essentially defensive strategy outlined by the author. On the other hand, even though the military concept is defensive, the Navy may play an increasing role in serving a broad range of Soviet political objectives. Moreover, the rapidly increasing Soviet merchant fleet can, in addition to its primary function of trade, provide a more tangible Soviet presence in far-flung areas.

While our main interest is focused on the present and future, the foundation for the future rests on the past. A comprehensive, documented, sound analysis and appraisal of the evolution of Soviet naval strategy is an important contribution to understanding current and prospective developments. No such study has been available. Now, the present volume should go far to fill that gap.

RAYMOND L. GARTHOFF

Washington, D.C.
October 20, 1967

Prologue ★

As early as 1925 the old school advocates of building strategically offensive high seas naval forces for the USSR are now revealed to have been roundly castigated by a regime spokesman for calling for the construction of aircraft carriers as essential to such a strategy. Denied aircraft carriers, the Soviet naval leaders had no alternative but to restrict Soviet naval strategy to a basically defensive young school (Jeune Ecole) strategy with regard to the Western naval powers, especially England, whom Soviet leaders considered as potentially their most likely future enemy throughout the twenties and early thirties. Under their "active defense" strategy, Soviet naval leaders were supposed to find ways of compensating for the great numerical inferiority of the USSR's naval forces. This they unrealistically hoped to do by somehow managing to refuse combat except under highly favorable conditions of advance intelligence warning, optimum conditions of sea and weather, and close off-shore areas in which the enemy would be exposed simultaneously to the hazards of minefields and to coordinated attack by coastal artillery, shore-based aircraft, light fast coastal torpedo boats, and submarines. In effect, this strategy meant that the duties assigned to the Soviet naval forces were limited to missions for coastal defense and for supporting the seaward flanks of the ground forces in any aggression against minor powers such as Finland or the Baltic states.

In the late twenties and early thirties, as the range of carrier aircraft increased and the reliability of carrier flight operations improved, naval aviation proponents predicted the emergence of the aircraft carrier as the successor to the battleship as the single most important warship type for offensive naval operations designed to contest for supremacy at sea. This, in fact, was to be demonstrated clearly to be the case in World War II. In the meantime, however, Nazi Germany emerged as an obviously expansionist power in the thirties and replaced England in Soviet defense planning as the most likely Soviet protagonist in a war that seemed increasingly likely after the mid-thirties. The Anglo-German Naval Agreement of 1935 had effectively abrogated the prohibition against significant warship construction imposed by the Versailles Treaty by authorizing Germany to build up to thirty-five per cent of England's tonnage. This allowed the German Navy to program two aircraft carriers in 1936, the first of which was completed in 1938 (the *Graf Zeppelin*). The second was to be completed by late 1941. Two more were to be ready by 1947, according to a ten-year plan adopted by Hitler in February 1939.[1]

Apparently motivated primarily by a determination to match the German program of aircraft carrier construction, Stalin reluctantly agreed to a comparable Soviet program of building four carriers under a ten-year program.[2] Hitler's invasion of the USSR in June 1941 effectively terminated both programs.

Not only did World War II demonstrate beyond question the emergence of the aircraft carrier as the ruler of the oceans but the Soviet naval leaders gained convincingly first-hand experience of the inadequacies of shore-based naval air support for providing timely and effective protection for surface naval forces even in such relatively small sea areas as the Baltic and the Black Sea. As a direct result of the severe limitations inherent in shore-based naval air support for surface warships, the Baltic and Black Sea fleets were unable to implement their long-standing strategy of "active defense." Instead, their major surface ships were either put out of action by the Luftwaffe's attacks or, especially in the Baltic, forced to retreat ignominiously into ports with adequate antiaircraft defenses and there be reduced to floating gun batteries with most of their crews used as troop replacements in the fighting on the land fronts.

Consequently, in the early postwar period, most Soviet naval strategists were more strongly convinced than ever of the military requirement for the construction of aircraft carriers. It appears reasonably clear now, however, that whatever Stalin's dreams of dominion may have been, they did not seriously envision a Soviet effort in his lifetime to challenge the sea supremacy of the Western maritime powers. Stalin continued in the

---

[1] Clark G. Reynolds, "Hitler's Flattop—The End of the Beginning," *United States Naval Institute Proceedings,* January 1967, pp. 43, 44, and 46.

[2] Former Soviet Naval Officer, "Soviet Naval Strategy," address to the U. S. Naval War College, October 31, 1964.

postwar period to want to build a big, balanced navy including all types of warships except carriers. Thus he contemplated a substantial number of medium-range submarines, destroyers, light cruisers, and battle cruisers. These he appears to have intended primarily for prestige and deterrence in peacetime and for defense in the event of any third world war. With the immediate threat of the German Navy eliminated and faced with the need to repair the great damage suffered by the Soviet Union in World War II, Stalin avoided making the major commitment of funds to build any aircraft carriers for five or six years after the end of the war. This meant that the strategy of the Soviet Navy reverted from the largely passive defense forced on it during the war by the lack of even shore-based air support for its surface ships to the prewar strategy of "active defense." As a result, the Navy's wartime missions were still limited to those of coastal defense and protection of the seaward flanks of the ground forces.

Even though the United States emerged in the Cold War as the USSR's most likely enemy in any future war, Stalin did not even increase the small proportion of his medium-range patrol submarines deployed to the Northern Fleet where they could have constituted a deterrent threat against the vital Atlantic shipping lanes. It appears that he was convinced that the great bulk of his large submarine force was required for purely defensive purposes, particularly in the Baltic with its direct sea access to the USSR's industrial vitals. Only in the event of a successful land war in Western Europe that secured the Baltic area and captured the Danish Straits would the large Baltic submarine force become available for use in a *guerre de course* against Western shipping in the Atlantic.

Finally in the early fifties, having brought about the USSR's development as the only other nuclear superpower, and so created a direct confrontation with the United States, Stalin again permitted himself to be persuaded to authorize an initial program for the construction of several aircraft carriers. Again fate intervened. The program died with Stalin in early 1953. Thus the renewed hopes of the old school proponents that were dominant in the Navy for building offensive, high seas fleets were again dashed. One of the first acts of Stalin's successors was to abolish the independent naval ministry that had been set up in 1950 to carry out the old school program and resubordinate the Navy to the Army-dominated Ministry of Defense. Admiral Nikolai Kuznetsov, the prewar and wartime naval minister whom Stalin had rusticated on a pretext after the war but brought back in 1950 to take charge of constructing the projected new navy, was forced to retire due to an obviously political "illness." He was replaced by Admiral Sergei Gorshkov, a former flotilla and fleet commander who had the reputation as a loyal Party man and an advocate of applying advanced nuclear and missile technology to the Navy.

Apparently at least partially in return for his support in overcoming the natural dissatisfaction of the old school adherents, Khrushchev overcame his own inclination to abolish the Navy as a separate service and provided it with a considerable number of submarines, surface ships, shore-based naval aircraft, and coastal missile batteries, all of them equipped with missiles and some of the submarines with nuclear propulsion. With these Gorshkov was expected to implement a neo-young school strategy of "active defense" under which the Navy's primary mission would be to destroy NATO's naval forces at the outset of another war, hopefully before the strike carriers and Polaris submarines could launch their missile strikes against the Soviet Union. Additionally, the Soviet Navy was to operate a substantial number of ballistic missile submarines as a relatively invulnerable supplement to the land-based intercontinental ballistic missiles that comprised the bulk of the USSR's national nuclear deterrent.[3] Moreover, the Navy was still charged with the usual wartime missions of defending the USSR from amphibious invasion, protecting the USSR's vital coastal shipping, and supporting the coastal flank of the Army. The Navy was also assigned the mission of interdicting Western shipping in the Atlantic in case of war. To make this threat credible as a deterrent, Khrushchev multiplied the Northern Fleet submarine force fivefold.

His successors have continued his neo-young school strategy of eschewing efforts to build forces that could contest for sea supremacy and settling for strategically defensive naval forces calculated to contribute to deterring a general nuclear war. Construction of the "colossally expensive" attack carrier-striking forces is still denied with accompanying propaganda charges that strike carriers are the weapons of aggression *par excellence* and, with typical inconsistency, that they have been outmoded by the military technological revolution.

There were some signs in 1962 and 1963 that the USSR's ballistic missile submarines might not share in the first strike role with Soviet ICBM's but might only have a second strike role and then only against coastal targets, primarily ports and naval bases. Despite the fact that Defense Minister Malinovskii was cited just two weeks before his death at

---

[3] "Nuclear-powered ballistic-missile submarines have an almost unlimited range, potentially higher speeds than surface ships, and the ability to engage directly in strategic missile warfare. This is not control of the seas; this is nuclear deterrence. It is not sea power either; it is strategic missile power." Nels A. Parson, Jr., *Missiles and the Revolution in Warfare* (Cambridge, Massachusetts: Harvard University Press, 1962), p. 144.

the end of January 1967 as having written that "the strategic missile troops and missile-carrying nuclear submarines . . . are the principal means of deterring an aggressor and smashing him in the event of war,"[4] it appears almost certain that Soviet missile submarines are not conducting the regular patrols off the U. S. East Coast that would be necessary for them to be accorded deterrent credibility in a first strike role.

Moreover, as has been related in some detail, there are even indications that the Soviet Party leaders may well have decided, perhaps on a cost effectiveness basis, that maintenance of a credible deterrent against NATO's major sea communications by means of a large force of submarines is no longer necessary.

Whatever the truth may be as to present and future assignment to the Soviet Navy of missions for submarine missile attacks on the U. S. or warfare against shipping, unquestionably the primary mission of Soviet naval forces for the present and the foreseeable future will remain that of defending the USSR as best they can against nuclear strikes from NATO's strike carriers and from Polaris submarines. It has been shown that, on balance, the military-technological revolution, especially the development of the long-range Polaris missile system, has combined with geographical factors to greatly disadvantage the Soviet Union, dependent as it is on shore-based naval aviation of limited range and endurance.

Unquestionably, the Soviet Navy today, particularly in its submarine force, poses the potent and technologically challenging threat of denying the NATO powers wartime use of the seas for shipping vital to the conduct of any protracted war. Yet, it must be remembered that although submarines have the potential capability to deny the free use of the seas to other nations' shipping, they are, by their nature, unable to exercise command of the sea for their own state's use. This point was stated by Mahan when submarines were primitive compared to contemporary nuclear-powered torpedo-attack or missile-firing classes. Admiral Arleigh Burke, U. S. Navy (Retired), has recently reaffirmed that, despite these technological advances, submarines are still unsuited and unable to exercise command of the sea.[5] This fact means that the Soviet Navy can neither adequately protect the USSR's own vital sea lines of communications, even along Soviet coasts, nor give protection to surface antisubmarine ships on the high seas, where Polaris submarines must be hunted; such ships comprise the surface components of the air-surface-submarine team required for the most effective antisubmarine warfare. These in-

---

[4] V. P. Razumov, "U serdtsa korablia" (At the Heart of a Ship), *Krasnaia Zvezda,* February 25, 1967.

[5] R. D. Crane (ed.), *Soviet Nuclear Strategy.* (Washington: The Center for Strategic Studies, Georgetown University, 1963), p. 56.

herent limitations become of immense significance in the present situation in which the greatest coalition of naval powers known to world history is confronted by a basically hostile continental power that has built up an unprecedentedly large submarine force, one many times greater than ever before constructed by a nation not at war. There is substantial evidence that the Soviet leaders understand quite well the unsuitability of their Navy for the strategic offensive although their propaganda not infrequently exploits Western gullibility on this point. In fact, Nikita Khrushchev clearly acknowledged the strategically defensive nature of the Soviet submarine force as intended to deny the sea approaches of the USSR to enemies. In a report to the Central Committee of the Party in October 1961, Khrushchev, making the standard ideological assumption that the "imperialists" would be the ones to initiate aggression, stated:

> The USSR is a continental power. Those who wish to unleash war against us [or use sea power to counter the USSR's superior land power] will be compelled to cross great expanses of water. This is why we are creating a powerful submarine force. . . .[6]

Regardless of this infrequently mentioned Soviet appreciation of the fact that their largely submarine navy is primarily a weapon of the strategic defense,[7] Western writers have repeatedly portrayed the Soviet Navy as an offensive, high seas fleet designed to contest for command of the seas.[8] It appears particularly difficult for United States and British

---

[6] N. S. Khrushchev, "Otchet Tsentral'nogo komiteta KPSS XXII s"ezdu Kommunisticheskoi partii Sovetskogo Soiuza; Doklad Pervogo sekretaria TsK tovarishcha N. S. Khrushcheva 17 Oktiabria 1961 goda" (Report of the Central Committee of the CPSU to the XXII Congress of the Communist Party of the Soviet Union; Report of the First Secretary of the Central Committee, Comrade N. S. Khrushchev, October 17, 1961), *Krasnaia Zvezda,* October 18, 1961.

[7] Soviet ballistic missile submarines are, of course, a weapon of the strategic offense *par excellence.* Since their military objectives are exclusively land targets rather than enemy naval forces or merchant shipping and hence do not directly affect the war at sea, they should be considered apart from other types of warships designed to play roles in the basic contest of naval warfare for command of the sea (even if only in limited coastal areas as in the Soviet case). Rather than being viewed as a weapon of naval warfare *per se,* ballistic missile submarines should be considered a component of the national nuclear deterrent along with intercontinental ballistic missiles and long-range, nuclear weapon-carrying bomber aircraft. Even though ballistic missile submarines operate in the oceans and so must be hunted there, if at all, by the opponent's naval air, surface ship, and submarine forces, nevertheless, their unique lack of primary design capabilities against an enemy's naval and merchant ships and their equally exceptional primary mission against land targets, even though ports and naval bases are included, make it unrealistic and inappropriate to consider them as other than components of a state's strategic nuclear deterrent and striking forces. (Parson, *op. cit.,* p. xxviii.)

[8] The following are typical examples of the similar misinterpretations of Soviet naval theory by British and Americans: "There is a drastic change in Russian defence philosophy since the war. Russia has always been regarded as a country exclusively of land animals. But she is that no longer. She has built up an enormous submarine fleet . . .

naval officers and writers, steeped as they are in the Mahanian tradition of naval operations by high seas fleets, to appreciate the position of a weaker naval power and think realistically about the problems involved in developing and implementing a strategically defensive strategy. Consequently, almost all of the thinking and writing on Soviet strategy in England and the United States overemphasizes the Soviet Navy's offensive capabilities at the expense of the defensive ones. It appears that this error is made under the assumption that, because the Soviet Navy is now second in tonnage only to the United States Navy and has made a considerable application of nuclear propulsion to its submarines and of nuclear missiles to its submarines, surface ships, and naval aircraft, it is basically the same kind of strategically offensive instrument of power as the United States' and British navies. Unfortunately, this erroneous assumption has led to an outpouring of misleading articles portraying the Soviet Navy as essentially a strategically offensive force, a blue-water, high seas fleet capable of actually contesting with the NATO navies for command of the sea. Soviet propaganda consistently and effectively exploits such misleading articles by trumpeting claims that the USSR has become a great sea power and, together with the military-technical revolution, has brought an end to the Western powers' command of the sea.[9] However, without aircraft carriers to provide air cover for surface naval forces when and where needed, the Soviet Navy is leashed to the short and quite inelastic umbilical cord of land-based aviation.

One unfortunate result for the Western world of this common failure to distinguish between naval forces built around aircraft carriers capable of the strategic offensive and those that have no carriers and are therefore forced to remain on the strategic defensive is that the great size of the naval forces which the Soviet Union would require solely to dis-

and a powerful and very up-to-date surface navy. She is moving out massively onto the oceans." (Admiral Sir Alexander Bingley, "A Fresh Look at Defence," *Daily Telegraph*, February 6, 1964.) "Communist Russia—its goal a Communist world—is trying to achieve as a means to that end, dominion over blue water . . . to strengthen materially the deep sea elements of the Soviet Navy, already the world's second largest fleet . . . The Soviet Navy . . . has been transformed from what was essentially a coastal defensive force into a blue water offensive fleet." (Hanson Baldwin, "Red Flag over the Seven Seas," *The Atlantic Monthly*, September, 1964, pp. 37–43.)

[9] The following examples are typical of the many that might be given to illustrate the propagandistic aspect of many Soviet statements on naval matters: "Our country is a very great land and also a mighty sea power." (G. I. Levchenko, "Velikii flot Sovetskoi derzhavy" [Mighty Navy of the Soviet Power], *Krasnaia Zvezda*, July 14, 1957); "Our Navy has become a completely modern navy capable of fulfilling any strategic mission in its field." (R. Ia. Malinovskii, "Vneocherednoi XXI s"ezd Kommunisticheskoi Partii Sovetskogo Soiuza, rech' marshala Sovetskogo R. Ia. Malinovskogo," [The Extraordinary XXIst Congress of the Soviet Union, Speech of Marshal of the Soviet Union R. Ia. Malinovskii] *Krasnaia Zvezda*, February 4, 1959.)

charge the essential *defensive* missions is either overlooked entirely or greatly underestimated. One must always keep in mind how inescapably and completely the Soviet Navy is committed to a largely deterrent and defensive posture and how very limited are its actual offensive capabilities. It is hoped that this dissertation, by tracing the offensive-defensive alternations through which Soviet naval strategy has evolved, will make it clear to its readers the essentially deterrent defensive nature of post-Stalin naval strategy and the factors that now greatly inhibit the possibility of changing it. Only through gaining such an understanding can one begin to appreciate what an extremely difficult defense posture the USSR now finds itself in due to its seemingly irremedial situation of naval inferiority. At the same time, it becomes apparent that Soviet naval strategy is a rational one if viewed in the context of "peaceful coexistence" and a Soviet policy aim of avoiding a general nuclear war at almost any cost.

SOVIET NAVAL STRATEGY

The Navy at its Nadir ★

I

W ell before the "October Revolution" *coup d'état* brought the Soviet Communist Party to power in Russia on 7 November 1917, the strong Bolshevik organization of Baltic Fleet sailors at Kronshtadt Naval Base[1] had refused to recognize the authority of the provisional government.[2] A Baltic Fleet cruiser from Kronshtadt, the *Aurora,* was given a key role to play in the Bolshevik's master plan, including signaling the start of the coup[3] by gunfire and firing her main battery guns on the Winter Palace, seat of the provisional government, to break the resistance of the ministers.[4] The Kronshtadt sailors, aided by the " revolutionary workers' Red Guards," are also credited by the official Party history with having put down an attempted counter coup of military cadets, allegedly led by a group of Social Revolutionaries.[5] For these and many other revolutionary services Lenin honored the sailors with the ultimate encomium for a Communist of constituting "the vanguard of the working masses."[6] Commensurate with the elevated status that the sailors then enjoyed, Lenin established a separate Naval Commissariat, with considerable autonomy within a unified defense ministry, when he officially disbanded the Tsar-

---

[1] Kronshtadt Naval Base was the headquarters of the Tsarist Russian Baltic Fleet. This base was, and still is, located on Kotlin Island near the eastern end of the Gulf of Finland about 15 miles west of present-day Leningrad.

[2] W. H. Chamberlin, *The Russian Revolution 1917–1921* (New York: Macmillan, 1952), I, pp. 239 and 279.

[3] *Ibid.,* p. 311.

[4] *Ibid.,* pp. 316–317.

[5] Central Committee of the CPSU, *History of the Communist Party of the Soviet Union (Bolsheviks), Short Course* (New York: International Publishers), 1939, p. 210.

[6] V. L. Selivanov, "Pervyi vserossiiskii s"ezd voennogo flota (1–8 dekabria 1917)" (First All-Russian Congress of the Navy, 1–8 December 1917), *Morskoi Sbornik,* February 1938, p. 96.

ist Russian Navy on 12 February 1918 and created the "Socialist Work-er-Peasant Red Fleet."[7] Moreover, although his actions may have been prompted largely by military considerations, Lenin showed a marked in-terest in restoring the Navy to acceptable conditions of operational read-iness. He drafted and secured adoption on 23 October 1920 of a resolu-tion calling for the prompt rehabilitation of the Baltic Fleet.[8] At about the same time, Defense Commissar Leon Trotsky summed up the Navy's deplorable situation in one short sentence: "The Red Fleet has been weakened to the last degree—but it exists."[9] The British writer, Anthony Courtney, summed up the new Soviet Navy's discouraging prospects:

> The period from 1921 to 1934 saw the Russian fleet . . . at its lowest ebb in Russian naval history. Its commanders were faced with all those problems which had been experienced by the French Revolution-ary navy in the 1790's, in addition to the natural handicaps which every Russian fleet must suffer when it lacks political support of the centre. Apart from this Soviet Russia had lost her former advanced base in the Baltic at Libau (Lepaya), Leningrad was within gun range of the Finn-ish frontier . . . and the bulk of Imperial Russia's maritime population had been removed at one stroke through the new-found independence of Estonia, Latvia and Lithuania. It was small wonder then that the Red Navy became an appendage of the Soviet Peoples' Commissariat of Defense, subordinate to soldiers such as Marshal Voroshilov.[10]

Nor was the Navy to retain its cherished revolutionary reputation for long. The Kronshtadt naval mutiny was impending with its long-term consequences of loss of confidence by the Party leadership and of more than a decade of negligibly small budgetary allocations for desperately needed ship modernization and construction. Some of the stringent

---

[7] "Khronika" (Chronicle), *Morskoi Sbornik*, February 1919, p. 135.

[8] "Proekt postanovleniia Soveta Truda i Oborony po voprosu o vostanovlenii Baltii-skogo flota" (Project of the Resolution of the Council of Labor and Defense for the Re-habilitation of the Baltic Fleet), *V. I. Lenin, Voennaia perepiska* (V. I. Lenin, Military Correspondence), (Moscow: VoenIzdat, 1966), Document No. 496, p. 297. Presumably Lenin limited his resolution to the Baltic Fleet for two reasons: 1) The Baltic affords much more direct access to the industrial heart of the country; and 2) All the major ships of the Black Sea Fleet had "defected" (See p. 13 *infra*.) and it was beyond the RSFSR's financial and industrial capabilities to replace them.

[9] V. Zof, "Krasnyi Voenno-morskoi flot" (The Red Fleet), *Krasnyi Flot*, January 1922, p. 4. Not the least of the reasons for the Baltic Fleet's disorganization was voiced as a complaint in 1920: "For a long time now every time the Soviet authorities need energetic and decisive workers their eyes turn to the Baltic Fleet. And the Fleet pro-vides them . . . combatants for the ground forces' front lines . . . river flotillas . . . merchant marine . . . and so on without end. In this regard our fleet is like . . . a cow that is milked, milked but never fed." M. Serebriakov, "Agitatory na liniiu!" (Agitators to the Front Lines!), *Krasnyi Baltiets*, June 1920, p. 6.

[10] Anthony Courtney, "The Background of Russian Seapower," *International Affairs* (London), January 1954, pp. 21–22.

budgetary limitations unquestionably were owing to the country's straight-ened circumstances after the years of war, revolution, intervention, and blockade. Yet, the Kronshtadt mutiny was to affect naval developments adversely for many years.

On 1 March 1921 the new Soviet Republic was shaken by the out-break of the Kronshtadt mutiny. The sailors of the Baltic Fleet based at Kronshtadt joined with other sailors and workers from the Kronshtadt Naval Base to demand that the monolithic Communist control of the So-viet government be broken.[11] Not only did the mutineers call for a shar-ing of power by non-Communist political parties, but they demanded ex-tensive economic and political reforms. Among the latter were demands for freedom of speech, press, assembly, and voting by secret ballot.[12]

Since such demands were wholly incompatible with the continuance in power of the Soviet Communist regime, the Party leaders refused to ne-gotiate with the Kronshtadt sailors and demanded their unconditional surrender. When the mutineers refused to surrender, the Red Army launched large-scale attacks across the ice of the Gulf of Finland. The first attack failed, partly because the attacking troops were so tightly massed that the ice broke beneath them. Two more daylight attacks were repulsed. Finally, a night attack by troops camouflaged in sheets suc-ceeded in breaching the Kronshtadt defenses. After a day and night of fierce street fighting, the last resistance was put down. The Soviet secret police, the dreaded Cheka, carried out summary executions of all who could be found alive of the five to six thousand sailors and workers who had supported the mutiny.

The excellent reputation for political reliability that the Navy had built up as a result of its leading role in the Communist seizure of power in November 1917 was destroyed in a few days by the mutiny at Kronshtadt. A. Bubnov, a full Politburo member and the top political com-missar of the armed forces at the time clearly indicated the adverse and lasting effect that the mutiny was to have on naval development:

> The building of the Soviet Navy has not proceeded at the same tempo nor by the same paths as that of the Soviet Army. The reason for this is understandable. It is connected with the cruel blow that was struck in March 1921.[13]

---

[11] Chamberlin, *op. cit.*, II, pp. 441–444.

[12] For the official Soviet version of the Kronshtadt Mutiny, see *History of the Commu-nist Party of the Soviet Union (Bolsheviks), Short Course* (New York: International Publishers, 1939) p. 250. A more detailed version is given in *Desiatyi s"ezd RKP(b), Mart 1921 goda, Stenograficheskii otchet* (Tenth Congress of the RKP(b), March 1921, Stenographic Record) 2nd ed., (Moscow: Gosizdatpolitlit, 1963), pp. 855–856.

[13] A. Bubnov, "Voennoe stroitel'stvo na novykh putiakh" (Military Construction on New Paths), *Krasnyi Flot*, January, 1925, p. 86.

The Tenth Party Congress, after several weeks' adjournment to permit its members to assist in quelling the Kronshtadt mutiny, passed a resolution "to strengthen the Navy with political workers, above all from the ranks of sailor-Communists working in other fields."[14] All Communist Party members with previous naval experience were recalled to duty.[15] Not satisfied with these two measures, the Party directed that a purge of naval personnel be carried out. About one out of every six persons was eliminated from the Navy.[16] To provide more politically conscious personnel to fill the enlisted ranks, mass recruitments of a total of nearly 7,800 "volunteer" Communist Youth League (Komsomol) members were conducted in 1921, 1922, and 1923.[17] By the end of 1923, 70 per cent of all naval personnel were members of the Komsomol.[18]

Since years would be required to train ideologically reliable cadres as naval officers, the Soviet Communist Party had no choice but to use former Tsarist naval officers temporarily. It was not until the Great Purge of 1937–38 that the major share of the former Tsarist officers could be replaced with younger officers of the Soviet generation. Up until that time a system of political commissars was used to watch over the reliability of all naval personnel, with the former Tsarist personnel automatically under continuing suspicion. Many of the Tsarist naval officers held over in the Soviet Navy were found intractable when the Party tried to implement strategic doctrines formulated in terms of Marxist theory.[19]

As it is described today to Soviet military and naval officers in a book from the *Biblioteka Ofitsera* (Officer's Library) series, "the Navy came out of the war weakened to the extreme."[20] A graphic description of Bal-

---

[14] USSR, Central Committee of the Communist Party. *KPSS v resoliutsiiakh i resheniiakh s"ezdov, konferentsii i plenumov TsK* (Communist Party of the Soviet Union in Resolutions and Decisions of the Congresses, Conferences, and Plenums of the Central Committee). (Moscow: Gosizdat, 1954), p. 571.

[15] *Ibid.*, p. 568.

[16] Up to 15,000 naval personnel were purged in this first major "chistka" (cleansing) of the Navy's ranks. (P. A. Smirnov, "Sozdam moguchii voenno-morskoi flot SSSR" [We are Creating a Mighty Navy], *Morskoi Sbornik*, April, 1938, p. 9). There were roughly 90,000 naval personnel at the time. (Ivan Ludri, "Desiat' let borby i stroitel' stva" [Ten Years of Struggle and Construction] *Morskoi Sbornik*, February, 1928), p. 28.

[17] N. A. Piterskii, *Znai flot* (Know the Navy), (Moscow: DOSAAF, 1956), p. 34.

[18] V. Zof, "Morskaia Khronika" (Maritime Chronicle), *Morskoi Sbornik*, November-December, 1924, p. 54.

[19] This was particularly true of old school adherents such as Gervais and Petrov who were to be officially disgraced for not accepting the young school in its Marxist guise. See pp. 10–11, 21 and 23.

[20] Strokov, A. A. (ed.), *Istoriia voennogo iskusstva* (History of Military Art), (Moscow: Voenizdat, 1966), p. 293.

tic Fleet conditions was provided by a Tsarist officer who had remained on active duty with the Soviet Navy until he fled the country in 1921:

> Wood and coal are totally lacking. There is not enough coal to heat the ships in the winter. A part remains unheated which destroys the piping. In the summer they repair the damage done in the winter. There is plenty of naptha [fuel oil] but . . . on account of this lack of coal only the six Novik Class destroyers and five submarines could possibly put to sea in the summer of 1921.[21]

The Soviet Navy was able to obtain enough repairs and supplies to conduct training exercises in the Baltic and Black Sea fleets in the summer of 1923.[22] The following year, the Frunze Military Reforms of 1924 included provisions for the regular supply of the military forces as well as an orderly, if exceedingly modest, program of replacing military equipment, including ships.[23] Just the same, material conditions remained only marginally satisfactory throughout the period of the New Economic Policy (1921–28).

In an answer to advocates of a major shipbuilding program for the Navy, the Navy Chief of Staff, A. V. Dombrovskii, declared in late 1921:

> Defense of the borders of the state from the side of the water boundaries is the cornerstone of our present day naval policy; for the time being we will relinquish broader tasks. . . . Any other interpretation of the direction of naval policy must be absolutely and categorically refuted as not corresponding with the present economic conditions of the country.[24]

Four years later, Defense Commissar K. I. Voroshilov attempted to allay the dissatisfaction of senior naval officers with the continued lack of warship construction:

> We must remember that the program of construction depends on the means which can be provided by the government. In the measure of these means we will carry on the further development of the Red Navy.[25]

Undoubtedly, the regime could have found enough money and materi-

---

[21] U.S. Embassy Helsingfors, *Military Information Bulletin*, March 15, 1921, p. 3. U.S. Archives, Alexandria, Virginia.

[22] I. Gordeev, *Krasnyi morskoi flot* (The Red Navy), (Moscow: Gosvoenizdat, 1925), p. 42.

[23] "Morskaia Khronika" (Maritime Chronicle), *Morskoi Sbornik*, February, 1925, p. 3.

[24] A. V. Dombrovskii, "Kakoi RSFSR nuzhen flot?" (What Navy Does the RSFSR Need?), *Morskoi Sbornik*, January-February, 1922, p. 82.

[25] K. I. Voroshilov, "Osnovnaia direktiva" (Basic Directive), *Krasnyi Flot*, February, 1926, p. 3.

als to build some submarines and destroyers, as well as to complete a few of the nearly-finished cruisers. It is equally clear, however, that the regime did not have at its disposal the money, material and facilities that would have been required to carry out an extensive warship building program, including battleships and aircraft carriers.

The Old School Strategy ★

II

In the early years of the Soviet regime, Defense Commissar Trotsky successfully opposed the desire of other Party leaders to reinterpret military and naval strategy in terms of Marxist concepts.[1] As a result, throughout the 1920's the naval strategic views that had been taught in the Tsarist Russian Navy before the 1917 Revolution continued to be taught to Soviet midshipmen and to form the general milieu of naval thought on naval missions and required types of ships. Professors Gervais, Petrov, and others at the Voroshilov Naval War College and the Frunze Naval Academy in Leningrad espoused a command-of-the-sea doctrine that was only slightly modified from the tenets of Mahan. The Soviet "old school" of naval strategy, formed by these Soviet pedagogues, held to the conviction that the battleships and cruisers of a traditional high-seas fleet were essential to exercise command of the sea in the maritime approaches to Soviet Russia. The old school advocates acknowledged that the advent of the submarine and airplane had made it more difficult for a surface fleet to gain and to maintain command of the sea. However, they held that for every new weapon that appeared, counterweapons soon followed in development.[2] In the case of the submarine, Gervais admitted that "submarines are an effective weapon of sea warfare which constitute a grave threat to the maritime communications of

---

[1] Leon Trotsky, *The Revolution Betrayed,* (New York: Doubleday, 1937), p. 214. See also D. Fedotoff-White, "Soviet Naval Doctrine," *Journal of the Royal United Service Institution,* August, 1935, p. 607.

[2] B. Gervais, "Flot segodniashnego dnia" (The Navy of the Contemporary Period), *Krasnyi Flot,* February, 1922, p. 26. For an interesting current Soviet reiteration of this view on weapons technology, see V. Abchuk, "Tsel'—v morskikh glubinakh" (Target—in the Seas' Depths), *Krasnaia Zvezda,* September 18, 1964.

9

any enemy with the outside world."[3] Nevertheless, he concluded, antisubmarine warfare can be successful:

> The struggle against this danger is not hopeless, but demands the expenditure of vast means . . . submarines are not a decisive factor under conditions in which appropriate numbers and types of weapons to combat them have been prepared for operating under control of the surface forces.[4]

The old school also gave Mahan's cogent answer to submarine enthusiasts who argued that the advent of the submarine had rendered obsolete all types of surface warships:

> . . . to cut the maritime communications of an enemy with the outside world . . . is only half of the wartime task. Yet another task remains, one that is not less if no more important: to secure one's own communications with the outside world. In what manner can this task be accomplished by submarines?[5]

Considering the vastly superior naval forces that England could deploy to the Baltic whenever the occasion demanded, Gervais asserted: "Our position would not be so hopeless if the [Soviet] Navy were to have a correct composition, that is, were to have the right share of battleships and cruisers, of destroyers, and of submarines."[6]

Professor Gervais and other members of the old school persisted in expressing their views despite some strong suggestions that their theories were of little help to a country and to a navy that, for at least a decade, could not hope to have the means to build major warships. For example, V. Zof, the Navy Commissar, personally took members of the old school to task in an address at the Naval War College in 1925:

> You speak of aircraft carriers and of the construction of new types of ships . . . at the same time completely ignoring the economic situation of our country and corresponding conditions of our technical means, completely ignoring the fact that perhaps tomorrow or the day after we will be called on to fight. And with what shall we fight? We will fight with those ships and personnel that we have already.[7]

---

[3] Gervais, *op. cit.*, p. 27.

[4] *Ibid.*, p. 29.

[5] *Ibid.*, p. 30.

[6] U.S. Naval Attache Berlin report No. 40, February 27, 1923. U.S. Archives, Alexandria, Virginia.

[7] V. Zof, "Mezhdunarodnoe polozhenie i zadachi morskoi oboroni SSSR" (The International Situation and the Tasks of Maritime Defense), *Morskoi Sbornik*, May, 1925, p. 16. For a more definitive indication that the Old School supported aircraft carrier construction, see the criticism of that school in I. Ludri, "Krasnyi Flot v sostave vooruzhennykh sil respubliki" (The Red Navy in the Composition of the Armed Forces of the Republic), *Morskoi Sbornik*, October, 1927, p. 26.

Eventually, Gervais and other members of the old school were to pay with their lives for having asserted the primacy of the battleship over the submarine and the need for building major warships to permit exercising command of the sea in Soviet maritime areas. Yet, this situation was not to occur for well over a decade. In the interval, a new generation of Soviet naval officers was being trained and was gaining the experience and seniority that would permit new appraisals of the naval strategy best suited to Soviet circumstances. Beginning in the late 1920's, this generation was to make itself heard in Party councils.

In 1921, a recommended approach to rehabilitating the Navy and providing Soviet Russia with a naval defensive capability was made by twenty-eight-year-old Fiodor Raskol'nikov, the commander in chief of the Baltic Fleet. He called for "eschewing broad and groundless plans for building a Grand Fleet." Instead, he recommended planning a reconstruction program that would "repair, outfit and provide regularly with fuel the most important units of the Baltic Fleet."[8] This sensible plan was adopted and permitted training exercises to be conducted at sea in 1923. In 1927, Navy Commissar R. Muklevich, in a review of the intervening years, admitted: "We have neither the means nor the possibility of throwing away a lot of money on military equipment."[9] The Navy Commissar went on to state the exact criterion for such expenditures as were made on military equipment (including ships): "We give the Army and Navy only that which is essential to defend our country from surprise attack."[10] England was the power most feared throughout the 1920's. This policy was justified on the basis that money which might otherwise be spent on the Army and Navy was needed "for the reestablishment and improvement of our economy."[11]

Available data on Soviet naval appropriations during the period of the New Economic Policy show that the Navy was given barely enough to survive, let alone to expand. For example, after a careful analysis of the 1922–23 naval budget, which revealed that the total expenditure for ship repair and construction was less than for clothing allowances, Soviet naval writer L. Gorbovskii concluded:

> Utilizing such a minor sum, the Naval Commissariat is not able to put into a condition of battle readiness even those remnants of the former

---

[8] F. Raskol'nikov, "Morskaia Khronika" (Maritime Chronicle), *Morskoi Sbornik,* January-February, 1921, p. 100.

[9] R. Muklevich, "Desiatiletie Oktiabrskoi Revoliutsii i morskoi flot" (The Tenth Anniversary of the October Revolution and the Navy), *Morskoi Sbornik,* October, 1927, p. 5.

[10] *Ibid.*

[11] *Ibid.*

navy which, with adequate means, might be repaired and put into combat condition.[12]

Similarly, Navy Commissar Muklevich complained in a top secret report on the 1928–29 naval budget, which he submitted to the Revolutionary Military Council of the USSR, that the Extraordinary Commission for War Readiness of Baltic Naval Forces, of which he was chairman, "considers it imperative to reexamine that part of the budget . . . which deals with the construction and repair of warships. . . . The sums assigned . . . do not in any degree correspond with the program laid down for the defense of the Union."[13] In effect, the Navy Commissar was rejecting a very modest program that provided for limited ship overhauls and the construction of up to five submarines. In the place of this projected program, he recommended completing the construction of four former Tsarist heavy cruisers and two light cruisers, as well as constructing six destroyers and four submarines.[14] The old school strategy underlying this program of building heavy surface ships as the basis for high-seas, offensive forces is quite apparent.

For the period from 1921 to 1924, the Navy was so weak that it was forced to adopt a strategy of passive defense, utilizing nearly immobile ships and coastal fortifications. This, of course, was the type of strategy traditionally described since the writings of Admiral Mahan as *"fortress fleet."* This strategy envisaged little more than improvised defense with the very limited means that were already available or could be prepared at little or no extra cost. In keeping with such a strategy, a "Commission for the Reorganization of the Navy," which convened in Moscow for six days beginning 15 July 1921, determined that only "one battleship having the best guns and propulsion plant was to be kept in fighting trim and used as a floating battery, with the remainder [of the major units of the Baltic Fleet] to be transferred to the reserve."[15]

The only other warships (besides the one battleship) to be kept in operational condition were eight destroyers and an unspecified, small number of submarines. The heavy caliber guns of the one battleship were to be backed up by greatly improved coastal forts at the eastern end of the Gulf of Finland. In that location, they would be most useful for defending the approaches to Petrograd. By late 1921, new and larger guns that could match the range of the main batteries of British battleships were installed in at least four coastal forts between Petrograd and the Estoni-

---

[12] L. Gorbovskii, "Morskie biudzhety 1922–23g" (The Naval Budgets for 1922–23), *Morskoi Sbornik,* September, 1924, p. 115.

[13] U.S. Military Attache Riga report No. 5862 of September 4, 1927, U.S. Archives, Alexandria, Virginia.

[14] Gorbovskii, *op. cit.,* p. 115. See also Bubnov, *op. cit.,* p. 57.

[15] U.S. Military Attache Riga, *op. cit.*

an border.[16] In 1923, Kronshtadt Naval Base, situated astride the near approaches to Leningrad, was also refortified.[17] Across the mouth of the Gulf of Finland, extensive mine fields, backed up by the eight subma- rines in a barrier, were intended to cause an initial attrition of attacking forces in wartime. Naval air support in this early period up to 1924 was limited to twenty-four seaplanes in the Baltic Fleet.[18]

In the Black Sea, no battleships or cruisers remained after the removal of most of the former Tsarist Black Sea Fleet to Bizerte, Tunisia, by General Pyotr Nikolayevich Wrangel, one of the "White" (anti-Bolshe- vik) leaders. Accordingly, the Black Sea Fleet improvised the best de- fenses it could, using offshore mine fields, six coastal submarines, coastal artillery, and six dredges on which a total of 18 six-inch guns had been installed.[19] Additionally, a few gunboats were retained in the Caspian Sea for use against the British in Persia.[20] The new Soviet Republic was too weak to maintain any significant defenses in the Arctic or in the Pacific. It was not to be until the early 1930's that the Northern and Pacific fleets were reestablished, and a few destroyers and submarines assigned to each.

By late 1923, Professor M. Petrov, Professor Gervais' most noted col- laborator of the old school of naval strategy, turned his attention to the practical requirements of a Navy in such poor condition that talk of command of the sea (except in selected, vital inshore areas of the USSR) was morale-shattering nonsense. From his writings came a strat- egy of "active" (offensive) defense by small naval forces designed to contest for command of the sea in the Soviet coastal areas within range of land-based naval aircraft. In contrast with the impracticality of the high-seas-fleet advocacy of the pre-1924 period, some sound advice was proffered by Professor Petrov after 1923 in what constituted a definite muting if not outright compromise of old school tenets. For example, writing in 1924, Petrov made the following observations:

> Setting ourselves the task of teaching all of the essential military quali- ties, we thereby acquire nothing original as compared with what the enemy receives from his training. We, the weaker, cannot be satisfied with this. Undoubtedly, if we had command personnel who were more

---

[16] U.S. Commissioner Riga report No. 312 of October 19, 1921. U.S. Archives, Alexandria, Virginia.

[17] USS *Scorpion* report No. 488 of December 10, 1923. U.S. Archives, Alexandria, Virginia.

[18] USS *Pittsburgh* report No. 1440 of August 27, 1923. U.S. Archives, Alexandria, Virginia.

[19] U.S. Military Attache Warsaw report No. 1271 of March 1, 1921. U.S. Archives, Alexandria, Virginia.

[20] USS *Scorpion, op. cit.*

expert under all circumstances than the enemy, then we would have an improved chance of success. Yet, to depend on this would be inadvisable. At the same time, we must have some superiority which the enemy most likely will not have. . . . Tactics must not be universal, especially not ours, the weaker one. More attention must be given to action against a stronger enemy. We must develop tactics for a small navy, learning all the weak sides of a stronger opponent.

From all that has been said, we can outline two directions which the tactics of a small navy should take: (1) the concept of the attack, and (2) exceptionally complete intelligence. (In the World War . . . we had absolutely no intelligence and, therefore, could not conduct any active operations with assurance.) [21]

A year later, Professor Petrov's ideas for a strategy of an active defense had been further developed. In November of 1924 he published the following conclusions:

Defense of the coasts is a complicated strategic operation. This defense is more difficult [than other types of naval operations] in that here the initiative is with the enemy. In view of the various possible plans of the enemy, there must also be various possible plans for his defeat. The first necessity for defense is intelligence in order to permit assembling the requisite means for defense. . . . Intelligence, concentration, combat— these are the stages of defense. [22]

In the main, the advice given by Professor Petrov was accepted and put into practice with good results. By 1925 a naval strategy of active defense using small naval forces designed to fight only limited engagements in coastal areas had become accepted doctrine in the Soviet Navy. For example, an article in an official Soviet naval journal of August 1925 stated:

Thus, for fulfillment of our general needs and shortages, it is desirable to occupy ourselves with the exploitation of the various [World War I] experiences with the idea of bringing up to date methods for further instruction of the Navy—the tactics of the limited engagement, active defense and the resolution of a series of specific tasks stemming from the conditions of a given theatre. [23]

Only two years later, by the summer of 1927, it appeared that the Soviet Navy was testing out a somewhat more ambitious strategy akin to the old school's original and fundamental doctrine of a high-seas fleet

---

[21] M. Petrov, "Zametki o taktiki malogo flota" (Notes on the Tactics of a Small Fleet), *Morskoi Sbornik,* September, 1923, p. 48.

[22] M. Petrov, "Stroitel'stvo flota; bol'she vnimanie morskoi aviatsii" (Construction of the Navy; More Attention to Naval Aviation), *Krasnyi Flot,* November 1924, p. 79.

[23] Iu. Rall, "Neskol'ko zamechanii po povodu pervoi poloviny kampanii 1925g" (A Few Comments on the First Half of the Campaign for 1925), *Morskoi Sbornik,* August, 1925, p. 5.

whose main strength would be composed of battleships. The Baltic Fleet maneuvers of 1927 were built around two old battleships that had been refitted and were operational by that time. One may safely conclude from the report of well-qualified naval observers quoted below that the Soviet Navy was not yet ready to progress beyond the recently adopted strategy of active defense of the Soviet maritime borders:

> The maneuvers [of 1927] proved once again that a gunnery duel on the high seas is not advantageous to the Red Navy, which is weaker than its probable enemy [England]. On the other hand, destroyer and submarine attacks, supported by the fire of the battleships, combats at night and in fog, and the use of mine barrages under protection of the coast batteries or of the battleships, are to be desired and further developed.[24]

Throughout the period from 1921 to 1928, the Navy's spokesmen alternately voiced their hopes and subsequent disappointments with regard to gaining the Soviet regime's support for a program of warship construction. As early as 1923, Navy Commissar Zof expressed what were to prove unrealized hopes: "I voice the belief that the improving material condition of the Soviet Republic permits our government to devote a corresponding amount of means to the building of the Red Navy."[25] The following year, a more realistic, if rather frustrated, chord from the same theme was struck: "In view of the current financial situation of the USSR, it is perhaps too early still to speak of new warship construction (even on a limited scale). Yet, it is impossible to be completely silent."[26] In 1925 the Navy Commissar openly complained of the continued failure of the Party to authorize and fund at least a few new ships for replacing those that were worn out:

> In the past year, the Soviet economy grew significantly stronger and our industry, which serves the Red Navy as a base for construction, was expanded. No matter how onerous and difficult for the government to provide the means for strengthening the Red Navy, we were counting on definite decisions since they are demanded by the defense interests of the Soviet Union and of the proletarian revolution.[27]

The Navy Commander in Chief in 1928, Ivan Ludri, summed up the Party's naval policy up to that time as follows:

> The period of the restoration of the Navy, which began in 1922 and

---

[24] U.S. Military Attache Riga report No. 6510 of April 16, 1928. U.S. Archives, Alexandria, Virginia.

[25] "G.2," "Tov. Zof o Chernomorskom flote" (Comrade Zof on the Black Sea Fleet), *Krasnyi Flot,* June-July, 1923, p. 24.

[26] A. Sobelov, "Na poroge novogo etapa stroitel'stva" (On the Brink of a New Stage of Construction), *Morskoi Sbornik,* January, 1925, p. 16.

[27] V. Zof, "Krasnyi Flot za 1924 god" (The Red Navy in 1924), *Morskoi Sbornik,* January, 1925, p. 16.

extended about to 1927, may be called the Rehabilitation Period, and was based on old, basic capital. During this time the Navy, just like industry, did not build anything new, but primarily rehabitated old and uncompleted ships.

> The tempo of development of naval forces coincided (and had to coincide) principally with the tempo of development of industry. . . . The Navy . . . more than any other type of military service, depends on the degree of industrialization of the country.[28]

Although only the most modest means had been devoted to the Soviet Navy during the period of New Economic Policy from 1921 to 1928, it can be seen that a definite shift away from the fortress-fleet concept of strategy took place as rapidly as the Navy found such a change practicable. The strategy of active defense that was developed in the 1920's should be considered as just the Soviet Navy's *"campaign" strategy* for the Baltic theater. From the point of view of *"grand" strategy,* the term *"fleet in being"* is applicable.[29] To illustrate this point, the Soviet Navy's plan for wartime employment of the Baltic Fleet, as of 1926, provided for the two battleships of that fleet to remain at the Kronshtadt Naval Base. In that rear-guard position, they would constitute a "reserve *point d'appui* for the active groups" (comprised of submarines, PT boats, and destroyers). These light forces would venture out towards the mouth of the Gulf of Finland to engage an attacking enemy.[30] One can readily appreciate that the avoidance of all unnecessary risk to the battleships that characterizes this general war plan is equally distinctive of a fleet-in-being strategy. Such a strategy continued to dominate Soviet naval thinking until planning was undertaken, about 1928, for the naval aspects of the First Five-Year Plan. The change that then took place will be discussed in the next chapter. Before turning attention to the ensuing shift in naval strategy, however, an effort to evaluate the old school strategy is in order. In this connection, it should be noted that the old school was criticized frequently by many senior naval officers on the basis that high-seas fleets would be of little use in the restricted seas in which such fleets would have to be based.[31]

---

[28] Ludri, "Desiat' let borby i stroitel'stva," p. 35.

[29] As it applies in the Soviet context, "fleet in being" may be explained as follows: "A nation may fight a limited offensive if its sea power is weak. . . . Normally, a nation weak in sea power has no alternative but to adopt the limited offensive. . . . The 'fleet in being' strategy is a modification of the limited offensive, exemplified in the stationing of the German Fleet idly at Wilhelmshaven in World War I as a constant menace which anchored the much larger British Navy to Northern Scotland." J. C. Shaw, "Naval Strategy," *Encyclopaedia Britannica* (Chicago: 1951), XVI, 169.

[30] U.S. Military Attache Riga report No. 5553 of October 31, 1926. U.S. Archives, Alexandria, Virginia.

[31] "USSR, Progress of Russian Naval Construction," *United States Naval Institute Proceedings,* March, 1939, p. 431.

The Tsarist command-of-the-sea strategy bequeathed to the Soviet regime met with scant appreciation by Party leaders. Lacking any understanding of sea power and immersed in the effort to restore and to expand the industry of the country, the Soviet political leaders failed to see and act on the potential for Soviet Russia of strong and balanced naval forces. The circumstances of shortages of supplies, material, and investment capital were exacerbated by the Party's preference for industrial expansion. These factors, added to the Army's dominance over the armed forces defense budget, ensured that the Red Navy was treated like an orphan.[32] Had the Navy been given a substantial share of the defense budget each year, as the leaders of the Navy repeatedly urged, the USSR could have undertaken an effective, if limited, expansion of her naval forces. Continued throughout the New Economic Policy period until 1928, such an orderly expansion of the Soviet Navy would have resulted in the creation of a small, but immensely valuable, force. Failure to adopt a policy of substantial naval reconstruction in 1921 facilitated the overthrow of the old-school strategists who could have led the Soviet state to the construction of the naval forces required to exercise command of the seas in the peripheral areas vital to its national interests.

Considering the miniscule naval appropriations that were doled out to the Red Navy during the New Economic Policy period, the former Tsarist naval officers (who continued to provide the bulk of the senior officer corps) deserved considerable credit for their accomplishments. They showed much resourcefulness in providing the fortress fleet defenses that served the Soviet state well in the 1921–25 period of unpredictable international developments. Similarly, the strategy of active defense adopted in 1925 was well-suited to domestic conditions and the foreign situation that confronted the USSR at that time. In view of the limited forces available to implement a fleet-in-being strategy in 1925, it is apparent that the former Tsarist officers lost no time in taking the first step away from the purely passive defense concept of a fortress-fleet strategy to an offensive (active) defense concept. Undoubtedly, the former Tsarist naval leaders saw this as a major step in the direction of their ultimate old-school goal of developing high-seas fleets in the Soviet Black Sea, Baltic, Northern, and Pacific Fleet areas. With a new generation of Soviet-trained naval officers receiving rapid promotion to commanding positions and senior rank, it is probable that the former Tsarist officers realized that they had only a short time left in which to provide a convincing demonstration of the value of building balanced, high-seas fleets. At

---

[32] "Various Notes," *United States Naval Institute Proceedings,* September, 1938, p. 1369: "Kalinin admitted that the Navy had been neglected [not only during the NEP period but also] during the first two five-year plans."

any rate, as early as 1927, they had gotten two of the old Tsarist battle-ships in operational condition and were trying to operate them in the Baltic as the backbone of a small, high-seas fleet. Unquestionably, the old school never was given the opportunity to put its theories to a fair test. It is conceivable that those who criticized the old school from the outset as unrealistic in trying to apply a command-of-the-sea strategy in the restricted seas around the Soviet Union might have been proved right had the Soviet Navy been allowed to test the old-school theories with strong, balanced forces. However, the test was never made. As a result, considerable doubt overshadows the ensuing practice of relying on "mos-quito" surface forces without cruisers, battleships, or aircraft carriers.

Certainly if one accepts the general Western assumption which was prevalent during the peak years of the Cold War that the USSR's grand strategy inalterably involves the eventual use of force to gain and main-tain world domination, it may then be concluded that it was unfortunate for the furtherance of such an aim that the USSR did not test out the old-school theories by building high-seas fleets. However, as will be brought out in the concluding chapter, one may reject this assumption and instead conceive of the Soviet aim as one of increasing its influence wherever power vacuums or vulnerabilities exist, but by "peaceful coex-istence" methods supported by an adequate nuclear *deterrent* force re-quiring minimum military expenditures. It may then be seen that Soviet strategy, even though inadequate for defense in any protracted general nuclear war, is far from being the irrational strategy it would be if Soviet policy were actually militantly offensive.

III

As mentioned in the preceding chapter, Trotsky had successfully opposed the wishes of other Party leaders to reinterpret military and naval
strategy in terms of Marxist concepts. Those wishes had taken the form
of a "School of Proletarian Military Doctrine" which held that the Red
Army and the "Naval Forces of the Red Army," as the Navy was then
constituted, "could have nothing in common with the national armies of
the capitalist countries. The new ruling class must in all respects have a
distinct military system; it remained only to create it."[1] Frunze, Tukhachevskii, Voroshilov, and other military leaders, attempted to derive a
unified military and naval doctrine from their experiences in the partisan
warfare that had characterized much of the Russian Civil War.[2] In their
Proletarian Military Doctrine, the principles of maneuver and particularly of the offensive were raised to dominating positions. It was these
efforts by Party stalwarts to pattern Soviet military and naval strategy and
tactics solely on partisan warfare that Trotsky opposed implacably. He
appeared to have temporarily silenced advocates of such a doctrinaire
Marxist approach with an article published in the Soviet press on 1 April
1922. In the article Trotsky stated, *inter alia:*

> I also do not doubt that if a country with a *developed socialist economy*
> found itself compelled to wage war with a bourgeois country, the picture
> of the strategy of the socialist country would be wholly different. But this
> gives no basis for an attempt today to suck a "proletarian strategy" out of

---

[1] Trotsky, *op. cit.,* p. 212.

[2] Frunze's classic statement of the highly controversial principles of Proletarian Mili-
tary Doctrine was published in 1921 in the first issue of *Voennaia nauka i revoliutsiia*
(Military Science and the Revolution) under the title, "Edinaia voennaia doktrina i
Krasnaia Armiia" (Unified Military Doctrine and the Red Army), p. 4–17.

our fingers. . . . By developing a socialist economy and raising the cultural level of the masses . . . we will undoubtedly enrich the military art with new methods. But for this, it is necessary to learn from the advanced capitalist countries, and not to try to "infer a new strategy by speculative methods from the revolutionary nature of the proletariat."[3]

In his final verdict on the School of Proletarian Military Doctrine, Trotsky gave its adherents credit for sincerity, but asserted that their views were not actually Marxist despite the consistent trappings of Marxist terminology used to embellish those views. Rather, Trotsky observed, those views were completely idealistic and unrealistic. They were, he alleged, derived "from motionless psychological abstractions, and not from real conditions of time and place."[4] Trotsky analyzed this unrealistic approach as resulting from the Soviet bureaucracy which, he said, "wanted to believe, and make others believe, that it was able in all spheres without special preparation and even without material prerequisites, to accomplish historic miracles."[5]

With such an effectively articulate opposition, it is understandable that the School of Proletarian Military Doctrine was unable to gain acceptance for its views as long as Trotsky remained active in the Party. With Trotsky's removal and replacement by Frunze in early 1925 as Peoples' Commissar for Military and Naval Affairs and especially with the defeat of Trotsky's thesis of permanent revolution by Stalin's policy of first building socialism in the USSR, and with Trotsky's expulsion from the Party in November 1927,[6] his powerful opposition to what he considered untried and manifestly unsuitable innovations in military and naval doctrine was brought to an end.

It was not long before ideas strikingly similar to those of the School of Proletarian Military Doctrine were to be voiced with ever increasing authority. In the same year that Trotsky was expelled from Party councils, there was formed a military section of the "Communist Academy" of the Central Committee of the Party. This organization was established to serve as the official oracle on Marxist-Leninist doctrine. The formation in 1927 of a military section of the Communist Academy provided an obvious warning that the earlier immunity of military and naval doctrine from theoretical tampering had been violated. No longer would military science be the exclusive, or even the main, province of the Red Army's

---

[3] Trotsky, *op. cit.*, p. 214.

[4] *Ibid.*, p. 213.

[5] *Ibid.*, p. 214. This Party proclivity for undertaking vast projects with poorly-conceived plans and inadequate resources was to become glaringly obvious in the 1939–41 effort of the Third Five-Year Plan to build a high-seas fleet rapidly with a Soviet industry which was inadequately equipped for the task.

[6] Leonard Shapiro, *The Communist Party of the Soviet Union* (New York: Alfred A. Knopf, Inc., 1964), pp. 283, 288, 306.

Frunze Staff College and the Voroshilov Naval War College. Final verdicts on such matters as strategy, tactics, and military organization were to come from the Communist Academy.[7] The experience gained from conventional warfare and the theory and practice of the other major powers of the world was to be distrusted completely. The new guiding principles were to be derived from the partisan warfare of the 1918–21 period of the Civil War and from such precepts of Marx and Lenin as dialectical materialism and Lenin's theory of revolution. Naval officers were officially advised that the final aim of all theoretical work in naval science was to develop strategy and tactics of naval warfare "based on the Marxist-Leninist methodology, in accord with the general line of the Communist Party."[8]

In the early months of 1932, the Commander in Chief of Naval Forces, V. M. Orlov, made merciless attacks on the proponents of the old school. Professors Gervais and Petrov were subjected to substantial fines for their "incorrect" theories. Orlov took a leading role in a vigorous discussion of naval strategy and completely discredited the concepts of the old school. Orlov was uncompromising in demanding complete conformity to the maxims of Communist theory and to the Party line. In view of this, it must have become clear to all naval officers that any concepts of naval strategy subsequently developed would have to be rationalized in terms of Marxian dialectics. Consequently, what was termed in the USSR as the young school (*molodaia shkola*) of naval strategy, which grew up in opposition to the old school, was confronted with *a priori* requirements to pay heed primarily to the lessons of the Russian Civil War; the Party line on Soviet industrialization, defense, and foreign affairs; and to express all views in approved Communist terminology. The success with which this was done, and the results for the Navy of implementing such a policy, constitute major elements of the analysis which is to follow.

Criticism of the old school, and of its particular views on the classical command of the sea doctrine, became increasingly vocal between 1927 and 1932. The leading personalities of the young school were largely Soviet-trained naval officers including Ivan S. Ludri, K. I. Dushenov, A. P. Aleksandrov, and a number of others. The basic tenet of the young school, when stripped of its Marxist theoretical baggage, was simply an assertion that the submarine had replaced the battleship as the main

---

[7] D. Fedotoff-White, "Soviet Philosophy of War," *Political Science Quarterly*, September, 1936, p. 347.

[8] M. Krupskii, "Za chistotu marksistko-leninskoi teorii v voenno-morskikh voprosakh" (For the Purging of Marxist-Leninist Theory on Naval Questions), *Morskoi Sbornik*, January, 1932, p. 18.

striking unit of the fleet. The young school theorists argued that, owing to the development of submarines and aircraft, close blockade no longer could be achieved against a modern navy. More importantly, no general surface fleet actions, such as the Battle of Jutland, would occur in future wars. Accordingly, the utility of the battleship supposedly had ended. Submarines, aided by aircraft and light surface ships and craft, were held to be the major weapons of contemporary naval warfare. A balanced naval force should consist of light units. No battleships or cruisers were required. Only submarines, PT boats, high-speed destroyers, and naval aircraft were essential.[9]

As the result of the unified command principle that evolved from the Leninist concept of the unity of military and naval strategy, the submarines, surface ships, coastal defense forces, and aircraft of the Soviet Navy all were required to coordinate their operations according to one plan.[10] Also, local Army troops were required to coordinate with all the naval units in the area, including coast artillery, naval infantry troops, naval aircraft, and naval surface and submarine forces.[11] The Marxist rationale for this requirement for such thoroughgoing coordination was simply that all arms of the military services, whether ground, air, or naval, "support the single idea of the defense of the interests of the workers" and, therefore, should not be permitted to go their separate ways in supporting accomplishment of those interests.[12]

The writings of the young school theorists reveal clearly the more practical considerations that underlay their strategic and tactical concepts. These considerations, not surprising for a country so devastated

[9] The Soviet "Young School" (Molodaia Shkola) resembles too closely to be coincidental the French "Jeune Ecole" originated by Admiral Aube in the 1880's. As summarized and criticized in 1930 by the noted French naval writer, Admiral Castex, the "Jeune Ecole" was presented as follows: "The strategic doctrine of the 'Young School' . . . denied the importance of organized force and of the battle which determines its fate. It asserted the strange belief that the principal objective at sea was not as on land the destruction of the main enemy force. It set up as a system the evasion of battle. It justified commerce raiding as the one and only method of operation. It pretended to employ coastal warfare offensively and defensively after a curious fashion. Offensively, it was to be carried on by bombardment followed by flight—in the safety of which it took a childish hope which took no account of the existence of the enemy fleet. Defensively, it proposed to assure the protection and security of the coast by spreading out our forces in a thin line . . . it believed in the very small warship, in naval dust, in fantastic tools like the floating gun, the mortar boat, etc., all unsuitable for an offensive task and incapable of remaining at sea." Raoul Castex, *Theories Strategiques,* Translated by R. C. Smith, Jr. (Newport, R.I., U.S. Naval War College, 1938), I, 57–58.

[10] "O zadachakh boevoi podgotovka voenno-morskikh sil RKKA na 1932 god" (On the Combat Training Tasks of the Naval Forces of the Red Army in 1932), *Morskoi Sbornik,* January, 1932, p. 3.

[11] Zof, "Mezhdunarodnoe polozhenie i zadachi morskoi oboronu SSSR," p. 6.

[12] Ludri, "Krasnyi Flot v sostave vooruzhennykh sil respubliki," p. 24.

and backward, were largely matters of basic economics. Soviet Russia was still too insufficiently industrialized to build battleships without substantial foreign assistance, even had the Party leadership been willing and in a position to make the great outlays of capital, material resources, and labor required to build them. Party leaders were determined to devote all possible resources to the successful completion of the First Five-Year Plan "for the reconstruction of the country's economy and in particular to create new branches of industrial production requisite for a highly developed heavy and defence industry in the shortest possible time."[13] Consequently, the Soviet regime had what it considered to be a compelling reason for minimizing the share of the national income spent on naval armaments. As a result of this economy-mindedness in matters of naval construction, it is not surprising that the Soviet Party and Army leaders who controlled the Navy succumbed to the attraction of the relative cheapness of submarines, PT boats, and destroyers. For example, twenty destroyers could be built for the price of a single battleship, the price of which had multiplied six times since pre-World War I days. The Soviet author of these statistics apparently had the price tag primarily in mind as the major "real condition" when he wrote that a British naval writer's "ideas of superiority of the battleship due to its greater gun range were abstract and scholastic" and "not in correspondence with the real conditions of modern war."[14] Old school strategist Professor Petrov was strongly condemned for having written in his textbook on naval strategy that battleships rather than submarines played the main attack role in naval warfare.[15] Battleships were considered as next to useless by the young school theoreticians for several years after 1932. Yet, by 1937, battleships were grudgingly recognized to be of some secondary value when used in cooperation with naval aircraft, submarines, and fast, light, surface striking forces.[16]

With the improvement in the Soviet economic position achieved by

---

[13] A. Baykov, *The Development of the Soviet Economic System* (Cambridge, England. The University Press, 1948), p. 157.

[14] "Bol'shie ili malye korabli?" (Large or Small Warships?), *Krasnyi Flot*, July 4, 1938, p. 3.

[15] "Protiv reaktsionnykh teorii v voprosakh boevogo ispol'zovaniia podvodnykh lodok" (Against Reactionary Theory on the Combat Employment of Submarines), *Morskoi Sbornik*, February, 1932, p. 59.

[16] Fedotov-White, "Soviet Naval Doctrine," *op. cit.*, p. 612. This probably was influenced by the battleship's return to favor in the major navies of the world after the end of quantitative treaty limitations in 1936. This awkward and ingenuous theoretical innovation had the practical benefit of permitting continued use of the existing three old battleships without attributing to battleships as a type enough importance as to logically require the heavy expenditures that would have been necessary for construction of new ones.

the First Five-Year Plan, and with the development of a doctrinally acceptable naval strategy that would be relatively inexpensive to implement, the Party approved sizable programs of light warship construction.[17] At the same time, a large program for naval aircraft production was approved.[18] With the beginning of the Second Five-Year Plan, on 1 January 1933, the USSR undertook a large submarine construction program that was to make the Soviet Navy the proud possessor of the largest submarine force in the world by the end of the plan period on 1 April 1937.[19] As Deputy Defense Commissar Marshal Mikhail Nikolaevich Tukhachevskii reported to the Central Executive Committee of the Party in January 1936: "We are creating a powerful navy. We are concentrating our forces primarily upon the development of a submarine force."[20] In the same month, Navy Commander in Chief Orlov reported to the Extraordinary Eighth All-Union Congress of Soviets: "If we take the ship composition of our fleet on January 1933 as one hundred per cent, then by the end of 1936 we have submarines to 715 per cent."[21] As to the numerical significance of this percentage, "one of the lowest estimates made by foreign experts in Moscow as to the number of Soviet submarines in 1933 was twenty; this should give a present total of 145. Some calculations run much higher."[22]

The remainder of the money allocated to the Navy for naval construction during the Second Five-Year Plan period accomplished the following increases over the levels at the end of the First Five-Year Plan period in December 1932: "Small surface ships—300 per cent; naval aviation—510 per cent; coastal guns—75 per cent; and naval base fortification—100 per cent."[23] It may be seen that these publicly reported expenditures were of a nature that was quite consistent with the young school strategy of building light forces of surface ships to supplement very strong submarine and naval air elements. Yet, certain inconsistent developments became apparent in early 1934. They signaled the

---

[17] A few, probably five, coastal submarines had been built in the First Five-Year Plan period (October 1, 1928 to December 31, 1932). Otherwise, naval expenditures on surface ships had been limited to repair and upkeep work: "During these years [of the First Five-Year Plan] all ships were repaired, some battleships overhauled, several submarines built, and our coastal defense strengthened." P. Zvonkov, *Kirov i Moriaki* (Kirov and the Sailors), (Moscow: Voenizdat, 1940), p. 75.

[18] Walter Duranty, "Youth Revitalizes the Soviet Fleet," *The New York Times,* October 23, 1932, p. 3.

[19] The French Navy's submarine force, which led the world's navies until the USSR took the lead, had 75 effective submarines at the end of 1936. By April of 1937, the Soviet submarine force was about twice the size of the French force. "Soviet U-Boat Fleet," *United States Naval Institute Proceedings,* December, 1937, p. 1810.

[20] Trotsky, *op. cit.,* p. 207.

[21] "Morskaia Khronika" (Maritime Chronicle), *Morskoi Sbornik,* December 1936, p. 3.

[22] "USSR," *United States Naval Institute Proceedings,* February, 1937, p. 281.

[23] *Ibid.*

end of the young school of strategy and the reemergence of the old school strategy in its prewar Stalinist form.

Soviet naval officers, like their Tsarist predecessors, had formed the habit of keeping fully alert to naval developments abroad. During the 1920's, a plentiful cause for sniping at the old school adherents was to be found in the international climate of opinion on naval strategy, particularly on the role of the battleship. Not a single battleship was under construction anywhere in the world in 1929 when the *United States Naval Institute Proceedings* reprinted a *New York Times* report from London saying that it would be "difficult to imagine a situation more favorable for doing away with capital ships."[24] The reason underlying this remarkable situation, and the resultant support it afforded to opponents of the old school, were well described in 1938:

> With her [the battleship's] curtailment at the Washington Conference, her critics waxed bold again. For a few years she was pictured, even by older officers of unquestioned ability, as headed for the scrap heap . . . while the airplane and torpedo craft [and the submarine] took over the trident.[25]

In view of the prevailing naval opinion favoring light, defensive forces over the offensive might of the battleship, one may well wonder how the old school managed to hold sway even until 1928 and not to be completely discredited officially until 1932. Had it not been for Trotsky's steadfast opposition from 1921 until 1927, the Marxist theorists would have completed the embodiment in theoretical formulae of the guerrilla experiences of the Red Army in the Russian Civil War, and the old school would have been supplanted by the young school not later than 1925 or 1926.

Had this situation occurred, the world's largest submarine force could have been created by the USSR even earlier than 1937. This accomplishment, in turn, might well have permitted the natural limitations of naval power based primarily on submarines to have become apparent to Stalin and other members of the Politburo considerably earlier than the Spanish Civil War, which demonstrated the USSR's need for strong surface forces.[26] With the additional six years that such a development would have made available to Stalin to build up the Navy, it is conceiva-

---

[24] "End of Capital Ships Foreseen in Accord," *United States Naval Institute Proceedings,* November, 1929, p. 1003.

[25] M. F. Talbot, "The Battleship, Her Evolution and Her Present Place in the Scheme of Naval War," *United States Naval Institute Proceedings,* May, 1938, p. 645.

[26] [Throughout] the events in Spain . . . we were unable to play a proper role in the naval control, conducted pursuant to a decision of the "Committee on Non-Intervention," [because] we lacked the necessary warships and logistic support ships. At that time it became particularly apparent how important the sea is for us and how we need a strong navy." N. G. Kuznetsov, *Nakanune* (On the Eve). (Moscow: Voenizdat, 1966), p. 257.

ble that by June 1941 strong and balanced naval forces could have been created, at least in the Baltic and in the Black Sea. Accordingly, considerable basis can be found for the view that the six-year delay in the evolution of Soviet naval strategy that resulted from Trotsky's opposition, actually had an adverse effect on Soviet naval development of far-reaching consequences.

Ironically, the application of Marxist theory to military doctrine which Trotsky had opposed so strongly turned out in practice to be nothing more than a veneer of Marxist terminology. In what must have been welcomed as a favorable coincidence by Party and Army leaders, the defensive concepts that were accepted generally by even the major naval powers lent themselves nicely to Marxist rationalization in terms of Frunze's "unified military doctrine." The "unification" achieved was actually the subordination of the naval forces to support the coastal flanks of the ground forces as "the faithful assistant of the Army."[27] By adopting this young school solution in order to replace the old school with its constant and importunate demands for major warship construction, the Soviet regime was able to put a good face on what was primarily a continued unwillingness to spend great amounts of money to build battleships and aircraft carriers.

In view of the climate of world opinion unfavorable to construction of battleships that existed, their continental orientation, and their first priority for expanding the USSR's heavy industrial base, it was not surprising that the Soviet leaders chose to expend the USSR's resources on heavy industry and the Red Army rather than on building strong naval forces. Nevertheless, it seems clear that the USSR, by forsaking the old school strategy of command of the sea, lost a major opportunity for building up strong, balanced naval forces in the Soviet fleet areas. Former Tsarist naval officers, who still had the greatest voice in the organization and operation of the forces afloat, did manage to restore the old, pre-1917 battleships to operational condition in an attempt to achieve a balanced force in the fleet area considered most critical—the Baltic. Yet, without a command-of-the-sea strategy accompanied by naval appropriations to build more battleships and cruisers, the Soviet Navy was prevented from developing modern, balanced forces. Such forces could have lent badly needed support to Soviet diplomatic efforts for achieving collective security against the Axis powers in the thirties and to Soviet military efforts for defeating the Nazis in World War II. For example, had the Soviet Navy had such forces during the Spanish Civil War, it could have accepted the Bay of Biscay as its share of the non-intervention pa-

---

[27] G. I. Levchenko, "Flot—Vernyi pomoshchnik Krasnoi Armii," (The Navy—Faithful Assistant of the Red Army), *Krasnaia Zvezda*, July 28, 1946.

trol instead of withdrawing in embarrassment,[28] and otherwise could have employed sea power with telling effect against Italian and German aid to the Franco insurgents. Instead, it could do no more than protest in a note to the Italian government and sign the Nyon Agreement when one of its merchant ships carrying arms to the Republican forces was sunk in the Mediterranean by a submarine attack carried out without warning.[29] A Soviet proposal, in effect, that the French and British navies provide the naval power that the USSR lacked to block Italian and German aid to Franco was not adopted, although Maxim M. Litvinov stated publicly that such action "would not only have put an end to the war in Spain, without arousing any international complications, but would have meant a shattering blow to aggression in general."[30] Certainly, had the Soviet Baltic Fleet been a modern, balanced force imbued with an offensive spirit rather than trained in "active defense," the Germans would have found it a serious deterrent consideration before launching Operation Barbarossa and a major, quite likely insuperable, handicap to the initial swift successes that the execution of that plan enjoyed in sweeping through the Baltic states and placing Leningrad under siege. So conscious was the USSR of its naval inferiority compared to Germany by 1939 that it took the unusual step of proposing that French and British naval forces join Soviet naval forces for joint fleet maneuvers in the Baltic.[31]

[28] Mairin Mitchell, *The Maritime History of Russia, 848–1948*. (London: Sidgwick and Jackson Ltd., 1949), p. 378.

[29] *Brassey's Naval Annual 1938* (London: William Clowes Ltd., 1938), p. 75.

[30] "Litvinov's Speech in Leningrad, June 23, 1938," Reprinted as Document No. 29, George F. Kennan, *Soviet Foreign Policy 1917–1941* (Princeton, New Jersey: D. Van Nostrand Company, Inc., 1960), p. 174.

[31] Max Jakobson, *Diplomacy of the Winter War* (Cambridge, Massachusetts: Harvard University Press, 1961), p. 59.

IV

Without taking any immediate action to silence the young school naval strategists, Stalin started a shift away from the concepts of that school. He moved toward a large, balanced fleet strategy that was basically in accord with the traditional theory of Mahan and that of the old school.[1] The limited resources available until 1928 and official disfavor thereafter had forced old school advocates of a command-of-the-sea strategy, as a matter of expediency, to compromise and mute their views. Limitations on available resources were to influence adversely the implementation of Stalin's naval strategy. Yet, there seems to have been no

---

[1] "Former Soviet Naval Officer" included among his comments on the first draft of this study that the author, in developing the evolution of the USSR's naval strategic theory, was likely to give the reader an exaggerated impression of the importance of theoretical considerations in the essentially pragmatic process of Soviet military policy-making as it was practiced, particularly, in the interwar period. In this view the shift to the young school of strategy related in the last chapter appeared to Former Soviet Naval Officer and his post-World War II contemporaries as merely a temporary and expedient shift to a defensive strategy corresponding to the USSR's position of great naval inferiority compared to England. The author recognizes that this view has considerable merit and, in fact, may well be wholly correct. However, a number of considerations have led to substantially preserving the original findings including: 1. The old school-young school cycle was so clearly documented in the contemporary literature as to require presentation as this weight of evidence indicated. 2. Former Soviet Naval Officer studied the interwar period only in the post-World War II period and the Soviet penchant for rewriting history is well established. Nevertheless, the author has made it a point from the title right through to the conclusions to show the dichotomy between theory and practice. He trusts he has made sufficiently clear his conviction that the Party and Army leaders who have dominated naval policy formulation have alternated between old and young school theory twice primarily to provide rationalizations for naval shipbuilding programs selected on the basis of practical and political considerations such as the need to limit the defense budget and the Navy's disrepute for over a decade after the Kronshtadt Mutiny of 1921.

initial recognition of the problems, many of which had become painfully familiar to the suppressed old school adherents and could have been recognized at the outset had Stalin taken the trouble to consult them.

By January 1934, when the Seventeenth Party Congress convened, Stalin had overcome much of the opposition to his personal dictatorship.[2] As a result, he was in a strong position to secure eventual adoption of such programs as he deemed necessary. Yet, Stalin's political control was not complete until after his great purge reached its peak in 1938. Accordingly, he cautiously resorted to a trial balloon at the Seventeenth Congress to advance a view of naval strategy that was a radical departure from the prevailing view of the young school. A junior naval officer named Seleznev, a submarine commanding officer from the Pacific Fleet, addressed the delegates with a dramatic appeal not to base the defense of the Soviet Union's coasts solely on submarines but to build up a high seas fleet with warships of all types.[3] This speech accurately espoused Stalin's subsequently disclosed views. Influenced by the aggressiveness and concentration on naval armaments of both Germany and Japan, Stalin had resolved to devote military appropriations in the Third Five-Year Plan primarily to building up the Navy.[4] Seleznev's speech sounded like a call for a shift in Soviet naval strategy from the defensive to the offensive. It marked the start of an all-out, warship construction effort seriously intended to make the USSR, if not the greatest naval power in the world as Soviet propaganda claimed, at least a major naval power.[5]

Although the fact was to be kept hidden from foreigners for several years, the naval program of the Second Five-Year Plan (1 January 1933 to 1 April 1937) was not limited to provisions for more submarines, naval aircraft, and light surface ships and craft. It also provided for modernization of the old battleships and construction of heavy cruisers. The three former Tsarist battleships that had been retained in the Soviet

---

[2] The Seventeenth Congress, which was called in Party circles "the Congress of Victors," recorded in its minutes that "the general line of the Party had triumphed along the whole front." *History of the Communist Party of the Soviet Union,* p. 320.

[3] P. A. Smirnov, "Moguchii morskoi i okeanskii flot" (Mighty Sea and Ocean Navy), *Pravda,* February 3, 1938.

[4] "Na strazhe interesov naroda" (On Guard of the Interests of the People), *Pravda,* January 18, 1938.

[5] In a speech to the Supreme Soviet, Premier Molotov stressed the necessity for the Soviet Union to build a powerful navy. ("Likhovanie narodov Sovetskogo Souiza" [Exultation of the Peoples of the Soviet Union], *Pravda,* December 16, 1937.) By February of 1938, perhaps primarily to encourage the production effort, nothing but "the most powerful high seas fleet in the world" would meet Soviet requirements. (A. Pukhov, "Partiino-politicheskaia rabota v voenno-morskom flote za 20 let" [Party-political Work in the Navy for 20 Years], *Morskoi Sbornik,* February, 1938, p. 56.)

Navy were substantially modernized, including the addition of larger caliber, main-battery guns.[6] Also, in the Second Five-Year Plan period, a program of cruiser construction was undertaken at shipyards in both the Baltic and Black seas. Ultimately, this program resulted in the completion of six heavy cruisers.[7] Whether or not any serious consideration was given to construction of aircraft carriers in the Second Five-Year Plan is not known definitely but seems unlikely since no hint of such consideration has appeared in Soviet media despite revelations about subsequent carrier construction programs in Admiral Kuznetsov's memoirs.[8] Doubtless naval leaders desired their construction, appreciating their necessity for providing mobile sea-based air support for effective surface naval operations on the high seas. However, the lack of sufficiently large shipbuilding ways alone would have prevented the construction of carriers for at least the period of the Second Five-Year Plan.

Major improvements were made to existing shipbuilding yards in the period of the First Five-Year Plan. A major expansion of the USSR's heavy industrial base was also accomplished during that period. Nevertheless, by 1933 the Soviet Union still lacked the shipbuilding facilities to construct battleships or aircraft carriers. Also lacking was the industrial capability to produce large-caliber naval guns, battleship turrets, armor plate, and main-battery fire control equipment. Extensive efforts were made in the Second Five-Year Plan period to remedy this major limitation on Soviet industrial capabilities for fulfilling Stalin's ambition to make the USSR one of the world's leading naval powers.[9] However, much remained to be done during the period of the Third Five-Year Plan to develop a capability for complete construction and equipping of capital ships.

A feeling of unbounded optimism concerning the Soviet Union's industrial capabilities for building big, balanced fleets pervaded Party and government circles in the first year of the Third Five-Year Plan, which began on 1 April 1937. This general optimism is clearly reflected in the following quotation from a Communist youth newspaper in 1938:

> A new stage in the construction of the Red Navy is now beginning. Now, when our socialist industry has developed and grown strong, when there are being established great factories which are specially designated [that

---

[6] I. Nosenko, "V bor'be za sozdanie bol'shogo flota" (In the Struggle for the Creation of a Big Navy), *Morskoi Sbornik*, August, 1939, p. 46.

[7] These were the Kirov Class cruisers. U.S. Naval Attache Copenhagen report No. R-552 of December 17, 1936. U.S. Archives, Alexandria, Virginia.

[8] See pp. 31–34 *infra*.

[9] Smirnov, *op. cit.*, p. 1.

is, as "naval plants"] and which will reinforce the Navy with powerful warships, creating a big Red Navy has become a completely realistic task.[10]

Some uncertainty still exists outside of the Soviet Union about the numbers and types of large ships, especially battleships and aircraft carriers, programmed for construction at the height of the "big Navy" enthusiasm in the Soviet Union in the second half of the 1930's. It appears reasonably certain that three large, heavily-gunned battleships were laid down by 1940, two in Leningrad and one in Nikolayevsk.[11] In the recently published memoirs of the Navy Commissar at the time, Admiral Nikolai G. Kuznetsov, the old school building program undertaken in 1937 to develop a "fleet of the open ocean" (as the Soviets term a high-seas fleet) was described as follows:

> It was decided to build battleships, heavy cruisers, and other classes of surface warships; that is, a big surface navy. A large number of submarines was also to be built. Not excluded either was the construction of aircraft carriers; rather they were only postponed to the last year of the [Third (1937–42)] Five-Year Plan. This was explained, I recall, by the complexities of construction of warships of this class and the aircraft designed especially for them.[12]

---

[10] *Komsomol'skaia Pravda,* March 15, 1938.

[11] A reliable source, who was in an excellent position to have gained correct information in the matter of Stalin's shipbuilding programs, has stated that three battleships of a class to be called "Soviet Union" (Sovetskii Soiuz) of 35,000 tons displacement and having 16-inch guns were programmed and construction of all three actually begun by 1940. (Former Soviet Naval Officer, "Soviet Naval Strategy," address to the U.S. Naval War College, October 31, 1964.) The Germans captured one large, uncompleted battleship hull at Nikolayevsk in 1941. (*German Naval Records,* ONI-T-80E, NID PG/ 49180, Office of Naval History, Navy Department, Washington, D. C.) That there were at least two building in Leningrad is indicated by Admiral Kuznetsov's use of the plural in the statement in his memoirs (as first published in serialized form but not in the book version) when he described his visit to Leningrad in August 1940: "On the ways of one of the shipyards towered the hulls of battleships." "Pered voinoi" (Before the War) (*Oktiabr',* No. 11, November 1965, p. 139).

[12] Kuznetsov, *Nakanune,* p. 258. One notes with marked interest that neither the statement of the 1937 shipbuilding program's objective being to build a big surface navy nor that the program was to include aircraft carriers appeared either in the initial version serialized in *Oktiabr'* (issues 8, 9, and 11 of 1965) or in subsequent publication in the USSR's English language journal *International Affairs* (beginning with issue no. 5 of May 1966 and ending in March 1967). The most plausible reason for this important substantive omission would seem to be a desire not to inform the Western reader (who would give most of his attention to the first publicized versions, particularly the English one) while not withholding the truth from the Soviet readership (many of whom would have been aware of the facts anyway) that any Soviet government had ever considered carriers so necessary that a program for their construction had actually been fully approved and undertaken. The undermining effect that such an admission has on Soviet arguments to justify their continued lack of carriers is not insignificant and forces them to fall back solely on the argument that the military-technical revolution has outmoded carriers. This argument will be considered in Chapter IX.

Kuznetsov's memoirs make it clear that the construction of an unspecified number of aircraft carriers actually was fully approved by the Defense Ministry and by Stalin; and until subsequently cut out of the program for unspecified reasons, was to have covered both the Third and
the Fourth Five-Year Plans.[13] According to the best information available, one carrier was to have been laid down in 1942–43,[14] after the
necessary shipbuilding facilities could be built, plans for a carrier
procured,[15] the necessary components such as hull plating and turbines
fabricated, and workmen trained. A total of at least four were planned
for completion by the end of the ten-year program in 1948.[16] Kuznetsov
went on to criticize Stalin and the Army marshals "for not attaching the
least significance to the construction of carriers."[17] He added, with clear
reference to carriers, "that those who undertook to plan the long-range
development of the Navy should have more clearly grasped the main direction of development."[18] The Admiral's frustration at the memory of
this anomalous situation and the wholly untenable position in which it
placed the future of the Soviet Navy were neatly summed up by his view

---

[13] Kuznetsov, "Pered voinoi" pp. 142–143. This information appeared in both the
serialized versions but not specifically in the book as far as concerns Stalin and the
Defense Ministry having cut out the carriers from the 1937 program—and apparently
from a second program in 1939, and Stalin personally from another program "somewhat later" than 1939 (postwar?) which included both large and small (for antisubmarine warfare?) carriers. *Ibid.*, p. 143.

[14] Former Soviet Naval Officer, *op. cit.*

[15] Between 1937 and 1939, the USSR made intensive but unsuccessful efforts to obtain
from the United States the designs, plans, working drawings, and specifications for the
newest design of American aircraft carrier. (U.S. Department of State, *Foreign Relations
of the United States, Diplomatic Papers, the Soviet Union 1933–39,* [Washington: U.S.
Government Printing Office, 1952], p. 490.) Whether or not the Soviet inability to
obtain such design information for the most modern aircraft carrier potentially available played a decisive role in the eventual cancellation of carrier construction for the
ten-year program undertaken in 1937 is not known. It is certainly conceivable that it
was seized on as a pretext for cancellation by Stalin himself or by the Army marshals
in the Defense Ministry who preferred to spend as much as possible of the defense
budget on the Army.

[16] Former Soviet Naval Officer, *op. cit.*

[17] Kuznetsov, *Nakanune,* p. 258. In the English version in *International Affairs* the
"not attaching any significance to the construction of carriers" underwent the small but
critical change that "the program made no provision at all for aircraft carriers." Thus
the English version not only did not include the information already cited from the book
to show that the program did provide for carrier construction, it also made a textual
change that could be interpreted to mean that the program, in fact, did not include
any carriers. The deceptive intent here would seem to be beyond question. There is
also the clear implication that even Stalin's initial approval had been given with major
reservations, probably over the objections of the Defense Ministry, and with the understanding that the naval leaders who advocated carriers would be held responsible for
their success. (N. G. Kuznetsov, "Before the War," *International Affairs,* No. 12,
December 1965, p. 95.)

[18] Kuznetsov, *Nakanune,* p. 258.

of the strategic scenario which the lack of carriers would have created for the end of the ten-year program of naval construction:

> Visualize for a minute that the program were to have been completed in the second half of the 'forties. We should have had large squadrons with battleships, but . . . without a single aircraft carrier. Then how far out to sea could they have gone?[19]

Kuznetsov next proceeded to describe the key role played by carriers in World War II and concluded: "Our program was drawn up long before these events. Yet, even then, it was obvious already that aircraft carriers were essential, if only to protect the capital ships."[20] He added that the two naval officers most directly involved with shipbuilding matters, Admiral I. S. Isakov, chief of the Main Naval Staff (the naval operations section of the Defense Ministry), and Admiral L. M. Galler, deputy naval commissar for shipbuilding, both "understood the true significance of aircraft carriers"; yet they were "unable to sustain their point of view" in the Defense Ministry and "were not particularly listened to."[21]

As a further consideration given to the USSR's prewar naval strategy in his memoirs, Kuznetsov tries to account for Stalin's negative attitude toward aircraft carriers:

> . . . Stalin, who usually reckoned with the opinions of the experts, tended for some unexplained reason to underrate the role of aircraft carriers. I had repeated proof of this during discussions on naval affairs, especially during the approval of the naval construction projects in 1939. . . .

> I think all this was due to a tendency to underestimate the danger to ships from the air.

---

[19] *Ibid.* This also constitutes, of course, the clearest possible recognition by an unimpeachable authority that shore-based air support is simply not adequate for naval operations on the high seas.

[20] *Ibid.,* p. 259. In the English translation, again, Kuznetsov's words have suffered a subtle sea change: ". . . but even at the time it was obvious that aircraft carriers had to be there to give protection to the battleships." (Kuznetsov, "Before the War" p. 95.) The difference between carriers being "essential, if only to protect the battleships" and the need "to be there [solely] to give protection to the battleships" is just sufficient to constitute a major denigration of the multiple roles of carriers in naval warfare and to establish a debating point for asserting that with the disappearance of the battleship the *raison d'etre* for the carrier also vanished.

[21] Kuznetsov, *Nakanune,* p. 259. Only in the final book version are Isakov and Galler said to have understood the "true significance" of carriers. In *Oktiabr* (No. 11–65, p. 142) they merely understood their "significance" and in *International Affairs* (No. 12–66, p. 95) their "importance" (which is an acceptable alternate translation for the Russian word "znachenie"). Such small indications in the more complete and candid book version suggest that Admiral Kuznetsov was so convinced of the overriding importance of the carrier that even at present he would give small credence to Soviet propaganda that the military-technical revolution has outmoded the carrier.

The surprising thing is that his view on this matter did not change, even after the Great Patriotic War.

. . . .

On the other hand, Stalin had a special and curious passion for heavy cruisers.[22]

Most revealing of all, perhaps, is the answer Kuznetsov cites Stalin as having given to a request for increased antiaircraft capabilities aboard ships of the Navy: "We are not going to fight off America's shores."[23] Obviously, Stalin considered that the fighter aircraft of the Soviet naval aviation could take care of enemy air attacks on fleet units. Clearly this implied that the Navy would not be expected to operate beyond the range of its shore-based air support—a few hundred miles at most. Since this was to be the case, i.e., that the Navy was to remain essentially a coastal defense force, what justification for building such expensive ships as aircraft carriers could possibly be made? From this line of reasoning, one is certainly warranted in raising questions regarding why Stalin wanted to build the big, balanced fleet forces that he undertook so energetically and at such great expense in 1937–38. Did he really think that they would be able to operate in a strategically offensive manner on the high seas without any mobile carrier-based air power to accompany them? Presumably not, since it should have been clear to all that aviation had come to stay for the foreseeable future of naval warfare, and that ships at sea had an undeniable requirement for immediately available and sustained air cover at all times. It should have been equally clear that shore-based naval aviation could not begin to meet such requirements, no matter how large the size of the force.

Perhaps the most trenchant criticism of Soviet naval strategy since the 1920's (and obviously directed against Stalin's failure to develop a realistic theory for winning command of the seas) was expressed by Admiral S. G. Gorshkov, commander in chief of the Soviet Navy:

At the end of the 1930's the Soviet state set out on the course of creating a high seas ["oceanic"] fleet capable of resolving tasks at a significant distance from their bases. Powerful capital ships were laid down; the fleets received new cruisers, destroyers, long-range submarines, and other ships.

---

[22] Kuznetsov, "Pered voinoi," p. 142. Kuznetsov, "Before the War," p. 95. The criticism of Stalin for not listening to the naval experts' injunctions to build carriers is omitted from the book version. This omission may have resulted not solely from a desire to tone down the importance assigned to carriers but also from the fact that by the time the book went to press in August 1966 the indiscriminate criticism of Stalin under Khrushchevian de-Stalinization had given away to an effort to assess his historical role less harshly.

[23] Kuznetsov, *Nakanune*, p. 259.

But the lag of our military-theoretical thinking behind the steady increase of the strength of the Navy, the adherence to the previous [young school] views of its [the Navy's] use near the coasts which had been worked out in the period of the Navy's rehabilitation continued to constitute a hindrance which retarded the growth of our combat strength. . . . But at that time our military thought, like that abroad, patently underestimated greatly the enhanced military capabilities of aviation which, already at the start of the war, had become a powerful striking force in armed struggle at sea. To it [aviation], at that time as at the outset of its development, were assigned roles only as a basic means of reconnaissance and as a safeguard for the surface ships. This [underestimation] was one of the important reasons why no aircraft carriers which could have carried aviation for active participation in the combat operations of the Navy were built for us at that time. We did not even have any fighter aviation which could provide cover for warships at sea far from our coasts. . . . Thus even our big surface fleet, which began to be created on the eve of the war, actually was doomed to operating solely in our coastal waters, protected by fighter aviation from shore. This would not have had to happen if our military doctrine at the end of the 1930's had been directed to the full use of such qualities of a fleet as high mobility, continuous operational readiness, great striking power, and the capability over a protracted period of time for striking powerful blows at the enemy at a great distance from one's base. These qualities of naval forces were not valued at the time. Even then when the country was creating a big oceanic navy, the strategic principles on which its use was based were not revised and, as a result, they were left just the same as those which guided our Armed Forces in the period of the rehabilitation of the Navy.[24]

From the foregoing comments of admirals Kuznetsov and Gorshkov then, it would appear that Stalin was content with the wartime strategy of "active defense" which Professor Petrov had elaborated in the 1920's.[25] But why the big ships, the heavy cruisers and battleships, when they were superfluous to such a strategy? The amphibious assaults in the Northern and Black Sea Fleet areas during the Allied intervention right after the Bolshevik Party seized power and the USSR's internationally noted naval impotence in the Spanish Civil War suggest two complementary reasons: deterrence and prestige. Inasmuch as the Spanish Civil War had demonstrated that even the world's largest submarine force was not enough to command respect as a naval power for the USSR, big ships would be built as necessary in an effort to acquire the international prestige considered to be a prerequisite to success for Soviet diplomacy. Moreover, a big ship deterrent force was calculated to make the price of future invasions by sea greater than any potential enemy would care to

[24] S. G. Gorshkov, "Razvitie Sovetskogo voenno-morskogo iskusstva" (The Development of Soviet Naval Art), *Morskoi Sbornik*, February 1967, pp. 12–13.
[25] See Chapter II.

pay. So, with the exception of aircraft carriers, Stalin was willing to build the types of ships needed for a large, balanced fleet; but he appeared to have no intention of operating it in wartime as a strategically offensive instrument of force in the only manner that holds promise of victory. Stalin was right, but for the wrong reason, in the general type of balanced forces which he undertook to build. Clearly, however, in neglecting to build aircraft carriers, he failed to understand the extent of the "military-technical revolution" brought to naval warfare by the appearance of mobile, carrier-based air power.

As early as November 1936, the USSR began a concerted effort to obtain from the United States the plans, material, and equipment for two, potentially three, large battleships.[26] It was obvious that the United States offered the only possibility of assistance, since Japan and Germany were hostile and England, France, and Italy were fully occupied with their own naval rearmament efforts.[27]

The Soviet Union set out to win U.S. governmental support for their plan. Such support was deemed an essential preliminary to convincing American shipbuilders of the propriety and desirability of entering into shipbuilding contracts to build battleships for the Soviet regime. This preliminary aim was accomplished successfully. Working through the Carp Corporation, an American firm owned by Sam Carp (a naturalized U.S. citizen whose sister was married to Soviet Premier Vyacheslav Molotov), the services of a former congressman from Oklahoma were engaged as a Washington lobbyist. The President and Secretary of State Cordell Hull soon approved the Soviet project, reportedly on the grounds that it was desirable for the United States "to do nothing that would drive her [Soviet Russia] further into the arms of Germany."[28] Unfortunately for the USSR, the Carp Corporation itself inspired a notable lack of confidence on the part of the U.S. shipbuilders.[29] Also, the U.S. Navy was extremely reluctant to undertake the extensive cooperation with representatives of a foreign power, including the declassification of a large amount of confidential technical information, that would have been required to make this unusual commercial venture a success. Several key officers in the Navy Department, notably the Chief

---

[26] *Foreign Relations*, pp. 490 and 694.

[27] *Ibid.*, p. 465.

[28] Cordell Hull, *The Memoirs of Cordell Hull*, (New York: Macmillan, 1948). I, 743. A State Department memorandum of March 24, 1937 rationalized this decision on the basis of the following assumption: "It is considered that, assuming the evolution of the Soviet Government into a purely national government, the strengthening of the naval forces of the Soviet Union would not run counter to the national interest of the United States." (*Foreign Relations*, p. 466.)

[29] *Ibid.*, p. 671.

of the Bureau of Ordnance and the Director of Naval Intelligence, took strong and continuing exception to helping a totalitarian regime. They particularly opposed any moves to strengthen the Soviet Navy.[30]

The Soviet battleship project was pushed aggressively. In a number of conferences with officials of the Department of State in May 1937, Soviet Ambassador Alexander A. Troyanovsky alternately employed insults and cajolery to gain Soviet ends. He even stated that all battleships built with U.S. assistance would be stationed in the Soviet Pacific Fleet where they would help the U.S. Navy keep the Japanese Navy in check.[31] Even Stalin, himself, made a personal bid to bring the negotiations to a successful and rapid conclusion. He unexpectedly walked in on U.S. Ambassador Joseph E. Davies while the latter was paying a routine courtesy call on Soviet Premier Molotov in June 1938. This was an unprecedented act. Stalin had avoided private meetings with foreign ambassadors in Moscow in order to maintain the fiction that he was only a Party, not a government, official. In his meeting with Ambassador Davies, Stalin gave his main attention to the battleship project. The only other subject he mentioned was that he was reconsidering paying the debt owed the United States for American claims against the Russian provisional government.[32] This remark had all the earmarks of an inducement to the U.S. to expedite the Soviet battleship project. So strong was Stalin's desire to further the project that he even went to the extreme of insinuating that President Roosevelt could not be sincere in his professed support for the project or he would have overcome the opposition of the military "technicians" who were holding up the awarding of contracts.[33]

Stalin's venture in personal diplomacy was followed up in March 1939 by the dispatch to the United States of a Soviet naval mission headed by the Vice Commissar of Naval Affairs, Admiral Ivan S. Isakov. After two months in the United States, in which he held initially encouraging meetings with the Secretary of the Navy and senior Navy Department officers, Isakov returned to Moscow with no apparent progress to report.[34]

---

[30] These naval officers were mentioned in State Department conferences and memoranda as engaging in "obstructive tactics" to prevent execution of the Presidential decision to assist the USSR to build battleships in the U.S. Allegedly, these naval officers had threatened American shipbuilders with loss of future shipbuilding contracts if they accepted contracts to build battleships for the Soviet Union. *Ibid.,* pp. 481, 491, 676, 692, and 894. This charge was later discounted by Secretary Hull. *Ibid.,* p. 700.

[31] *Ibid.,* pp. 473 and 897.

[32] As a condition of U.S. diplomatic recognition accorded the Soviet regime in 1933, Stalin had promised to settle this debt.

[33] Joseph E. Davies, *Mission to Moscow.* (New York: Simon and Shuster, 1941), pp. 208–210. See also *Foreign Relations,* p. 572.

[34] *Foreign Relations,* pp. 871, 875, 881 and 886.

After Isakov's departure, Ambassador Troyanovsky continued to plump for the battleship proposition. Little came of his efforts other than to reveal that Stalin's ambition was to build battleships of much larger tonnage than those of any other navy.[35] As described by Admiral William D. Leahy, who acted for the Secretary of the Navy in this matter, the Russians wanted a battleship "nearly twice as big and half again as powerful as any war vessel afloat."[36] Moreover, as Navy Commissar Kuznetsov had announced, all new Soviet warships were to be designed, constructed, and fitted out with equipment of "the highest technical level."[37] Once the United States had made it clear that the USSR would be given no American assistance to build ships over the anticipated new treaty limits of 35,000 tons and 16-inch guns, the Soviet representatives acquiesced and continued negotiations on that basis.[38] However, they would not compromise on obtaining the latest U.S. technical advances, even though the details were still considered confidential. As a result, an impasse was reached, and by June 1939 negotiations had broken down completely. On the subject of this breakdown of negotiations with the Russians, Secretary of State Cordell Hull wrote in his memoirs ten years later:

> The Russians insisted, however, that the very latest American devices and inventions should be incorporated in it [the first battleship the USSR was trying to order]. The Navy was agreeable to permitting the construction of a battleship at least as modern as those we already possessed but was rightly unwilling to give away to the Russians all the latest secrets that American research had amassed over a period of years, some of which were being embodied in our new battleships then under construction.[39]

Thus, after two and one-half years of fruitless negotiations, the Russians lost all hopes of persuading the United States to build the battleships needed to form the backbone of the large, balanced fleet that Stalin envisioned.

The impending breakdown of negotiations with the United States for providing plans for the latest U.S. aircraft carrier design and for building one battleship and providing the material for one or two more apparently was anticipated by the Soviet leaders as early as February of 1939. By that time, the Soviet government had undertaken the construction of the

---

[35] *Ibid.*, p. 688. The USSR persisted in efforts to buy a Gibbs and Cox design for a 62,000 ton, 18-inch gunned ship even after it became clear that the U.S. would not build such a ship for the USSR.

[36] *Ibid.*, p. 682.

[37] *Ibid.*, p. 465.

[38] *Ibid.*, pp. 694, 696, and 702.

[39] Hull, *op. cit.*, I, 743.

first of its reported program of three battleships.[40] As Admiral Isakov stated in November 1938, the USSR had decided to build conventionally-sized battleships [within the treaty limits of the London Naval Conference of 1936] of 35,000 tons and 16-inch guns.[41] Subsequent developments supported Isakov's statement. The first battleship to be laid down reportedly was to displace 35,000 tons and have 16-inch guns.[42] Moreover, it was learned that the Soviet government had approached a French munitions concern regarding placing orders for 16-inch, 45-caliber naval guns.[43]

Every effort was made to speed up the construction of large warships. The widespread terror resulting from the Great Purge of 1936–38 was exploited to lend weight to threats such as the following:

> The workers in industry are obliged, as Bolsheviks, to fulfill the demands for faster construction by the responsible shipyards and, in the shortest possible time, to start the construction of still further [warships] of large tonnage and to raise still further the tempo of construction of the fleet.[44]

The speaker of the foregoing words, P. A. Smirnov, added that the successful accomplishment of the tasks he had enumerated would require the exercise of "revolutionary iron discipline," but would be accomplished at all costs.

No panacea was to be found, however, for achieving the speed-up that was demanded. At the Eighteenth Party Congress, which was held from 10 to 21 March 1939, Navy Commissar Nikolai G. Kuznetsov reported in a speech on the seventeenth that "ship construction rates are not satisfactory and Comrade Tevosyan [the Minister of Shipbuilding] was correct in saying that they need to be expedited until they catch up and surpass the rates of capitalist countries."[45]

All of this public and Party oratory appeared at least to have had the effect of spurring the normally lethargic Soviet bureaucracy to herculean efforts. This development was not surprising when the certain alternative to superlative performance was being shot or imprisoned. Setting down his observations and conclusions about the prewar period of intensive shipbuilding, David Dallin wrote:

---

[40] See p. 31 *supra*. Reportedly named *Tretii Internatsional*. "USSR, A Survey of Russian Fleets," *United States Naval Institute Proceedings*, May, 1939, p. 760.

[41] *Foreign Relations*, p. 707.

[42] "USSR, A Survey of Russian Fleets," *op. cit.*, p. 761.

[43] *Foreign Relations*, p. 707. The French firm was the Schneider-Creusot works of St. Etienne, France.

[44] Smirnov, *op. cit.*, p. 1.

[45] N. G. Kuznetsov, "Rech' tov. Kuznetsova," (Speech of Comrade Kuznetsov), *XVIII s"ezd vsesoiuznoi Kommunisticheskoi partii (b), 10–21 marta 1939g; Stenograficheskii otchet* [XVIIIth Congress of the All-Union Communist Party (Bolsheviks), March 10–21, 1939; Stenographic Record], (Moscow: Gosizdatpolitlit, 1939), p. 477.

Shipbuilding was pushed with utmost energy, since it was known that Stalin personally was directing the effort. There was "not a single plan of a naval vessel, of a naval gun, or a great or small problem in general, which did not pass through the hands of Comrade Stalin," reported Tevosyan in 1939. The main task was the acceleration of the shipbuilding program. . . . "Everything [again quoting from Tevosyan] must be subordinated to the task of accelerated shipbuilding."[46]

Even as late as 1939, the Soviet Union had only enough large shipbuilding ways to construct a very few major warships simultaneously. The Eighteenth Party Congress, in its March 1939 resolutions on "the most important construction work" for the Third Five-Year Plan, called on the Soviet government "to accelerate the construction of shipyards already begun for the building of ships for the high-seas fleet."[47]

In March 1940, it was learned reliably that Soviet battleship construction still depended on the import of material from abroad. A battleship slated to be named the *Stalin,* which was under construction at the Marti Yard in Leningrad, had all work on it suspended in early 1940 owing to nondelivery of armor plate from the United States.[48]

By mid-1940 the shipbuilding rate was still too slow to satisfy the Soviet regime. In his Navy Day speech of July of that year, Admiral Kuznetsov revealed that "the number of ships built annually is insufficient. It is imperative that their quality be improved and their construction period be shortened."[49]

Even foreign naval observers came to note the wide gap between Soviet proclamations and performance in warship construction:

There have been numerous high sounding statements by Soviet officials concerning the might of the Red Navy. When analysed, there is found to be a certain vagueness about these boasts, which is explained when examination reveals the slow progress made in the delivery of important new ships.[50]

In his speech at the Eighteenth Party Congress in March 1939, Navy Commissar Kuznetsov had noted that modern navies included ships of all types. He had mentioned battleships, heavy cruisers, and aircraft car-

[46] David Dallin, *The Big Three: The United States, Britain and Russia.* (New Haven: Yale University Press, 1945), p. 96.

[47] *XVIII s"ezd vsesoiuznoi Kommunisticheskoi partii (b), 10–21 marta 1939g; Stenograficheskii otchet* (XVIIIth Congress of the All-Union Communist Party [Bolsheviks], March 10–21, 1939; Stenographic Record) (Moscow: Gosizdatpolitlit, 1939), p. 145.

[48] U.S. Naval Attache "L" report No. 81–40 of March 18, 1940. U.S. Archives, Alexandria, Virginia.

[49] "Da zdravstvuet sovetskii voenno-morskoi flot!" (Hail to the Soviet Navy!), *Pravda,* July 28, 1940.

[50] *Brassey's Annual—Yearbook of the Armed Forces, 1940.* (London: Wm. Clowes and Sons, Ltd., 1940), p. 39.

riers, as well as submarines, destroyers, and other lighter ship types. Kuznetsov had gone on to state that the Commissariat of Shipbuilding already had delivered to the Navy "ships of large tonnage [undoubtedly a reference to the Kirov-class cruisers] and that the construction of the remaining types of ships [i.e. battleships and aircraft carriers] is being organized."[51] By mid-1940, the new Commissar of Shipbuilding, Kosyenko, claimed that the Soviet Union had undertaken construction of "warships equal to those of any foreign power."[52] Obviously, this statement was intended to give the impression that by that time the USSR had both battleships and aircraft carriers under construction.

Whether Stalin's expressed determination to build the greatest navy in the world was mostly propaganda,[53] or was sincere but had been daunted by the many difficulties encountered by his shipbuilding program, is not known. It is known, however, that by February 1941, Admiral Kuznetsov was not following the lead of earlier Soviet officials in speaking of building "the largest" navy. Instead, he mentioned only that the Soviet Union was engaged in building "a large" navy.[54]

Reflecting in 1945 on the continuing force of the Stalinist naval strategy despite the interruption of World War II, David J. Dallin concluded:

> The concept of a big Soviet Navy is by no means dead. The idea of a navy as a prerequisite to a successful world policy took deep root in the Soviet government in the last five years preceding the war.[55]

From the foregoing considerations, Dallin accurately predicted that the Stalinist naval strategy, based on development of a big, well-balanced fleet, would be continued in the post-1945 period. Dallin clearly foresaw that, "There cannot be any doubt that among the first objectives of the postwar period the rehabilitation and construction of a powerful Soviet Navy will occupy a prominent place."[56] That this strategy would not long outlive Stalin and that a reversion to the young school strategy of submarine supremacy would take place were developments that remained shrouded in the unpredictable future of Soviet politics.

The considerations that underlay Stalin's decision to build a big, bal-

---

[51] Kuznetsov, "Rech' tov. Kuznetsova," p. 478.

[52] Dallin, *op. cit.,* p. 97.

[53] Theodore Ropp has given several historical examples of possibly comparable Tsarist Russian claims: "As advertisers, the Russian Navy far surpassed the British Admiralty, and all sorts of wonders were always being announced as ready to come forth from [the shipyards of] Sevastopol and Cronstadt." Theodore Ropp, "The Development of a Modern Navy: French Naval Policy, 1871–1904" (Unpublished Ph.D. dissertation, Dept. of History, Harvard University, 1937), p. 115.

[54] N. G. Kuznetsov, "Na strazhe granits Sovetskogo Soiuza" (On Guard at the Borders of the Soviet Union), *Morskoi Sbornik,* February, 1941, p. 3.

[55] Dallin, *op. cit.,* p. 99.

[56] *Ibid.*

anced navy have never been officially revealed. Yet one cannot help but
ponder the reasons that led Stalin, immediately upon his ascendance to
unrivaled power, to steer the Soviet ship of state on a course marked
with such plainly visible rocks and shoals. What about the enmity that
such an effort would be bound to stir up with England?[57] She was the
greatest sea power of the day and basically hostile to the Soviet regime.
(However, might not the United Kingdom have welcomed a strengthened Soviet Navy as the counterpart to a German Navy undergoing a
rapid rearmament?) What about Japan in the Pacific? Germany in the
Baltic? France, Italy, and Turkey in the Black Sea? None of these countries could be expected to accept passively such major naval expansion
by the Soviet Russians any more than they had the recurring naval armament programs of the Tsarist Russian Navy.

The answer to Stalin's fateful decision appears to lie in a combination
of factors. Many of these involve the external threats to the USSR that
existed in 1934. Other factors relate to Stalin's estimate of the USSR's
existing capabilities and potentialities for responding adequately to those
external threats. One may conclude that the factors set forth below contributed to Stalin's fateful decision:

1. The rise of expansionist militarism in Japan, fascism in Italy, and,
particularly, of naziism in Germany since the early 1930's indicated the
probable outbreak of another general war before many years.

2. A world-wide naval armaments race of unprecedented proportions
had developed since the expiration of the Washington Treaty limitations
in 1936. Among other countries, the USSR's two most probable antago-
nists, Germany and Japan, were putting major emphasis on the construction of battleships and aircraft carriers.[58] To the coldly realistic Stalin it
must have seemed certain that those two aggressive powers would not be
making the vast outlays required to build such ships without entertaining
great expectations of using them in a war.

3. The Soviet experience in the Spanish Civil War had educated Stal-

---

[57] One can legitimately speculate that England was the prewar reason and the United
States the postwar one that Stalin was unwilling to go ahead with the various programs
for constructing carriers. That is, Stalin might quite conceivably have reasoned that as
long as he postponed construction of the one type of capital ship essential to high seas
operations to contest for command of the sea he would not offend the leading naval
powers by building other capital ships for fleets whose strategy, lacking carriers, would
necessarily be defensive. Such speculation is consistent with the known facts of the
matter but evidence as to Stalin's long-term intentions regarding carrier construction
is lacking. Hopefully, he shared his views with some of his top Politburo colleagues or
left documentary evidence so that all possibilities for answering the question central to
an historical appreciation of Stalin as a naval strategist did not disappear with Stalin's
death.

[58] P. W. Rairden, Jr., "The Soviet Sea Power," *United States Naval Institute Proceedings*,
January, 1948, p. 65.

in to the fact that sea power played a major role even in continental warfare.[59]

4. The 1936 London Conference further enlightened Stalin to the fact that the Western powers were totally unimpressed by a navy, such as that of the USSR, that had its main strength in submarines rather than in battleships, cruisers, and aircraft carriers.[60] From this experience, Stalin came to realize that Soviet diplomacy could not be effective until backed up by naval power (in the form of modern, balanced naval forces) of great enough strength to rank the Soviet Union high among the major naval powers and at least to make her capable of exercising wartime command of the seas in the maritime areas along her lengthy seacoast.

5. Enthusiasm engendered by the notable successes of the Second Five-Year Plan period adversely affected the objectivity of Soviet estimates of their ship construction capability.[61] The Soviet planners greatly overrated their ability to overcome the major financial, industrial, and international obstacles that lay in the path of fulfillment of plans to construct battleships and aircraft carriers. From the outset, the odds were against the rapid building of naval forces that would be powerful enough to exercise command of the sea in even one of the four Soviet fleet areas.

6. Since the establishment of the Pacific and Northern forces in 1932 and 1933, respectively, the Soviet Navy had gained considerably less restricted access to the open oceans through those two fleet areas. Having naval forces in these two areas, rather than having all Soviet warships bottled up in the Baltic and Black seas, should have widened Stalin's horizons in regard to the potential for further expansion of Soviet naval power beyond the confines of contiguous seas and coastal waters. At the

---

[59] Dallin, *op. cit.*, p. 88. Dallin writes: "The Spanish Civil War had begun and immediately naval power attained great importance. . . . Soviet assistance to Spain was limited because of her naval weakness, and the course of events in Spain meant, as far as Soviet intervention was concerned, a naval defeat." Admiral Kuznetsov has recently given strong support to this conclusion in commenting on the need for long-term shipbuilding programs for developing a high seas Navy: "I believe that the events in Spain were instrumental in accelerating this process. We had been unable to take an effective part in the naval control carried out under a decision of the Non-Intervention Committee; we were short of the necessary ships and floating depots. At that time it became especially clear that the sea was vital to us, that we needed a strong Navy." Kuznetsov, "Pered voinoi," p. 142. (Note similar quote from book version, fn. 26, p. 25.)

[60] Quoting further from *The Big Three*, Dallin writes on pages 88 and 89: "It was clear to Moscow that the Soviet voice in the London Conference of the powers was feeble because of her utter weakness as a sea power. . . . Is it true, it was asked now, that the Soviet state does not need a navy other than a defensive force of small vessels? If it is to enhance its importance in international affairs, submarines are obviously not sufficient."

[61] "These were the successful years of the second Five-Year Plan . . . the Soviet Union had become, people in Moscow believed, one of the most powerful industrial countries in the world, and there were no obstacles to her development as a great naval power." *Ibid.*, p. 90.

same time, Stalin may well have failed to take into consideration the geopolitical limitations on the safe exit of his naval forces from their fleet areas onto the high seas.[62]

7. Stalin considered himself a superior strategist compared to the professional naval officers who served in his armed forces. In fact, as early as 1919, Stalin had expressed contempt for Russian naval strategists.[63]

8. Stalin also considered himself a great diplomatist, capable of shrewd and tactful management of Soviet foreign relations under conditions of extreme international tension. In conducting Soviet foreign affairs, Stalin was indebted to two men whose downfall he had brought about: M. P. Tukhachevskii and Zinoviev. They had provided the theoretical underpinnings for completely opportunistic diplomacy that Machiavelli would have admired. From Tukhachevskii's writings Stalin was provided with the principle that judiciously selected diplomatic ties should be made to ensure that the USSR only get involved in war on the stronger side. Moreover, any such involvement should be effected under circumstances that not only would prevent the Soviet state from being subjected to maritime blockade but would ensure continuing trade with those countries on whom the USSR was dependent for strategic war materials.[64] Stalin was particularly indebted to the former head of the

---

[62] A critique of Stalin's naval strategy, published by the USSR in 1962, stated: "It was not taken into account that two of our fleets [in the Baltic and Black Seas] were based in inland seas and it was difficult to bring out [even] the Northern and Pacific fleets onto the high seas." (V. D. Sokolovskii, ed., *Voennaia Strategiia* [Military Strategy], [Moscow: Voenizadt, 1962], p. 98.) Although much of this critique, as part of the de-Stalinization process, was overly critical of the Stalinist strategy, the writer finds that available evidence gives substantial support to this particular charge.

[63] "At the time of [General N. N.] Yudenich's advances on Leningrad in 1919, Stalin attacked and captured from the sea the powerfully armed forts of Krasnaia Gorka, in spite of expert advice from naval members of his staff. He [so the story goes] telegraphed Lenin at the time: 'Have captured Krasnaia Gorka . . . naval specialists are asserting that the taking of Krasnaia Gorka from the sea amounts to tearing asunder all naval science. I can only bemoan the so-called science. In the future will act likewise.' " (Fedotoff-White, "Soviet Naval Doctrine," *op. cit.*, p. 614.) A Soviet naval historian, writing in 1963 while the de-Stalinization campaign was still being carried on actively, recounted this same story in order to refute Stalin's claim to fame as a naval strategist by adducing Lenin's alleged reaction: "On this telegram he [Lenin] put three question marks and wrote 'Krasnaia Gorka was captured *from the land*'." (Leninskii Sbornik [Leninist Collection], Vol. 36, p. 77. Cited in B. I. Zverev, "Lenin i nachalo stroitel'stva Sovetskogo Voenno-morskogo flota" [Lenin and the Start of Construction of the Soviet Navy], *Morskoi Sbornik*, April 1963, p. 20.)

[64] M. P. Tukhachevskii, "Voina kak problema vooruzhennoi bor'by" (War as a Problem of Armed Struggle), *Bol'shaia Sovetskaia Entsiklopediia* (Great Soviet Encyclopaedia), Moscow, 1928), XII, p. 596. "Tukhachevskii sounded a new note in Soviet writings on war in stating that the plan of war should find support in international treaties and agreements, which would make possible the concentration against the enemy of the largest possible force, or, at least, facilitate the complete isolation of the

Third International, Zinoviev. In his book on *The Teachings of Marx and Lenin on War,* Zinoviev had developed an adequate Marxist rationalization to justify a Communist state in entering into military alliances with non-Communist states.[65] Stalin seemingly counted heavily on his presumed ability, through diplomatic maneuverings, to keep the Soviet Union out of war until he could build up the powerful naval forces that he considered essential, or until his enemies were so weakened by fighting among themselves that little naval power would be required to bring them to terms.[66]

The controversy in the 1929–34 period which led to the replacement of the command-of-the-sea doctrine of the old school by the preference of the young school for a small, defensive naval force became a political issue. It was not until 1938 after Stalin carried out his purge of the Navy and the young school that he could go ahead with building the big navy that he had decided was necessary as early as 1934.

The 1938 purge of nearly all of the former Tsarist naval officers left the Soviet Navy without the knowledge and experience needed to command it effectively in World War II. In view of the purge of the Navy that he conducted and the huge warship construction program that he undertook, it seems warranted to conclude that Stalin considered a large number of technically superior, heavy warships (primarily to provide prestige and deterrence) as comprising the only essential element of naval power. In this misconception, he followed in the footsteps of an earlier, continental military leader who showed an immense ignorance of the fundamentals of naval power:

> Napoleon, genius for war ashore, bungler at sea, sought the easy solution of increased numbers and increased armament, "viewing naval affairs through the distorting prism of pure arithmetic." He failed for there was no one to use the fleet he created.[67]

---

enemy. Diplomacy should obtain guarantees for the maintenance of economic relations with other countries during the war and prevent an economic blockade." Cited by Fedotov-White, "Soviet Philosophy of War," p. 343.

[65] *Ibid.,* p. 349. Fedotov-White noted in 1936 that Zinoviev "advanced the theory that a socialistic state would be justified in entering into a military agreement with a group of capitalistic states in order to form a block against other bourgeois countries, presumably more dangerous to the Soviet state. This theory, which to all intents and purposes forms the stock in trade of Soviet diplomacy today [1936], was attacked as heresy as late as 1932 . . . Zinoviev's plan of military understandings with capitalist countries is being freely adapted by Stalin and executed by Litvinov." *Ibid.*

[66] Kuznetsov, "Na strazhe granits Sovetskogo Souiza" *op. cit.* "This policy [for enhancing the USSR's power position] is derived from those principles which were formulated with great clarity by Stalin in his report to the XVIII Congress of the Bolshevist Party [in March 1939]: (1) Peace and strengthening relations with [other] countries; (2) Avoiding involvement; (3) Strengthening the Army and Navy by all measures; and (4) Strengthening ties with workers of all countries." *Ibid.*

[67] Talbot, *op. cit.,* p. 653.

Clearly, Stalin entertained no illusions about being able to exercise any significant degree of command of the seas in wartime against the major naval powers. He could realistically expect to exercise a considerable command of the sea only against the smaller powers in the Baltic and Black seas.

It may be stated, in summarizing the prewar Stalinist naval strategy, the Stalin appears to have committed four major blunders: he destroyed almost all of the experienced and capable naval leaders; he prevented rather than promoted the construction of aircraft carriers; he overestimated the industrial capacity of the USSR to rush the warship construction program to completion; and he had an exaggerated opinion of his own ability, through diplomatic activity, to keep the USSR out of war for a prolonged period.

The Navy in World War II ★

The Nazi invasion of Soviet Russia in June 1941 soon brought an end to all capital ship construction in the USSR for the duration of the war. Caught in a period of transition from a young school to an old school strategy (without aircraft carriers yet built) and bereft of its most competent leaders, the Soviet Navy proved unable to adapt its naval strategy to the combination of strategic defense and tactical offense that the circumstances required. Instead, Soviet naval forces were relegated to a purely defensive strategy in which they either supported the coastal flank of the ground forces, escorted coastal convoys, acted as a "fortress fleet" to defend key cities, or as armed merchant vessels to provide logistic support to besieged ports. Even the contemporary Soviet version of the Navy's role in World War II does not find it propagandistically practicable to go further than to cite the two less discreditable of these tasks:

> During the Great Patriotic War our Navy conducted limited military operations . . . aimed, mainly at support of the ground forces . . . and for the protection of maritime communications, mainly in the North.[1]

Writing in the February 1967 *Morskoi Sbornik,* the Navy's Commander in Chief S. G. Gorshkov ruefully characterized the results of the type of operations that the Soviet Navy conducted in World War II as having only "consolidated the Navy's role as merely an assistant of the ground forces."[2]

Fortunately for the Russians, Hitler made an equally grave mistake in failing to take advantage of the German Navy's great potential for sup-

---

[1] V. D. Sokolovskii (ed.), *Voennaia Strategiia,* (2nd ed., Moscow, Voenizdat, 1963), p. 396.
[2] Gorshkov, "Razvitie Sovetskogo Voenno-morskogo iskusstva," p. 16.

porting his ground operations in the Baltic theater. So overconfident was Hitler of the ability of his Panzer troops, supported by the aircraft of the Luftwaffe, to overrun Lithuania, Latvia, and Estonia and to reach Leningrad without delay that he paid little attention to providing naval support.[3] The German naval forces assigned to oppose the Soviet Baltic Fleet were composed solely of thirty-eight motor torpedo boats, ten mine layers, and five submarines.[4] By contrast, the Soviet Baltic Fleet in June 1941 consisted of two modernized battleships, two new and one old heavy cruiser, thirty-seven destroyer-type vessels, twenty mine layers, and over eighty submarines.[5]

At the time of the Nazi attack, the Soviet Baltic Fleet and its two new heavy cruisers were based on the ports of the Baltic states, which the USSR had absorbed in 1940 under threat of military invasion.[6] Hitler's invasion plan, "Operation Barbarossa," envisioned rapid overland thrusts to capture Leningrad, Moscow, and Kiev—Soviet Russia's three most important cities—so as to knock Russia quickly out of the war.[7] However, the blitzkrieg of Hitler's ground forces through the Baltic States to Leningrad was delayed for several weeks by the defense of the Baltic ports—most notably Libau (Lepaya), Riga, and Tallin—that was made by the naval forces based there.[8] When these bases were captured, the two new Soviet cruisers, along with destroyers and smaller craft, were forced to retire to the eastern end of the Gulf of Finland. There, with the two old battleships, they were based on the naval facilities at Kronshtadt and Leningrad.[9] Prior to this retirement, German and Finnish mine layers had succeeded in laying extensive mine fields in the northern Baltic and the Gulf of Finland.[10] In crossing the mine fields, both new cruisers were damaged, and nine new destroyers were sunk, as were a large number of smaller craft.[11]

At this time, the Germans temporarily stationed in the northern Baltic

---

[3] I. S. Isakov, *The Red Fleet in the Second World War* (London: Hutchinson and Company, 1947), pp. 25–26.

[4] C. J. Smith, *An Outline of Russian History.* (Washington: Office of the Chief of Naval Operations, 1958). Mimeograph. p. 92.

[5] *Ibid.*

[6] *Ibid.,* p. 91.

[7] *Istoriia velikoi otechestvennoi voiny Sovetskogo Soiuza, 1941–1945* (History of the Great Patriotic War of the Soviet Union, 1941–1945). Institute of Marxism-Leninism of the Central Committee of the C.P.S.U. (Moscow: Voenizdat, 1961), I, pp. 351–356; II, p. 64.

[8] Smith, *op. cit.,* p. 92; *Istoriia,* II, p. 44.

[9] Smith, *op. cit.,* p. 93.

[10] *Ibid.,* p. 92; *Istoriia,* II, p. 84.

[11] Smith, *op. cit.,* p. 93; the official Soviet history acknowledges the occurrence but admits only that the mines sank "several destroyers, patrol craft, and minesweepers." *Istoriia,* II, p. 85.

two battleships, four light cruisers, and three destroyers.[12] With these major German naval forces backing up the mine fields, which were further reinforced to the point that surface naval backup was no longer required, the Soviet Baltic Fleet surface forces were effectively bottled up in the Gulf of Finland.[13] There, however, during most of the crucial fall of 1941, the battleships and cruisers provided invaluable coastal gunfire support to the Soviet ground forces.[14]

As a direct consequence of its reversion to a defensive naval strategy, the Soviet fleets and fleet air forces came under the over-all command of the Army "front" commanders adjacent to the various fleet areas.[15] The first unfortunate result of this situation was that the Soviet naval air forces were for the most part commandeered by the Red Army commanders at the outset of the German onslaught.[16] In the Baltic, moreover, the German Army's rapid capture of most of the territory in the Baltic States deprived the Soviet Baltic Fleet Air Force of almost all of its twenty airfields.[17] So the few aircraft which were left to the Baltic Fleet Air Force were handicapped in not being able to operate from the

---

[12] Smith, *op. cit.,* p. 93. See also Isakov, *op. cit.,* p. 25.

[13] C. J. Smith, "The Soviet Navy in World War II, 1941–1945," *ONI Review* (Washington: Office of the Chief of Naval Operations), October 1952, p. 7; Isakov, *op. cit.,* pp. 31–32; this disastrous development for the Baltic Fleet was treated in the official Soviet history with a delicate touch: "A new stage of combat activity began for the Baltic Fleet—participation in the direct defense of Leningrad." *Istoriia,* II, p. 85.

[14] Smith, *Outline,* p. 93; "In the first days of August were undertaken preparations for utilization of the artillery of warships and coastal defenses of the fleet in the ground defenses of the city [Leningrad]." *Istoriia,* II, p. 86.

[15] *Istoriia,* II, p. 62.

[16] At the time in the late summer of 1941 when the planes of the Baltic Fleet Air Force could have been used to best advantage to provide the necessary air cover so that the cruiser-destroyer forces at Tallin and Riga could have operated offensively against German offshore and coastal logistic lines along the Baltic coast, the official history records: "Practically all of the aviation of the fleet was enlisted for the operations against the German ground forces." *Istoriia,* II, p. 44. For three other typical examples of this unfortunate use of naval air power under the pressure of military necessity, see *Ibid.,* pp. 80, 81, and 86.

[17] *Istoriia,* I, p. 274. The same volume of the Soviet official history of World War II makes some noteworthy admissions regarding the fleet air forces which reveal that it was prewar neglect as well as wartime necessity that deprived the surface forces of their air cover and thus doomed them to futility: 1) "However, the qualitative composition of Naval Aviation did not correspond to the tasks assigned. The tactical-technical characteristics of the seaplanes, which comprised a significant part of the fleet air forces, did not meet the demands of the times. In the air forces of the fleet were few strike aircraft, that is, mine-torpedo and bomber aircraft." (*Ibid.,* p. 450.); 2) Naval aviation received "practically no new aircraft" but were given some obsolescent ones on the eve of the war when the army air forces were being built up rapidly with the latest aircraft types. (*Ibid.,* p. 455). This information is followed with the marvelous bit of solemn understatement: "The lack of reliable air cover can make more difficult the operations of naval forces in wartime." (*Ibid.*)

coastal air fields close to the forces afloat. Consequently, the German Luftwaffe was able to exercise unchallenged air superiority over the Baltic Sea from the early days of the war.

In air attacks on the naval base at Kronshtadt in September 1941, the Luftwaffe sank one of the two battleships, damaged the other badly, and sank the one old heavy cruiser.[18] At this point a second consequence of Army dominance over the joint armed forces of the USSR and subordination of each fleet commander to the nearest Army "front" commander made itself felt. The large ships were moved into permanent anchorages in the Neva River, off Leningrad, where the ships' main batteries could protect the sea approaches and could also be used against German ground forces then beginning the long, but unsuccessful, siege of Leningrad.[19] The remainder of the ships' companies were used as infantry replacements in the defense of the city.[20]

After the winter ice melted in the Gulf of Finland in April 1942, the Germans and their Finnish allies renewed the mine fields across the mouth of the Gulf.[21] Nevertheless units of the Soviet Baltic Fleet Submarine Force, assisted by a few naval aircraft, some mine sweepers, and PT boats, ran the mine fields and gained the open Baltic where they operated against German shipping.[22] For the loss of ten Soviet submarines and seven others damaged, the Germans were forced temporarily to adopt a convoy system in the Baltic.[23] By the following year, in the summer of 1943, the Germans increased their mine warfare and antisubmarine patrol activities, and prevented units of the Soviet submarine force from even getting out of their bases at Leningrad and Kronshtadt.[24] The German ASW barrier was maintained until the summer of 1944, and effectively prevented any major operations by the Baltic Fleet Submarine Force.[25]

As in the Baltic, the Nazi plan of attack in southern Russia was to capture the naval bases and ports by the use of ground forces supported by the Luftwaffe.[26] Unlike the situation in the Baltic, the Germans had

---

[18] Smith, "Soviet Navy," p. 7.

[19] *Istoriia*, II, p. 86; Isakov, *op. cit.*, p. 26.

[20] "In the fall of 1941 the command of the Baltic Fleet formed seven naval brigades and several other units for the defense of Leningrad. In their ranks fought more than 80,000 enlisted and officer personnel of the fleet." *Istoriia*, II, pp. 91–92.

[21] D. I. Kornienko, *Voenno-morskoi flot Sovetskoi sotsialisticheskoi derzhavy* (The Navy of the Soviet Socialist State). (Moscow: Voenizdat, 1949), p. 232.

[22] Smith, "Soviet Navy," p. 7; Kornienko, *op. cit.*, p. 232.

[23] Smith, *Outline* p. 98.

[24] *Ibid.*, p. 99.

[25] *Ibid.*

[26] Isakov, *op. cit.*, p. 67; *Istoriia*, II, p. 45.

no way of even temporarily providing any substantial naval forces for use in the Black Sea.[27] The Romanian and Bulgarian forces available to the Nazis in the area were of minor value[28]—only two operational destroyers and one submarine. By comparison, at the outbreak of the war, the Soviet Black Sea Fleet dominated the area with one modernized old battleship, six cruisers, twenty-seven destroyer-type ships, twelve mine layers, and about fifty submarines.[29]

As the Nazi troops swept into the Ukraine and the Crimea, the Black Sea Fleet concentrated almost completely on the defense of the seaports, shipyards, and naval bases.[30] The main commercial port of Odessa and the main naval base at Sevastopol were subjected initially to heavy bombings.[31] Activity of the Black Sea Fleet Naval Air Force was limited to one bombing attack on Romanian ports at the start of the war.[32] As for surface-ship offensive activity, two destroyer leaders attacked the German naval headquarters at the Romanian port of Constanta. Little was accomplished by this attack, and one of the two destroyers was sunk.[33] Finally, to complete the list of the few early offensive actions by the Soviet Black Sea Fleet, during the siege of Odessa in the fall of 1941, surface forces staged a successful night attack behind the lines of the Romanians. Again the cost was high. One battleship and one cruiser were heavily damaged while five destroyers and a considerable number of small naval craft and merchant ships employed as naval auxiliaries were lost in the attack.[34] Starting in the fall of 1941, the Submarine Force of the Black Sea Fleet conducted antishipping operations that inflicted fairly substantial, but far from critical, losses on Axis shipping in the Black Sea.[35]

After their initial use on the offensive, the bulk of the destroyers and remaining cruisers were only employed defensively in ferrying men and supplies into besieged Sevastopol.[36] By the time Sevastopol fell in July 1942, the Black Sea Fleet surface forces had suffered heavy losses.[37] These losses were primarily caused by the prolonged exposure of these

---

[27] G. E. Blau, *The German Campaign in Russia—Planning and Operations (1940–1942)*. U. S. Department of the Army Pamphlet No. 20–261a, March, 1955, p. 110; Isakov, *op. cit.,* p. 66.

[28] Isakov, *op. cit.,* p. 66.

[29] Blau, *op. cit.,* p. 110.

[30] Smith, "Soviet Navy," p. 9.

[31] Smith, *Outline,* p. 93.

[32] Isakov, *op. cit.,* p. 70.

[33] Smith, *Outline,* p. 93.

[34] *Ibid.,* p. 95.

[35] *Ibid.*

[36] *Ibid.*

[37] *Ibid.*

forces to German air attacks without provision of any air cover.[38] Two cruisers were sunk and the remaining three heavily damaged and rendered inoperable.[39]

With the fall of Sevastopol, an alternate Black Sea headquarters was established at Novorossiisk at the eastern end of the Black Sea. By the fall of 1942, the Nazi ground forces overran even Novorossiisk.[40] As a result, the Black Sea Fleet was forced to rely on inadequate port and repair facilities of the small Caucasian ports of Sukhumi, Poti, and Batum in the southeastern corner of the Black Sea.[41]

In January 1943, with the defeat of the Germans at Stalingrad, the tide of battle turned and the Black Sea Fleet attempted an amphibious landing north of Novorossiisk.[42] No gunfire support was supplied by the remaining destroyers of the Black Sea Fleet which remained passively in port. For the lack of gunfire support and air cover, the landing was repelled.[43] However, by September 1943 the naval infantry of the Black Sea Fleet was able to carry out a sizable amphibious landing and recapture Novorossiisk.[44]

Significant activities of the Black Sea Fleet came to an end in the spring of 1944 with the conduct of another successful amphibious landing that retook Kerch, at the eastern tip of the Crimea.[45] By July 1944, the Germans had been cleared from the Crimea[46] and the Black Sea coast, the Romanians and the Bulgarians had surrendered, and the war in the Black Sea was over.

At the outset of the war there were no significant German naval forces in northern Norway or Finland to contest with the Soviet Northern Fleet Forces for control in Arctic waters.[47] These Soviet naval forces amounted to eleven destroyer-type ships, twenty-seven submarines, a large number of motor torpedo boats, and numerous other small craft.[48] Operation

---

[38] Boris Voyetekhov, *The Last Days of Sevastopol* (New York: Alfred A. Knopf, 1943), p. 217.

[39] Smith, *Outline*, p. 98.

[40] Smith, "Soviet Navy," p. 11; Isakov, *op. cit.*, p. 87.

[41] Isakov, *op. cit.*, p. 88.

[42] Smith, "Soviet Navy," p. 25.

[43] *Ibid.*

[44] G. Kholostiakov, "Flag nad Novorossiiskom," (Flag over Novorossiisk), *Trud*, September 16, 1966; Isakov, *op. cit.*, p. 90.

[45] Isakov, *op. cit.*, p. 91; see also I. I. Markov, *Kerchensko-Feodosiiskaia desantnaia operatsiia* (The Kerch-Feodosia Landing Operation) (Moscow: Voenizdat, 1956).

[46] Isakov, *op. cit.*, p. 103. See also V. M. Kononenko, *Chernomortsi v boiiakh za osvobozhdenie Kryma i Odessy* (Black Sea Sailors in the Battle for the Liberation of Odessa and the Crimea) (Moscow: Voenizdat, 1954).

[47] Smith, "Soviet Navy," p. 15.

[48] *Ibid.* Reinforcement of the Northern Fleet submarine forces by five boats from the Pacific Fleet was completed between January and May 1943. (Arseni Golovko,

Barbarossa called for the Nazis to capture Murmansk with ground forces after an initial air bombardment.[49] As in the Baltic and the Black Sea, no significant naval campaign had been envisioned by Hitler, and no provisions for naval warfare in the Arctic were made in Operation Barbarossa.

Defense of Murmansk against the five divisions committed to take the most important city in the Soviet Arctic was assigned to the Soviet Northern Fleet.[50] Using the Soviet naval infantry forces of the Northern Fleet, backed up by naval surface units operating in the Kola Inlet between Murmansk and the attacking forces, and aided by winter weather, a successful defense of Murmansk was conducted.[51] The Germans had to abandon their plan to take Murmansk by land, and so to cut off the vital flow of military supplies that could be brought in to this year-round port to support the entire Soviet war effort. In the meantime, the twenty-seven units of the Northern Fleet Submarine Force began attacks on the German shipping being used to support the Nazi forces in northern Norway.[52] As in the Baltic, these attacks had fair success until April 1943, when increased Nazi antisubmarine warfare measures[53] greatly reduced the number of Soviet sinkings of German merchant ships operating in the Arctic.

The main role played by the Soviet Pacific Fleet in World War II, of course, was that of a deterrent force against attack by Japan. The Japanese Navy was fully committed to the war against the United States, so it was in no position to attack the Soviet Pacific Fleet. Consequently, that Fleet saw no action until the Soviet Union declared war on Japan on 8 August 1945. Even then, the Soviet Pacific Fleet's active role was only to last for seven days until the Japanese surrendered to the U.S. on 15 August.

Although the Soviet Pacific Fleet included two new heavy cruisers, two dozen destroyer-types, and more than sixty submarines,[54] by August of 1945 there were no remaining missions against the Japanese Fleet that urgently called for their use to supplement the ships of the U.S.

With the Red Fleet [London: Putnam, 1965], pp. 148–149). In mid-1944 an additional four submarines, nine destroyers, and one battleship were received from the United Kingdom while a cruiser and many minesweepers were contributed by the United States. (David Woodward, *The Russians at Sea*, [London: William Kimber, 1965], p. 214.)

[49] Isakov, *op. cit.*, p. 45.
[50] *Ibid.*, p. 46.
[51] *Ibid.*
[52] *Ibid.*, p. 47
[53] *Ibid.*, pp. 48, 50.
[54] Smith, *Outline*, p. 108.

Pacific Fleet in its assault on Japan. In the end, the Soviet Pacific Fleet Forces were used solely to occupy the territory which Soviet Russia was to acquire as a reward for her week's participation in the war in the Pacific. Soviet Pacific Fleet units and personnel made two landings on southern Sakhalin and occupied the larger islands of the Kurile Islands.[55] They also made landings at four points in North Korea.[56] Japanese resistance to all of these landings was light. Some U.S.-laid mine fields at two ports in northern Korea at which Soviet amphibious forces made landings provided the most difficult obstacles.[57]

The experience gained in combat in the Baltic, Black Sea, and Northern Fleet areas taught the Soviet leaders a number of lessons. Some of these lessons were reflected in wartime changes to Soviet naval strategy and tactics. First and probably foremost of the lessons was that of the indispensability of naval air support for surface naval forces when strong enemy air opposition might be encountered.[58] After the initial depletion of the naval air forces to support fighting on the land front, these forces were built up again as the Navy's vital dependence on them became abundantly clear. A lesson of equal importance, as far as the survival of surface forces was concerned, was the need for providing sufficient air reconnaissance and patrol forces to prevent extensive mine warfare activity by enemy forces.

Another lesson was that amphibious landings were highly effective, but only when sufficient gunfire support by surface ships was provided during a landing opposed by ground forces. A similar lesson concerned the necessity for close air support for amphibious landings when air opposition might be encountered.

There are, however, other important lessons that top Party and Army leaders, but not the Navy's leaders, obviously failed to learn sufficiently

---

[55] Kornienko, *op. cit.,* p. 261.

[56] *Ibid.,* p. 261.

[57] Smith, "Soviet Navy," p. 104.

[58] Writing in 1963 about the lessons of World War II, the Soviet Navy Commander-in-Chief stated *inter alia:* "During World War II it was determined that operations of large surface ships far from their shores without reliable protection from air attack had become practically impossible." (S. G. Gorshkov, "Zabota partii o flote" [Concern of the Party for the Navy], *Morskoi Sbornik,* July, 1963, p. 14). Of even more significance, in view of the Army's dominant role in defense matters, is that a prominent Army marshal has also acknowledged the importance of air superiority for naval as well as other types of combat operations: "The most favorable condition for the successful conduct of operations of air forces, ground forces, and naval forces is supremacy in the air, maintained throughout the entire operation." (Marshal P. Rotmistrov, "O sovremennom Sovetskim voennim iskusstve i ego kharakternykh chertakh" [On Contemporary Soviet Military Art and its Characteristic Features], *Voennaia Mysl',* February 1958, p. 82).

well from the experience of World War II. Major among these is that of the absolute necessity of mobile, sea-based air support for surface naval task forces intended for operations on the high seas. The Soviet Navy Commander in Chief had publicly acknowledged the need in WW II for carriers to provide an adequate mobile combat-air-support capability.[59] Even had the land-based naval aircraft of the fleets not been largely commandeered by the Army initially and deprived of most of their coastal airfields, it is highly unlikely that they could have provided effective close air support against attacks from any quarter of the compass.

Probably the most important single lesson that could be learned by the USSR from Soviet naval participation in World War II is that of the superiority of the tactical offensive over the defensive, even on the part of fleets forced to take a strategically defensive posture. It is unlikely that the addition of most of the Soviet Navy's aircraft to the fighting on the land front made any vital difference in the outcome of the ground fighting. On the other hand, depriving the fleets of their air forces just when they were most desperately needed did make a vital difference in the ability of the fleets to maintain the tactical offensive despite Nazi air opposition. Even after the fleet air forces were built up in the later stages of the war, they were used almost exclusively for the defense of Soviet naval bases. Had the Baltic and Black Sea fleets had their own carrier-based air cover to protect the forces afloat, including the carriers themselves, from the Luftwaffe attacks, there is every possibility that those fleets could have continued offensive operations and greatly retarded the Nazi offensive, to say the least.

It is customary for writers on Soviet naval matters to point out how greatly the Soviet Navy's geographic position was improved as a result of World War II. This observation is true when considered primarily from a defensive standpoint. In the Baltic, the Navy's defensive position unquestionably was strengthened greatly by the permanent acquisition of the Karelian Isthmus (to give Leningrad a northern land buffer), of the Baltic States, and of the former East Prussian base of Baltiisk (near Kaliningrad, formerly Koenigsberg). Baltiisk provides a year-round, ice-free base which has been made the headquarters for the Soviet Baltic Fleet. These acquisitions, plus the availability for use of the Polish and East German naval bases on the Baltic, have effectively given the USSR control of the entire southern coast of the Baltic Sea. Yet, nothing was

---

[59] "In all cases when line ships and cruisers were found to be without strong air cover, enemy aviation was able to reach them quite easily. When cruising in the ocean or open sea, large surface ships could count on success only when they operated in coordination with aircraft carriers." Gorshkov, "Zabota partii o flote," p. 14.

changed substantially to improve the Baltic Fleet's strategic offensive capability against nonriparian powers. The single fact of overriding importance is that the Soviet Baltic Fleet is locked into the narrow confines of the Baltic by NATO control of the Danish Straits.

Similarly, the acquisition of Bessarabia and Bucovina, in addition to the development of Romania and Bulgaria as Soviet allies whose naval bases are available for use by the Soviet Black Sea Fleet, have expanded Soviet control along the entire western coast of the Black Sea. Nevertheless, the Soviet Black Sea Fleet is confined to the Black Sea as long as Turkey and her NATO allies dominate the Black Sea Straits at the Bosphorus or Dardanelles.

In the Soviet Northern Fleet, the Soviet takeover of the former Petsamo region of Finland and the port and naval base at Pechenga do nothing to solve the Northern Fleet's wartime problem in regard to taking the strategic offensive: that of gaining access to Atlantic shipping lanes for her submarines. They still would have to penetrate the surface, submarine, and air barriers which could be thrown up across the Greenland–Iceland–United Kingdom line.

Finally, in the Pacific theater, acquisition of Southern Sakhalin and the Kurile Islands has made the Sea of Okhotsk a Soviet lake. Yet, the failure of Soviet arms and diplomacy to gain unimpeded egress to the Pacific from the Sea of Japan and the Sea of Okhotsk means that the Soviet Pacific Fleet is still denied the free access to the Pacific that would be required before the Pacific Fleet could play a significant offensive role in wartime. Unfortunately for the USSR, the one naval base in the Pacific that does have open access to the Pacific, Petropavlovsk, cannot be supported logistically overland, but is totally dependent on shipping for its existence. Consequently, Petropavlovsk is extremely vulnerable and can only be useful in peacetime.

On balance, it can be concluded that Soviet maritime defense capabilities were, in fact, greatly strengthened by the USSR's territorial acquisitions at the end of World War II, but that those gains have done virtually nothing to improve the Soviet Navy's offensive posture vis-à-vis the naval forces of NATO.

The Stalinist Postwar Period ★

VI

In the early postwar years from 1946 until Stalin's death in 1953, his prewar big navy views and the old school views of the senior Soviet naval officers were confirmed and strengthened by the bitter World War II experience of the Soviet Navy. The Party-Army line on the importance, even in the new nuclear age, of profiting from the lessons of World War II was reiterated in mid-1963 by the Soviet Navy Commander in Chief: "Only on the basis of such analysis [of the experiences of combat operations at sea during World War II] could one draw the necessary conclusions, both for the development of naval theory and for the practical construction of our Navy."[1] This formulation, in addition to containing the proforma genuflection to the Army-dominated experience of World War II, seems to constitute an implicit but clear admission that practice can differ from theory in building the Soviet Navy. So construed, it contradicts the Marxist tenet of an essential unity between the two.[2] The differences between Soviet theory and practice, as illustrated in preceding chapters, are often very marked.

As noted above, poor results were obtained in World War II by Soviet surface warships, owing to their strategic misuse as mere seaward extensions of the ground forces rather than their being used for the "active" defense (including cutting the enemy's sea lines of communications) for which they had been built and trained. Yet, the continuing requirements for surface combatant ships, as well as the strategically defensive nature of the USSR's early postwar naval missions in face of the naval superiority

---

[1] Gorshkov, "Zabota partii o flote," p. 14.
[2] "Soviet military science . . . is built on the basis of the genuine unity and creative interaction of theory and practice." *Istoriia voennogo iskusstva*, p. 5.

57

of the Atlantic powers, were given authoritative expression in 1946 by a leading Soviet naval theorist, Admiral V.A. Alafuzov:

> The surface forces have always been, and still are, the basic and most universal element of the navy. . . . They can operate on the near and far approaches to our shore, and therefore they are capable of defending against enemy efforts to invade from the sea, or against separate strikes at our coasts.[3]

The necessity for including aircraft carriers in the composition of the immediate postwar navies was also stated explicitly in 1946 in the highly reputable Soviet journal *Military Thought:*

> The conditions of modern war at sea demand the mandatory participation in the combat operations of navies of powerful carrier forces, using them for striking devastating blows against the naval forces of the enemy as well as for the contest with his aviation. Both at sea and near one's bases these tasks can only be carried out by carrier aviation.[4]

From the foregoing remarks it can be seen that the early postwar naval strategic thinking and ultimate aims, despite the passing of the battleship and regardless of whether or not Stalin could be persuaded of the need for eventual construction of aircraft carriers, remained basically unchanged from the old school strategy of the 1937–41 period of building balanced fleets with ship types ranging all the way from heavy cruisers through large destroyers down to PT boats and submarines. Whether Stalin might have eventually adopted a true Mahanian concept of contesting for command of the high seas once the USSR possessed a powerful surface fleet is impossible to say on the basis of the available evidence. To have done so would have required aircraft carriers, of course. The generally assumed obsolescence of the battleship in the new era of nuclear warfare was not contradicted by Soviet leaders who may safely be presumed to have been relieved at the disappearance of a class of warship in which Western navies had such a great lead and which was so expensive to build. An equally warranted presumption would be that the Soviet leaders fervently hoped that the West could be persuaded that aircraft carriers were similarly outmoded.

Only in the context of the over-all political and military situations and of the measures taken by Stalin in the early postwar years in a concerted effort to offset the United States' atomic monopoly can Soviet postwar naval strategy and shipbuilding policy be fully understood. The USSR

---

[3] V. A. Alafuzov, "O sushchnosti voenno-morskikh operatsii" (On the Fundamentals of Naval Operations), *Morskoi Sbornik,* August, 1946, p. 26.

[4] I. Schner, "Avianostsi i ikh rol' v operatsiakh flota" (Aircraft Carriers and their Role in the Operations of a Navy), *Voennaia Mysl',* June, 1946, p. 82.

was in a strategic situation of such obvious military inferiority that it was imperative to find ways "to deter the West from using or deriving great political advantage from its nuclear strength before Soviet science could break the Western monopoly."[5]

Stalin's success in accomplishing this feat, although unquestionably owing in part to the severe limitations on U.S. nuclear capabilities in the early postwar period, was based primarily on a high degree of Western credulity and the Soviet leader's shrewd practical use of the limited assets available to him. The bulk of the divisions of the huge Soviet Army were stationed in East Europe and in the western part of the USSR in positions most threatening to the security of Western Europe. A strategic bomber force was developed by the Soviet Union, and Soviet air defenses were modernized. Additionally, Stalin decided that he must rapidly build up deterrent and defensive naval forces in the four Soviet fleet areas (in the Black Sea, Baltic, Northern, and Pacific).

After America's initial isolationist reaction of "Bring the boys back home!" Stalin had observed the resurgence of America's global interests from 1947 onward. Under the Truman policy of containment of any subsequent Soviet efforts at further territorial expansion, U.S. aid was given to Greece, Turkey, and Iran to block Soviet efforts of expansion in the Balkans, at the Turkish Straits, and in the Middle East. Further curtailment of Soviet expansion was made through the Marshall Plan, which helped to rebuild the devastated economies of the Western European countries that were threatened more by internal Communist subversion than by direct military threats.

The deployment to the Mediterranean of the U.S. Sixth Fleet and the maintenance in the western Pacific of the U.S. Seventh Fleet constituted credible deterrents to Soviet expansion in the Middle East and in the Far East, and gave strong support to the Truman Doctrine from 1947 onward. These readily visible supports to the U.S. containment policy, deployed within atomic striking range of the Soviet Black Sea and Pacific coasts,[6] were augmented by the less visible but also highly credible deterrent constituted by the U.S. Strategic Air Command, with its intercontinental atomic striking force of long-range bombers.

Stalin's appreciation of the USSR's naval inferiority, compared to that of the major powers of the free world, was revealed by his 1948 ultimatum to the Yugoslav leaders concerning the Communist-inspired Greek Civil War:

---

[5] Marshall Shulman, *Stalin's Foreign Policy Reappraised* (New York: Harvard University Press, 1963), p. 22.

[6] Hanson W. Baldwin, *The Price of Power* (New York: Harper Brothers, 1947), p. 76. E. B. Potter and C. W. Nimitz (eds.) *Sea Power* (Englewood Cliffs, N. J.: Prentice-Hall, Inc., 1960), p. 855. Cf. Similar French critique of 1930 in fn. 9, p. 22.

What, do you think that Great Britain and the United States—the United States the most powerful state in the world—will permit you to break their line of communication in the Mediterranean Sea? Nonsense! And we have no navy. The uprisings in Greece must be stopped and as quickly as possible.[7]

As already implied in Chapter IV, Stalin's aims in building balanced fleets were unorthodox if considered from the Mahanian point of view that such fleets are fundamentally intended to contest for command of the seas.[8] As a major continental land power but a weak sea power, Stalin apparently was convinced that the correct naval strategy for the USSR was one of deterrence and defense. His probable views on what the Navy should contribute toward furthering Soviet aims might be formulated as follows: a credible deterrent against seaborne enemy attack; an adequate wartime defense of the USSR's extensive maritime borders; and a prestigious position of readily apparent naval strength (tonnagewise), from which to conduct the political, economic, psychological, and paramilitary programs of the USSR's long-term policy of "peaceful coexistence."

Eventually to provide the naval forces required for purposes of prestige and to constitute a deterrent sufficient to discourage the major Western sea powers from taking advantage of their sea supremacy, Stalin planned to build up a big navy, including strong components of large surface ships, submarines, and shore-based naval aviation. In the interval of the several five-year plans that such an ambitious semi-old school naval strategy would require for implementation, it was decided not to rely solely on the strategically defensive young school strategy of *la guerre de course* against merchant shipping employing submarines and "mosquito fleets" of light, fast surface ships and PT boats. Rather, Stalin chose an unorthodox strategic mixture of naval forces that combined with the

---

[7] Milovan Djilas, *Conversations with Stalin* (New York: Harcourt, Brace and World, 1962), p 182.

[8] Writing before Stalin's death in 1953, Raymond L. Garthoff recorded his understanding of Soviet naval strategy as follows: "The Soviet conception of naval functions and missions is essentially in accord with 'traditional' naval doctrine as reflected in the writings of Mahan, Corbett, Castex, Brodie, *et al.*, with the single important difference that the Soviets do not contest for 'command of the sea'." (R. L. Garthoff, *Soviet Military Doctrine* [Glencoe, Illinois: The Free Press, 1953], p. 363.) Dr. Garthoff was prompted to this important observation, in all probability, by the obvious discrepancy between Stalin's predilection for building a big-ship navy but without any apparent intention of using it to contest for command of the seas. To avoid a misunderstanding on the nature of Mahan's "traditional" doctrine, it should be kept in mind that the concept of the command of the sea lies at the very heart of that doctrine so it cannot be an exception, even an "important" one. "Naval strategy *is* the art of gaining and retaining command of the sea." (Admiral Sir Reginald Bacon and F. E. McMurtrie, *Modern Naval Strategy* [Brooklyn, N. Y.: Chemical Publishing Co., 1941], p. ix. Italics added.

forces suitable for a young school strategy major elements of the two other strategies of "fortress fleet" and "fleet in being."

The "fortress fleet" elements consisted of the forces of the Soviet Navy's Coastal Defense Service, including coastal artillery, fortifications, antiaircraft artillery, Naval Infantry troops (Marines), shore-based fighter aviation, and coastal patrol craft. These were forces intended primarily to provide a last-ditch, largely immobile, and passive defense against amphibious invasion.

The "fleet in being" elements were to be the destroyer leaders and cruisers that Stalin was intent on constructing to serve initially as strategically defensive but tactically offensive naval forces, to be kept in Soviet coastal waters but concentrated in the fleet areas considered to be most vulnerable or threatened at any given period of international relations. Ultimately, at least according to the Navy's plans, the large destroyers and cruisers were to serve as the major screening and supporting elements of the carrier task forces envisioned as the main striking forces of the large balanced fleets.[9] Construction of the aircraft carriers, however, would have to wait until considerably later, not only until the immense destruction of World War II had been repaired and the economy restored, but also until the funds, shipbuilding personnel, construction facilities, and blueprints could be made available to undertake the enormously expensive and vastly complex task of building, manning, and operating aircraft carriers.[10] Not until several carrier task forces could be brought to operational status could the USSR conceivably have been realistic in progressing to the adoption of a strategically offensive old school strategy of employing large, balanced fleets to contest on anything like an equal basis with the great sea powers for command of the seas, even in the peripheral European areas considered vital to Soviet state interests. Pending the development of such naval forces capable of challenging the command of the seas enjoyed by the NATO powers, Stalin's naval strategy clearly remained that of the same "active" defense that had characterized his prewar strategy.

The significant new element in the strategic theory implicitly underlying Stalin's postwar ship construction program—in all probability one which with the benefit of hindsight may be retroactively read into his "big navy" construction program of 1937–40—was that no longer were the submarines, aviation, and light "mosquito" surface forces of young school theory considered adequate; rather the larger, more heavily gunned, surface ships then in vogue (i.e., destroyer leaders and cruisers,

---

[9] Former Soviet Naval Officer, *op. cit.*
[10] *Ibid.*

the battleship having been consigned to limbo) were to be added to the other forces advocated by the young school to once again establish the "active" defense concepts first worked out by Professor Petrov in the mid-1920's. A highly edifying critique[11] of Stalin's post-war strategy, written by Admiral Gorshkov, the Soviet Navy's Commander in Chief since 1955, points out the logical fallacy in the "active" defense strategy of assuming that a stronger enemy would be willing to fight in well-defended inshore areas of Soviet choosing. Gorshkov described the Stalinist strategy as presupposing that the enemy forces could be drawn into "combat at mine-artillery positions, that is, into sea areas having strong [Soviet] mine fields and that could be taken under fire by [the USSR's] long-range coastal artillery." Once Soviet naval forces had been used so artfully as to inveigle the enemy's surface forces into "the mined area" and "place him in an unfavorable situation for combat," then those enemy ships that avoided the mines would be attacked and destroyed by the coordinated efforts of naval aviation, surface ships and craft, and coastal artillery. This comforting Stalinist postwar scenario of a successful defense against any attack by the NATO naval powers was effectively discredited by Admiral Gorshkov by the simple expedient of showing the limited extent of its applicability:

> Of course, such actions could have taken place in opposing strikes of the enemy fleet against coastal objectives, and also in the course of operations to prevent amphibious landings, so that their working out in the process of combat training was [properly] given marked attention. But the fixed objective of conducting all combat against surface ships by counting on the main strike being in one's own coastal waters . . . was unwarranted.[12]

Admiral Gorshkov's critique went on to a fascinating explanation, and one not without contemporary relevance, of Stalin's strategy of "active" defense being the direct result of the Soviet Army and Party leaders' postwar fetishization of the USSR's World War II experience:

> But at that time [in the Stalinist postwar period] the continental character of the last war, in which the main forces which had opposed the Soviet Army and Navy were the ground troops of fascist Germany, had left its mark on our naval art.

> By force of the specific conditions which developed, it was necessary for our armed forces to concentrate their main strength in order to destroy the basic striking groups of the enemy along a front of more than two thousand kilometers. Naturally, the basic burden of this struggle fell on the shoulders of the Soviet Army. All the other branches of the armed

[11] Gorshkov, "Razvitie Sovetskogo Voenno-morskogo iskusstva," pp. 15–17.
[12] *Ibid.,* p. 17.

forces, among them the Navy, directed their strength at supporting and cooperating with the ground troops. . . .

All that served, needless to say, as the major basis for recognizing co-operation with the ground troops in defense and offense as the main mission of our fleet in the last war. Nevertheless, the acceptance of these views as a basis for the postwar period without taking into account the changes in the relation of forces in the international arena consolidated the dominating position of the defensive tendencies among views on the strategic employment of the Navy; these were propagated in the postwar years so that the Navy was tied down even more than it had been before to the coastal zone which is controlled by the ground forces. In this man-ner, the role of the Navy as merely an assistant to the Army was con-firmed.[13]

The complete disregard of the war experience of the major naval pow-ers and the purblind application of the Soviet Union's World War II ex-perience to the postwar period is described by Admiral Gorshkov, in an unprecedented exhibition of frankness on his part, as a "stagnation" in naval theoretical development, at a time of revolutionary technological advance, which derived from "schematism" and "formalism" on the part of the top (Army and Party) leaders:

The strengthening of these erroneous conclusions also aided at that time the selection of the direction of scientific work for the generalization of the military experience of the Soviet Armed Forces in the Great Patriotic War. In this the main attention of military researchers was devoted to the operations which were larger in scale and in results and to ground warfare in which the Navy was not allotted a role. According to these views the wartime experience of the great maritime powers was consid-ered inapplicable since they were considered of little relevance for us.

[All] this fostered the establishment of rigidity in the combat employ-ment of naval forces, engendered schematism, and tied the hands of the commanders—the organizers of combat.

To just this, above all, was due the lag in the level of naval art behind the possibilities which appeared in connection with the development of technology and the growth of the economic power of the country. The achievements of science, which by the end of the war had given a new stimulus to the activization of fleet operations and to the raising of its combat capabilities, were not taken note of in a timely manner because of the element of stagnation and formalism in naval theory.[14]

By 1950 the Navy had proposed and had gained Stalin's acceptance for a ten-year plan that provided for the construction of big surface fleets. According to a reliable source this plan was definitely known to

---

[13] *Ibid.*, pp. 15–16.
[14] *Ibid.*, p. 16.

have included four aircraft carriers,[15] presumably an initial one for each of the four fleet areas. However, before undertaking carrier construction, the shipbuilding plan called for constructing a number of *Stalingrad*-class heavy cruisers, the first of which was shortly laid down in a Black Sea shipyard.[16] Concurrently, a number of light cruiser hulls of the *Chapayev* class, which had been laid down in 1939 and were unfinished when Hitler invaded the USSR, were taken in hand and completed.[17]

---

[15] Former Soviet Naval Officer, *op. cit.* Interviewed by telephone on January 22, 1967 as to Admiral Kuznetsov's statements regarding Stalin's negative views on aircraft carrier construction for the Soviet Navy, "Former Soviet Naval Officer" stated that, although it was conceivable that the Navy's prewar projects for aircraft carrier construction had been blocked by the Defense Commissariat and by Stalin's personal objections as Kuznetsov claimed, it was nevertheless certain that Stalin had at least acquiesced to the Navy's postwar importunings for construction of at least four aircraft carriers. Whether or not Stalin took into account the potentially great value of carriers in wartime or had any thoughts of employing them in the optimum manner for the strategic offensive, it seems unlikely that he would have been completely impervious to the lessons of World War II as to the necessity for carriers in the composition of a modern Navy that would constitute a credible deterrent to the Western naval powers as well as a persuasive backup for Soviet advances on the international chessboard. In his memoirs Admiral Kuznetsov repeated what may well have been the same lessons of the Great Patriotic War which were used by the Navy to influence Stalin to permit carrier construction:

> In December 1941, the Japanese destroyed the American Fleet at Pearl Harbor by means of extensive use of carrier aircraft. . . . In 1942, following the Battle of Midway in the Pacific, it became quite clear that the nature of naval warfare had changed, and that a new strike force—the air arm—had made its appearance at sea. . . . The Japanese admiral, Yamamoto, was forced to retreat, although his battleships had not lost their fighting capacity. Without an air arm he could not hope for success. (Nakanune, p. 258.)

"Former Soviet Naval Officer," when apprised of Kuznetsov's comments on Stalin's negative attitude toward carrier construction even after World War II pointed out that it would have been a typically Stalinist method to have permitted the construction of carriers, ostensibly at the urging of his naval advisers, but without incurring the political risks of personally endorsing a project without definitely favorable prospects until and unless the success of the project had been "demonstrated by life itself." It seems highly probable that Stalin's prewar approval of a similar initial construction program for four carriers was based on an equally tenuous basis of personal noninvolvement, particularly since he subsequently canceled carrier construction entirely. "Former Soviet Naval Officer" went on to relate Admiral Kuznetsov's appearance at a meeting of ship commanders of the Baltic Fleet in Riga in mid-1951. Kuznetsov told his receptive audience, including "Former Soviet Naval Officer," that the Soviet Navy was slated to receive some aircraft carriers before long. To his listeners the fact that Kuznetsov would make such a flat assertion was taken to mean beyond any question that the carrier construction project had already been approved by the "Government" (i.e., by Stalin).

[16] Former Soviet Naval Officer, "Soviet Naval Strategy."

[17] Unless otherwise indicated all subsequent data on types, armaments, and numbers of ships is based on the standard open-literature sources, namely *Jane's Fighting Ships, Flottes de Combat, Marinekalendar, Flottentashchenbuch,* and *Brassey's Annual,* covering the 1939–65 period. Since Soviet security often effectively concealed for several years the construction of new ships, it has been necessary in some cases to project their construction backward chronologically to develop the data given.

Additionally, construction of twenty-four of a new, large class of light cruisers, the *Sverdlov* class, was undertaken and probably at least six were completed with six more under construction by March 1953.

Concurrent with cruiser construction as a first step and preparation for building carriers, the Navy's postwar naval construction program called for large numbers of the other primary types of ships required for a balanced fleet: destroyers and submarines. As many as fifty large, seagoing destroyers of the *Skoryi* class were completed during the three years from 1950 to 1953, while about one dozen more were under construction. During these same three years, production of submarines was shifted from about twelve per year, of which ten were small-tonnage coastal submarines, to a tripled program exclusively of medium-range patrol submarines of the W-class.[18]

It is readily apparent that Stalin's long-frustrated vision of creating big, balanced fleets was just beginning to take shape when his death in March 1953 brought an end to both the concept and the guiding will that had made eventual realization of a high seas Soviet Navy an actual possibility.

Stalin reportedly took a personal interest in even the details of naval ship development and construction. Certainly, it was due to his personal views that the construction of a conventionally-weaponed high seas fleet was again undertaken in the postwar period. Stalin has been criticized by others before Admiral Gorshkov's February 1967 article previously mentioned for the time lag that took place in the application of missile technology to the Navy.[19] This lag probably should not be attributed to Admiral I. S. Iumashev who temporarily replaced Admiral Nikolai Kuznetsov from 1947 to 1950, since Iumashev was able to do little but carry out a holding operation for the Navy while the World War II ravaged Soviet economy was repaired. However, once Stalin had again established an independent naval ministry in February 1950 and rehabilitated Admiral Kuznetsov, there does seem to have been a considerable further delay in production of naval missile weapons beyond even the

---

[18] For details on Stalin's retention of most of his medium-range patrol submarines in the Baltic and Black Sea for defensive purposes rather than in the Northern Fleet, where they could have threatened the Atlantic sealanes, see pages 131–132.

[19] For example, this sarcastic statement by 3 Soviet naval writers is an obvious reference to Stalin's postwar direction of naval developments along conventional, nonmissile lines: "Originally [speaking of the postwar period], successes in the development of missile weapons did not influence naval armaments and operations to any noticeable extent. It was considered that the artillery of large ships fully conformed to the missions executed in naval warfare." I. Argunov, I. Zheltikov, and V. Larionov, "Rayketnye oruzhiia sovremennykh vooruzhennykh sil" (Missile Weapons of Modern Armed Forces), *Krasnaia Zvezda,* January 10, 1962.

very considerable period of time required for research and development. This delay may well have been caused by the inhibiting effect of the USSR's World War II experience in the development of Soviet naval strategy as Admiral Gorshkov has recently asserted.[20] Whatever validity this criticism may have, and it appears credible, Stalin found Admiral Kuznetsov's experience and inexhaustible energy of great value in again undertaking the construction of a big, balanced Navy.[21]

Stalin had hardly been interred before the independent naval ministry was abolished and the Navy subordinated to the Army marshals who dominate the Soviet Defense Ministry in the postwar period. This organizational step signaled the impending shift in naval shipbuilding back to one of constructing only submarines, aircraft, and light, fast surface forces—i.e., back to a young school strategy.

Georgi Malenkov, Stalin's immediate successor, served as chairman of the Council of Ministers ("Premier") for almost two years until replaced by Marshal Bulganin in February 1955. From this fact it might be concluded that he played a major role in the shift in naval strategy that followed Stalin's death. However, such was not the case since the key role in the Soviet system at that time, as now, was played by the chairman of the Politburo of the Communist Party. Although Malenkov had taken over this position upon Stalin's death, he was ousted from it only eight days later. In the "collective" exercise of Party leadership that followed for six months until Khrushchev was formally recognized as Party chairman, the latter was able to exert himself as *primus inter pares*. Consequently, it is to Khrushchev's record that one must turn for initiatives in naval matters from Stalin's death in March 1953 until Khrushchev passed into living obscurity in October 1964. Accordingly, it is appropriate to consider next what could well be termed "the Khrushchev Era of Naval Strategy."

---

[20] See p. 63 *supra*.

[21] George Katkov and Jan Kowalewski, "The Russian Navy and the Revolution, 1921–1928," *The Soviet Navy*, (New York: F. A. Praeger, 1958), p. 99.

Khrushchev and the Nuclear Navy ✹

VII

For reasons that will become apparent in this chapter, Mr. Khrushchev gave every indication of having brought with him to the leadership of the Party and the government a virtually complete lack of comprehension of sea power. The obviously great nuclear strike capabilities of the NATO naval forces should have made it readily apparent to all Soviet Party and Army leaders that if they hoped to develop even an adequate defense against carrier and Polaris strikes there existed an inescapable requirement for large naval forces, including aircraft carriers with both fighter and antisubmarine aircraft. Yet, Khrushchev and Marshal Zhukov, defense minister in the critical 1955–57 period of technological transition, both managed to delude themselves that just as long as these forces were armed with nuclear missiles they need only comprise relatively inexpensive types, notably submarines, light surface craft, and land-based naval aircraft. Khrushchev was ultimately to announce publicly, during his visit to the United States in 1959, that the Soviet Navy was scrapping 90 per cent of its cruisers and was revising its naval program to concentrate on submarines and small surface ships.[1] That not only some of the submarines but also some of the surface ships were being armed with missiles was further publicized by Khrushchev at about the same time.[2]

---

[1] Wm. J. Jorden, "Premier Strolls Through City," *New York Times,* September 22, 1959, p. 22. Khrushchev took advantage of the good propaganda hearing afforded by his visit to the United States and even waited for what to him must have seemed like an appropriate "sea power setting" aboard a Coast Guard boat before revealing what he termed his "secret."

[2] "N. S. Khrushchev has noted, 'We are retaining in service coastal defense vessels and patrol ships which have missiles on board, the submarine fleet which is also armed with missiles, and destroyers and minesweepers." "Udarnaia sila flota" (The Striking Power of the Navy), *Sovetskii Flot,* January 31, 1960.

From the most recently published article by Admiral Gorshkov, it is now apparent that the Soviet Navy had a hard fight in the mid-fifties against the missile enthusiasts to save the Navy from virtual dissolution as a separate service and to gain decisive support even for a young school strategy of submarines, surface ships and craft, shore-based naval aircraft, and coastal batteries, all armed with missiles. As in the case of the Navy Commander in Chief's critique of the postwar Stalinist strategy, the comparable critique of the Khrushchev-Zhukov naval strategy is of such importance as to warrant being quoted at some length:

> In the course of the discussion which developed over the path of future development of our Navy in the mid-fifties, there abruptly appeared a . . . struggle of the old views with the new ones not yet proved by life. At that time, too, were expressed even extreme "leftist" views. It turned out, unfortunately, that we had some very influential "authorities" who considered that with the appearance of atomic weapons the Navy had completely lost its value as a branch of the armed forces. According to their views, all of the basic missions in a future war allegedly could be fully resolved without the participation of the Navy, and even in those circumstances when to do so would require the conduct of combat operations on the broad expanses of the seas and oceans. At that time it was frequently asserted that only missiles emplaced in ground launching sites were required for the destruction of surface striking forces and even submarines.

> In opposition to the views which were accepted in the early postwar years as to the significance of joint operations of the Navy with ground troops as one of its [the Navy's] primary missions, views were advanced which were completely divorced from any necessity for the Navy to co-operate with ground troops in the conduct of coastal operations. According to these [views] it was considered that, for ground troops having nuclear weapons, support from the sea was unnecessary since, with their own forces, they could overcome any water obstacles in the way or even fight with an enemy fleet which attempted to strike blows against them from the sea.

> It was even considered that amphibious landings had completely lost their importance and that the tasks which they had carried out formerly allegedly could be accomplished in nuclear war by air assaults or the armored amphibious carriers of the ground troops.

> Obviously, the spreading of such ideas in addition to the still existing defensive tendencies not only interfered with the determination of the correct directions for the further development of the Navy but also held back the forward movement of our military-theoretical thought.[3]

It seems a warranted view that the high price tag of carrier task forces was a major and indeed the primary consideration in the decision of the

---

[3] Gorshkov, "Razvitie Sovetskogo Voenno-morskogo iskusstva," pp. 19–20.

Khrushchev regime to revert to a young school strategy requiring only a submarine, naval aircraft, and "mosquito fleet" Navy. This conclusion is based on consideration of the competing demands of other sectors of the Soviet economy (such as agriculture, consumer goods, heavy industry, and the space race), on Khrushchev's one-sided emphasis on intercontinental missiles and air defense at the expense of repeated cuts in conventional forces, and on frequent references not only to cruisers but also to carriers as being too "expensive"[4] and to the amount spent by the U.S. on its aircraft carrier forces as "colossal."[5]

With the reversion in 1955 to a deterrent-defensive naval strategy based primarily on submarines, the Soviet leadership voluntarily gave up their only two naval bases on foreign soil noncontiguous to the USSR— naval bases of strategically great value for the operation of naval forces. One was the Porkkala naval base in Finland that could control the entrance to the Gulf of Finland; the other was the Port Arthur base near Dairen on the Liaotung Peninsula of Communist China, a potentially invaluable Pacific base outside the confines of the Sea of Japan. The contrast between the Stalinist neo-old school and the Khrushchevian neo-young school views on the importance of large fleets and adequate numbers of strategically-located bases is pointed up nicely by the contrast between Khrushchev's voluntary surrender of the Port Arthur base only three years after Stalin had exploited the Chinese Communists' need for material assistance in the Korean War to force them, in September 1952, to concede an indefinite extension of the provision of the 1950 Sino-Soviet Treaty of Friendship, Alliance, and Mutual Assistance that had legalized the USSR's occupation of Port Arthur.

In announcing Soviet surrender of these base rights in early 1956, Defense Minister Zhukov went on to stress the threat constituted by U.S. capabilities for transoceanic amphibious invasions. It appeared that the Soviet leaders were intent on cutting their commitments to protect "overseas" bases that were, in the face of NATO naval supremacy, impossible to support logistically in wartime.[6] The USSR's subsequent failure to ex-

---

[4] "An aircraft carrier is a most expensive ship. . . . The present-day U. S. aircraft carrier *Enterprise* has a crew of 4,000 men. . . . [and] they are [all] highly trained personnel." I. Isakov, "Problemy voina na more" (Problems of Warfare at Sea), *Izvestiia,* June 3, 1962.

[5] I. I. Borzov, "Groznaia krepost' nad morem" (Threatening Fortress Over the Sea), *Krasnaia Zvezda,* July 18, 1964.

[6] "We have withdrawn troops from the military bases in Port Arthur and Porkkala-Udd and have inactivated them. In readying the [U.S.] Navy, primary attention is being given to creating the means for executing long-range naval transport and amphibious operations. . . . "XX s"ezd KPSS, rech' tovarishcha Zhukova" (XX Congress of the KPSS,

tort naval base rights in even a single one of such strategically located places as Indonesia, Zanzibar, Yemen, Egypt, Syria, Algeria, Guinea, and Ghana, all places where Soviet aid has been very substantial, gives some support to the thesis that the USSR still is wary of overextending its defense commitments to areas not contiguous to Soviet territory and, consequently, not subject to the pre-eminent power of the Soviet Army. A clear statement of the Soviet rationale that overseas bases are not required by the USSR in this age of intercontinental missiles was made incident to Khrushchev's rationalizations concerning the Cuban missile crisis of October 1962:

> Certain people depict the matter thus: that we placed the missiles for an attack on the U.S. This, of course, is not sensible reasoning. Why would it be necessary for us to place missiles in Cuba for this purpose when we had and have the capability to deliver a strike from our own territory, having the necessary number of intercontinental missiles of the necessary range and power?

> We have, as a matter of fact, no need for military bases on foreign territory. It is known that we have liquidated all our bases abroad. People with the least understanding of military affairs know that in the age of intercontinental and global missiles, Cuba, this small, remote island . . . has no strategic importance in the defense of the Soviet Union.[7]

To carry out what was tantamount to a shift to a neo-young school naval strategy, Khrushchev replaced Stalin's favorite naval minister, Admiral Kuznetsov, in late 1955 and along with him deliberately shelved the Stalinist old school naval strategy of building up powerful balanced surface fleets and of acquiring strategically-located naval bases overseas. In place of Kuznetsov, Khrushchev installed Admiral Sergei Gorshkov, a faithful Party man, a World War II flotilla commander, and a postwar Commander in Chief of the Black Sea Fleet. Gorshkov was known to have a strong interest in naval applications of missile technology. No more was to be heard for 12 years in favor of aircraft carriers. Marshal Zhukov, writing in *Red Star* in early 1957, tried a transparently flimsy if rather effective propaganda argument to explain the Soviet government's failure to provide the Navy with aircraft carriers: he said that carriers were only useful for first-strike missions since they were so vulnerable.

Speech of Comrade Zhukov), *Krasnaia Zvezda*, February 21, 1956. Max Beloff, *Soviet Policy in the Far East 1941–51* (London: Oxford University Press, 1963), p. 265.

[7] N. S. Khrushchev, "Sovremennoe mezhdunarodnoe polozhenie i vneshnaia politika Sovetskogo Soiuza; Doklad tovarishcha, N. S. Khrushcheva na sessii Verkhovnogo Soveta SSSR 12 dekabria 1962 goda" (The Contemporary International Situation and the Foreign Policy of the Soviet Union; Report of Comrade N. S. Khrushchev to the Session of the Supreme Soviet of the USSR of December 12, 1962), *Krasnaia Zvezda*, December 13, 1962.

Accordingly, they were only of interest to aggressor states like the United States and Great Britain.[8] This has become the standard Soviet line in a persistent effort to discredit aircraft carriers.

Although clearly not in accord with the neo-young school strategic theory which denied the utility of large surface ships and that had been imposed on the Navy by the Party leaders, Admiral Gorshkov neverthe-less contrived not only to keep the six postwar cruisers of the *Sverdlov* class that had already been completed from being scrapped, as Khrushchev had claimed they would be, but was able to continue the program for three years and so complete ten more.[9] However, in 1956 the cruiser building program was terminated with subsequent surface ship construc-tion concentrated in large destroyer leaders.[10] Only four of the cruisers that still were under construction in Leningrad in 1956 were eventually scrapped.[11]

Although none of the fourteen *Sverdlov* cruisers have been armed with the surface-to-surface missiles with which several classes of destroy-ers have been equipped, two of them have been fitted with surface-to-air missiles that would give them increased survivability in wartime opera-tions beyond the range of shore-based naval air cover.[12]

To prevail on Khrushchev not to carry out his publicly-announced in-tentions of scrapping 90 per cent of the Soviet Navy's cruisers, Admiral Gorshkov conducted a well-conceived and adroit but cautious, step-by-step campaign over a period of more than two years. Gorshkov's goal, politically speaking, was an ambitious and audacious one—not only just to complete and retain a large percentage of the cruisers but to gain

---

[8] L. Kitaev and G. Bol'shakov, "Vizit druzhby" (Visit of Friendship), *Krasnaia Zvezda*, March 23, 1957.

[9] The rationale for the downgrading of cruisers under conditions of nuclear war was stated explicitly by Admiral Vladimirskii in 1955: "The destructive power of missiles . . . has decreased the role of large ships . . . since comparatively small ships equipped with missile weapons can successfully defeat the largest battleships and cruisers equipped with conventional artillery . . ." L. Vladimirskii, "Novaia tekhnika na korabliakh" (New Weapons on Ships), *Komsomol'skaia Pravda*, July 23, 1955.

[10] *Jane's Fighting Ships 1963–1964*, p. 417. Actually, Gorshkov must have obtained a considerable reprieve for scrapping the unfinished cruisers. It was not until 1959, also during his U.S. visit when propaganda could best be accrued, that Khrushchev announced: "Military ships are good only to make trips for state visits. From a military point of view they have gone out of fashion. They have become obsolete! Now they are only a good target for missiles! Just this year we have permitted the scrapping of our cruisers which were almost completed." Iu. Stvolinskii, "Kreiser vycherknut iz spisok" (A Cruiser is Struck from the Lists), *Leningradskaia Pravda*, March 23, 1960.

[11] Hanson Baldwin, "Strategic Background 1958," *The Soviet Navy* (New York: F. A. Praeger, 1958), p. 116.

[12] *Jane's Fighting Ships 1966–1967*, p. 437.

practical, if not theoretical, acceptance of the continuing importance of large surface warships in the nuclear era.

In 1960 when Khrushchev informed the Supreme Soviet that "the submarine forces assume great importance while surface ships can no longer play the part they once did,"[13] Gorshkov was quick to affirm the Party line as laid down by Khrushchev, but with words just sufficiently qualified as to start a campaign for restoring surface ships to respectability without giving offense to Khrushchev. He said that ". . . surface ships can no longer play *as* important a role as they played in the past."[14]

Most significant of all the outwardly visible steps taken by Gorshkov to restore the good name of cruisers was his announcement in early 1961 that "large surface ships which have lost their combat value under contemporary conditions have been scrapped."[15] Although this statement might be considered to apply to four older cruisers and to the four unfinished *Sverdlov* cruisers that had all been scrapped, it appears that the Navy Commander in Chief was primarily speaking of the old battleships as the one general type that had lost their potential value. Since not only fifteen of the *Sverdlov* cruisers (one was provided Indonesia), but up to four of the older cruisers had been retained in service,[16] Gorshkov's words clearly reflected a conviction that cruisers still have significant roles to play in modern naval warfare. It has been reliably reported, for example, that one wartime role envisioned for the cruisers would be to disperse barriers of surface antisubmarine ships set up in locations such as the Greenland–Iceland–United Kingdom gap to prevent Soviet submarines from reaching the Atlantic shipping lanes.[17]

In January 1962, an unsigned editorial in *Red Star* very pointedly emphasized the importance of conventional ships: "Conventionally-powered and armed ships hold an honored position and are assigned a great role in naval combat operations. These ships and their armaments are very complex and are still being perfected in order to acquire new and modern capabilities."[18]

---

[13] N. S. Khrushchev, Speech to the USSR Supreme Soviet, January 14, 1960. "Razoruzhenie—put' k uprocheniiu mira i obespecheniiu druzhby mezhdu narodami" (Disarmament—Road to Peace and Friendship among People), *Izvestiia*, January 15, 1960.

[14] S. G. Gorshkov, "Nadezhnyi strazh na bezopasnosti rodiny" (Faithful Guard over the Security of the Homeland), *Sovetskii Flot*, February 23, 1960. Italics added.

[15] S. G. Gorshkov, "Na strazhe nashei rodiny" (Guarding Our Homeland), *Trud*, February 23, 1961. A month later a senior officer of Soviet Naval Aviation criticized those naval aviators who believed that surface war at sea was obsolete. S. M. Ruban, "Tri tochki opory" (Three Points of Leverage), *Krasnaia Zvezda*, April 1, 1961.

[16] *Jane's Fighting Ships 1966–1967*, p. 438.

[17] Former Soviet Naval Officer, "Soviet Naval Strategy."

[18] "Boevaia vakhta Sovetskikh moriakov" (Combat Watch of Soviet Sailors), *Krasnaia Zvezda*, January 9, 1962.

In the same month, one of Admiral Gorshkov's junior flag officers, Rear Admiral Prokof'ev, published a politically brash, if doctrinally sound, formulation of the need for surface ships. Quite possibly inspired by Admiral Gorshkov as a political test of strength by proxy with the Party theorists who were developing the neo-young school strategy,[19] Prokof'ev's statement included what can only be considered a gratuitous slap at those theorists if not, by implication, at Khrushchev himself:

> Soviet naval thought opposes the one-sided exaggeration to an extreme of any particular arm [of the Navy]. Naval combat operations will develop over enormous ocean and coastal areas and will require the cooperation of all forces as well as comprehensive combat support for the main striking forces—the submarines. Surface ships in particular will have to solve a large number of tasks which in contemporary warfare conditions have become exceptionally complex.[20]

Despite several derogatory public remarks about the Soviet Navy in general and surface ships in particular, Khrushchev made what for him was tantamount to a public bid for reconciliation after a visit to a Leningrad shipyard in the spring of 1962:

> Comrades, a few days ago I visited Leningrad, acquainting myself with the work of shipbuilding. Naval vessels . . . are very good. In the past we frequently criticized our naval comrades for shortcomings in the development of the Navy, and demanded that it be improved. This criticism has not been wasted. What I saw were ships which fully conform to contemporary naval development, to the modern developments in military science and technology.[21]

It would seem from the foregoing remarks that the Navy Commander in Chief had scored a really remarkable success in changing Khrushchev's unfavorable opinion of surface ships. Admiral Gorshkov's final step in withdrawing surface ships from the obscurity to which the Party's military theorists seemed determined to relegate them was taken two months later. He stated in an article published in *Pravda* that surface missile ships armed with missile weapons are equally as important as

---

[19] "The Communist Party and its Central Committee probe deeply into all the important problems of the strengthening of the maritime defense of the country, defining the path of further modernization of the Navy." "Partiia—Stroitel' flota i vospitatel' ego kadrov" (The Party—Builder of the Navy and the Instructor of Its Cadres), *Sovetskii Flot,* July 25, 1958.

[20] V. Prokof'ev, "Glavnaia udarnaia sila v voine na more" (Principal Striking Power in Warfare at Sea), *Krasnaia Zvezda,* January 13, 1962.

[21] N. S. Khrushchev, "Za novye uspekhii, rech' tovarishego N. S. Khrushcheva na vsesoiuznom soveschanii rabotnikov zheleznodorozhnogo transporta 10 maia 1962 goda" (Toward New Successes, Speech of Comrade N. S. Khrushchev at the All-Union Conference of the Workers of Railroad Transport, May 10, 1962), *Trud,* May 11, 1962.

submarines.[22] This would have been considered heresy two years earlier when Khrushchev was carried away by his initial overenthusiasm for missile submarines to the virtual exclusion of all other types of ships.

With the victory won in gaining acceptance for surface ships, Admiral Gorshkov, in mid-1963, seemingly completed his surface-ship sales campaign with a general statement of the roles of such ships in the Soviet Navy in the nuclear age. His statement was prefaced, as usual, with the requisite genuflections to the Party-line view of the hallowed pre-eminence of submarines which by then had been joined by missile-carrying aircraft:

> Modern submarines and missile-carrying aircraft comprise the principal striking forces of the Navy and are the essence of its power. Yet, there must be other forces besides the long-range strike forces both for active defense against any enemy within the limits of the defense zone of a maritime theatre and for the comprehensive support of the combat and operational activities of the main striking forces of the Navy. To such forces belong surface missile ships and small craft, warships and aircraft for antisubmarine warfare, minesweepers, warships and merchant ships of special [KGB or naval auxiliary] designation, coastal missile units, etc.[23]

In consideration of these exceptionally important surface-ship aspects of current Soviet naval strategy, a comment would seem to be in order on the circumspection and success that attended Admiral Gorshkov's efforts to reverse Khrushchev's initial low opinion of surface ships, especially cruisers, and gain open acceptance of them on a practical, if not on a theoretical, basis. In addition to being intrinsically interesting as an example of how political opposition, even to top Party dictates, by gradual theoretical changes can sometimes be successfully carried out in the USSR, this achievement by the Soviet Navy Commander in Chief has merited examination because of another reason. It is important as the major significant exception made by the Party's leadership as a practical matter to the largely impractical concepts of the neo-young school of

---

[22] "On a level with submarines in the armament of our Navy are surface ships carrying missile weapons and the latest equipment." S. G. Gorshkov, "Vernye syny rodiny" (True Sons of the Homeland), *Pravda,* July 29, 1962.

[23] Gorshkov, "Zabota partii o flote," p. 16. A year before the only other Soviet Fleet Admiral, Ivan Isakov, had made an emphatic case for a surface navy to protect Soviet maritime communications. In the process, Isakov admitted that Soviet naval operations would have to be strategically defensive: "As long as the population of our planet continues to move freight along sea lanes and as long as there is a merchant navy in existence nothing but a navy can insure the security of these movements along sea communications lines. Certainly, under special conditions, there will be a possibility of protecting sea communications by means of missiles, aircraft, and other means [that is, submarines]. Yet, a surface fleet cannot be dispensed with. Even in the case of strategic defense, it will be necessary to make use of maritime communications." Isakov, "Problemy voiny na more."

Party theoreticians. A recent article reveals how completely the Communist Party theorists dominate the formulation of military doctrine, and how they make pretensions to having completely worked out comprehensive military and naval doctrine right down to the types and numbers of weapons systems to be provided to each of the armed services:

> The strengthening of our Army and Navy in significant measure depends on the development of military-theoretical ideas. Military scientific cadres of the Central Committee of the Party deeply study and elaborate the new process of armed combat, the character and characteristics of contemporary war. On this basis has been worked out Soviet military doctrine, that is, the objective and complete system of views on the essence and character of contemporary warfare, on the means, equipment, and methods of successful defense of our state and of the entire socialist camp from imperialist aggression, which has been adopted by the Party and government. In correspondence with them, new regulations and procedures have been worked out which teach the characteristics of possible nuclear-missile warfare.[24]

In view of the formidably complete control of strategy formulation exercised by the Party,[25] Admiral Gorshkov's accomplishment in restoring surface ships to a state of practical, if not doctrinal, respectability takes on added luster.

Khrushchev revealed that it was in 1954, the year after Stalin's death, that the Party decision was made to shift from "obsolete" surface ships to a Navy based mainly on submarines.[26] In mid-1955, Admiral Vladi-

---

[24] L. Sytov, "Vooruzhennye Sily SSSR v poslevoennyi period" (The Armed Forces of the USSR in the Postwar Period), *Kommunist Vooruzhennykh Sil,* February, 1964, p. 69.

[25] Although the leading U.S. specialists on Soviet military affairs are undoubtedly aware of the Party's dominance in military decision-making on strategic matters, the effects of this dominance on naval strategy have not been generally understood. For example, Thomas Wolfe has shown an unawareness of how very little Soviet naval leaders have to say about naval policy formulation by his misunderstanding of the reason that motivated a *naval* writer, Admiral Alafuzov, to limit his consideration for the use of missile submarines to the primarily *naval* role of cruise missile-launching submarines against aircraft carriers rather than to take up the role of ballistic missile submarines as a component of the USSR's strategic nuclear deterrent forces. (Thomas W. Wolfe, *Soviet Strategy at the Crossroads* [Santa Monica, California: The Rand Corporation, 1964], Memorandum RM-4085-PR of April, 1964, p. 232.) Similarly Dr. Herbert S. Dinerstein has shown the same lack of appreciation in making the assumption that the fact that Soviet naval officers put a high value on a particular ship type was tantamount to its enjoying equally great appreciation and support by Party and Army leaders. For the ship type in question in this case—ballistic missile submarines—there is good reason to distinguish between naval approval and that of the Army and Party leaders, as will be brought out subsequently. (H. S. Dinerstein, *War and the Soviet Union* [New York: F. A. Praeger, 1962], p. 237.)

[26] Khrushchev was quoted by Admiral Kasatonov on the making of the fateful decision in 1954 to abandon plans for building big, balanced fleets in favor of building a Navy whose striking power would be concentrated largely in submarines: "Coming to

mirskii reported that "great attention is being paid to increasing the combat power of the Navy."[27] He also accurately forecast the main direction which the modernization of the Soviet Navy was to take initially as one of primarily a submarine-surface-air defense of employing missiles against NATO aircraft carriers.[28]

However, it was not until after the Twentieth Party Congress in 1956 that the modernization program for the Navy was given maximum emphasis.[29] The Defense minister, Marshal Zhukov, supported this program by informing the delegates to the Congress that "in building the Navy we hold that warfare in naval theaters of a future war will acquire immeasurably greater significance than was the case in the last war."[30] What underlay this change was clearly stated in the revised edition of *Military Strategy* in 1963: "The Navy's overall importance in a future war is determined by the new missions assigned it, especially combat with the enemy's navy, whether the latter is at sea or in port."[31] This modernization primarily involved providing jet aircraft to Naval Aviation[32] and missilizing the Navy's submarines, aircraft, light surface ships and craft, and coastal defense batteries.[33]

By 1958 there was a virtual cessation of the Soviet submarine construction program of as many as 60 new underseas craft per year.[34] As

---

the reception of graduates of the military academies of the Armed Forces of the USSR on 8 July of this year [1964], Nikita Sergeevich Khrushchev related how ten years ago arose the problem of the necessity for transforming the armaments of our Navy, which were based in the main at that time on cruisers, destroyers, and other surface ships. Those armaments largely had become obsolete for the conduct of war under contemporary conditions. It was then that the decision was made to create a submarine fleet as the main basis for our Navy." V. A. Kasatonov, "Boevaia vakhta Sovetskikh moriakov" (Combat Watch of Soviet Sailors), *Krasnaia Zvezda*, July 26, 1964.

[27] L. Vladimirskii, "Moguchii Voenno-morskoi flot Sovetskogo gosudarstva" (Mighty Navy of the Soviet State), *Leningradskaia Pravda*, July 24, 1955.

[28] "The answer to the capital ships [i.e., aircraft carriers and cruisers] is the guided missile launched from an aircraft, a submarine or a small, fast surface ship." Vladimirskii, "Novaia tekhnika na korabliakh."

[29] The full technical modernization of the armament of the Army and Navy was particularly increased after the XXth Congress of the Communist Party of the Soviet Union (1956) and related to the revolution in military affairs." Sytov, *op. cit.*, p. 68.

[30] Zhukov, *op. cit.*

[31] Sokolovskii, *op. cit.*, 2nd ed., p. 248. On page 312 of the same edition, the view is repeated: ". . . the Navy's basic mission in a contemporary war will be combat with the naval forces of the enemy at sea and at bases."

[32] "[By 1956] the forces of aviation were completely equipped with modern jet aircraft." Vooruzhennie Sily SSSR" (The Armed Forces of the USSR), *Bol'shaia Sovetskaia Entsiklopediia, Ezhegodnik 1957g.* (Moscow: Gosnaukizdat, 1957), p. 45.

[33] Sokolovskii, *op. cit.*, 1st ed., p. 400.

[34] Adjusting *Jane's* data of the 1951–61 period with data in subsequent issues of *Jane's* and other published releases, it is apparent that the construction of conventional submarines nearly doubled over the 1951–53 high of about thirty-six per year. See Claude Huan, "The Soviet Submarine Force," *Naval Review 1964* (Annapolis: U. S. Naval

this lull continued into 1960 it became clear that it was incident to a partial shift to missiles and nuclear propulsion.[35]

An article in the Navy's newspaper pointed out that all future U.S. submarines were to have nuclear propulsion, clearly implying that the USSR should have made the same decision.[36] Later statements by top Soviet defense ministry officials confirmed that diesel-powered submarines would continue to be maintained since they could be employed against aircraft carriers as well as used in an anti-shipping role in any future war.[37] In fact, the USSR has continued to build substantial numbers of diesel-powered submarines not only of torpedo-attack types but also others armed with either ballistic or guided missiles.[38] Obviously, nuclear propulsion plants are too expensive to be installed in all new Soviet submarines despite the exceptionally great advantages to be accrued in underwater endurance and speed.

Progress in applying missile technology to the Navy was far enough along that, by May 1960, Khrushchev could report to the Supreme Soviet that the Navy's forces "are in the process of converting to missile weapons and, strictly speaking, have already made the changeover."[39]

The most recent reliable data publicly available credits the Soviet

---

Institute, 1964), p. 55. In *Flottes de Combat 1962*, p. 357, the rate of Soviet submarine construction in 1954 is given as fifty-two per year. See also John W. Finney, "Soviet Held Shifting to Atomic Submarines," *New York Times*, December 19, 1957, p. 1.

[35] "Both [Vice Admiral W. V.] Davis [Deputy Chief of Naval Operations for Air] and [Rear Admiral H. G.] Rickover agreed that Russia . . . now has slowed down submarine construction. Davis said that the Soviets' frantic submarine construction program has practically halted. Davis said this meant that the Soviets planned to revise their program." Thom Nelson, United Press release, *Washington Post*, April 10, 1958, p. 1.

[36] "Nadezhnyi strazh sovetskikh morskikh rubezhei" (Faithful Guard of the Maritime Borders), *Sovetskii Flot*, July 20, 1960.

[37] V. Sokolovskii and M. Cherednichenko, "Voennoe iskusstvo na novom etape" (Military Art at a New Stage), *Krasnaia Zvezda*, August 28, 1964: "Even diesel-electric submarines with modern weapons have not lost their significance [against aircraft carriers]." Also, "Diesel-electric submarines will obviously still be used against lines of communications." Sokolovskii, *op. cit.*, 2nd ed., p. 401.

[38] *Jane's Fighting Ships 1966–1967*, pp. 433–435. This edition of *Jane's*, which was published late in 1966, credits the Soviet Navy with forty recently-constructed, long-range, conventionally-powered torpedo-attack submarines of the F-Class.

[39] N. S. Khrushchev, "Zakliuchitel'noe slovo tovarishcha N. S. Khrushcheva na zasedanii Verkhovnogo Soveta SSSR 7 Maia 1960 goda" (Concluding Remarks of Comrade N. S. Khrushchev to the Supreme Soviet Session of May 7, 1960), *Krasnaia Zvezda*, May 8, 1960. Whatever the reservation was that caused Khrushchev to use the "strictly speaking" qualifier, a senior military officer put the application of missiles to all of the armed forces into the past tense when he wrote on the subject two days after Khrushchev's speech: ". . . the USSR Armed Forces have been equipped with first-class, formidable modern weapons. On the decision of the Soviet state, the Army and Navy have shifted over to missile weapons." F. I. Golikov, "Velikie plody velikoi pobedy" (Great Fruits of a Great Victory), *Krasnaia Zvezda*, May 9, 1960.

Navy as having about 385 modern submarines, plus obsolescent coastal units.[40] Additional data from *Jane's Fighting Ships 1966–1967,* although not generally as reliable as more official sources, indicate that, as of the beginning of 1967, the Soviet Navy had roughly 82 missile submarines of which 28 were estimated to be nuclear-powered.[41] Of the 82 missile submarines, 53 carry ballistic missiles but with only 13 of them nuclear-powered.[42] Soviet strategists acknowledge that ballistic missile submarines are designed for use against land targets.[43] The other 29 missile submarines, of which 15 reportedly are nuclear-powered, are armed with guided (air-breathing cruise) missiles.[44] These types, Soviet writers admit, are primarily designed as antiship weapons,[45] although they could be used but with markedly less accuracy against coastal targets.

Of the total of 385 modern Soviet submarines 25 are of the medium-range Q-class suitable only for operations in coastal waters or in the Baltic, Black Sea, or Caspian, largely for training and experimental work. Subtracting the 25 coastal units and the 82 missile submarines from the 385 figure, the remaining 278 are long-range torpedo attack classes, including 12 or so with nuclear propulsion.[46] After probable use during the nuclear-exchange period of any general war, along with other suitable forces, in efforts to forestall nuclear strikes by NATO carrier forces and Polaris submarines, it would be whatever part of these 278 submarines not required for the continuing large defensive tasks to counter NATO's Polaris submarines, strike carriers, torpedo attack submarines, and amphibious forces that could be used subsequently against Free World shipping (should the war be a protracted one).

The Soviet Northern Fleet is estimated to include from 150 to 175, or up to 44 per cent of the total number of 400 Soviet submarines.[47] One

---

[40] By dropping the 15 M-V coastal submarines given in *Jane's Fighting Ships 1966–1967,* p. 436, the 400 total Soviet submarine figure given by Vice Admiral C. B. Martell, U.S. Navy, to a Pentagon news conference on December 20, 1966, according to UPI, may be reduced to 385 modern submarines, including those with nuclear propulsion and missiles.

[41] *Jane's Fighting Ships 1966–1967,* pp. 433–434.

[42] *Ibid.*

[43] "Ballistic missiles are mainly designed for the destruction of land targets such as naval bases and industrial centers. . . ." N. V. Isachenkov, "Novoe oruzhie korablei" (New Weapons of Warships), *Krasnaia Zvezda,* November 18, 1961.

[44] *Jane's Fighting Ships 1966–1967,* pp. 433–434.

[45] "The most effective means for combat on the seas and oceans . . . are homing missiles. Armed with homing missiles, Soviet warships have the capability to destroy at sea, from hundreds of kilometers away, the merchant ships and warships of the enemy, in particular his aircraft carriers. . . ." Isachenkov, *op. cit.*

[46] *Jane's Fighting Ships 1966–1967,* pp. 433–435.

[47] The 150 figure is given in "Soviet Naval Power Cited," *United States Naval Institute Proceedings,* March, 1964, p. 153. The 175 estimate, the latest available, is from *The Military Balance 1966–1967* (London: The Institute for Strategic Studies, 1966), p. 5.

might logically expect that the 82 missile submarines would be stationed primarily in the Northern Fleet and, to a considerably lesser extent, in the Far East in order to have relatively free access to the Atlantic and Pacific to carry out their cold war deterrent missions or their general war missile strike missions. The latter missions would be against land targets in the case of the approximately 53 ballistic missile submarines and primarily against NATO naval forces for the 29 guided missile submarines. However, the latter could be used against land targets or merchant convoys as exigencies of the situation might require. So, of the roughly 150–175 submarines in the Northern Fleet, it can be estimated that not more, and perhaps considerably fewer, than 100 torpedo attack submarines could be made available for a protracted war campaign against Atlantic shipping.

In addition to the fourteen *Sverdlov* cruisers mentioned previously, the Soviet Navy still has up to four older cruisers in at least limited service for a maximum total of eighteen.[48] None of these eighteen cruisers has nuclear propulsion or carries any nuclear armament.

As for the numbers of destroyers fitted with surface-to-surface antiship missiles, the Soviet Navy was estimated to have 24 by the beginning of 1967.[49] Their mission, according to *Military Strategy,* is "to *try* to defeat enemy naval formations, his carrier task forces. . . ."[50] For antisubmarine defense and general purpose work the Soviet Navy reportedly has 179 other destroyers and frigates.[51] In general, they have a poor antiaircraft defense. In addition, the Soviet Navy is credited with about 300 coastal escorts, 300 minesweepers, and 450 motor torpedo boats, including 100 armed with short-range surface-to-surface missiles.[52] Use of these shallow-draft missile gunboats would have to be limited to coastal work, either defensively against attack by amphibious forces or ground forces along the coast or offensively to support the advance of the Soviet ground forces along their coastal flank.

During Khrushchev's tenure in office three substantial reductions in the over-all strength of the Armed Forces were announced. In August 1955 an initial reduction of 640,000 men was declared for completion by the end of the year.[53] Marshal Georgi K. Zhukov, the Soviet defense minister, reported to the Twentieth Party Congress in early 1956 that

---

[48] *Jane's Fighting Ships 1966–1967,* p. 438.
[49] *Ibid.,* pp. 439–440.
[50] Sokolovskii, *op. cit.,* 2nd ed., 1963, p. 251. Italics added.
[51] *Jane's Fighting Ships 1966–1967,* pp. 440–443.
[52] *Ibid.,* pp. 432, 445–447.
[53] *Ezhegodnik 1957g., op. cit.,* p. 45.

this cut was carried out in full and on time.[54] Despite the fact that this cut was carried out in the same period as the Soviet disestablishment of its "overseas" naval bases at Porkkala and Port Arthur, there were no public claims or other indications that this first cut reduced naval personnel strength below an estimated 600,000.[55] In May of 1956, the second reduction of the Armed Forces—1,200,000 men—was announced for completion by 1 May 1957.[56] The same announcement stated that 375 warships would be laid up, but said nothing about any reduction in the number of naval personnel. An official U.S. Navy public information release in January 1958 stated despite the fact that, "the Soviet press and radio have publicized numerous 'evidence' and 'examples' of the extent to which the claimed reduction in strength of their naval forces have decimated or deactivated operational units and returned former servicemen to civilian occupations," no actual reductions in naval personnel strength had been made.[57] The same source went on to explain that the announced laying up of 375 ships was not significant since "by so doing, at least 400 ships and submarines which are obsolete, of nonstandard design and of little value in modern naval warfare, could be laid up with virtually no loss in combat effectiveness."

On 15 January 1960 the Supreme Soviet approved a plan for a third cut in military personnel strength, again of 1,200,000; this was claimed to amount to one-third of Soviet armed forces personnel strength at the time.[58] Defense Minister Malinovskii hastened to reassure the public that "we are reducing the Armed Forces not because of economic and budgetary weakness but because of the strength and power of our

---

[54] Zhukov, op. cit. The significance of the reduction on naval expenditures is not readily apparent, but indicates a qualitative change, not just a quantitative one. Even such an authority in Soviet military matters as Raymond Garthoff has written: "Zhukov, supported by his Army associates, and Khrushchev decided to cut sharply investment in a conventional navy and Admiral of the Fleet Kuznetsov—who evidently objected— was replaced by Admiral Sergei Gorshkov." (R. L. Garthoff, Soviet Strategy in the Nuclear Age [New York: F. A. Praeger, 1958], p. 50.) One can agree with Dr. Garthoff that the cut in naval appropriations most likely was the result of Zhukov and Khrushchev jointly and that Kuznetsov may have objected, although it isn't "evident"; the more important point at issue, however, is that the cut in investment was not made possible merely by cutting investment in a conventional (i.e., old school, high seas fleet) but by a shift to a young school strategy requiring much less costly ship types.

[55] N. Galay, "The New Reduction in the Soviet Armed Forces," Bulletin, Institute for the Study of the USSR, July, 1956, p. 48.

[56] "Zaiavlenie pravitel'stva SSSR po voprosu o razoruzhenii" (Announcement of the Government of the USSR on the Question of Disarmament), Krasnaia Zvezda, May 15, 1956.

[57] U. S. Navy Department, Office of Information, Answers to Questions Concerning the Soviet Navy. Washington, Chief of Information Notice 5720 of January 31, 1958, p. C-1.

[58] I. Grundinin, "Ot chego zavisit chislennost' armii" (On What the Size of the Army Depends), Krasnaia Zvezda, February 16, 1960.

government."[59] As in the other services, an all-out effort was made to justify this third reduction to the Navy. Meetings were held in the various fleet areas to placate the mass resentment of the personnel threatened with being abruptly returned to civilian life and, in the case of the officers, to less remunerative labor.[60] The official Navy newspaper editorialized on the "profound concern for the working and living arrangements of military personnel being discharged" that allegedly was being shown by "the Party, the government, and the entire country."[61] So unpopular was the third reduction, not only with the personnel involved but with the military high command, that one can believe that Khrushchev was vastly relieved when the Berlin crisis provided a reason for calling it off.[62] Apparently, this was done before the Navy had suffered any substantial further reduction.[63] Published estimates of current Soviet naval strength still place it at about 500,000.[64]

Just after the third reduction in conventional forces was announced in mid-January 1960, a pair of seemingly dissident Soviet military theorists stressed two relevant points in public print. First, a Marxist-Leninist precept was "rediscovered" to the effect that the development and introduction of new weapons to the armed forces depended on the economic resources available.[65] Second, they argued with unimpeachable logic that

---

[59] "Pust' gromche zvuchit golos propagandista!" (May the Voice of the Propagandist Resound More Loudly!), *Krasnaia Zvezda*, January 21, 1960.

[60] "Vse strana edinodushno odobriaet resheniia Verkhovnogo Soveta SSSR" (The Entire Country Approves of the Decision of the Supreme Soviet), *Sovetskii Flot*, January 17, 1960. See also: "Vse nashi sily—sluzheniiu rodine" (All Our Strength—At the Service of the Homeland), *Krasnaia Zvezda*, January 21, 1960; N. Emel'ianov, "Kurs na novoe—peredovoe" (Course Toward the New, the Progressive), *Sovetskii Flot*, January 24, 1960.

[61] "Large changes will be effected in the number of naval personnel in accordance with the [Fourth] Session of the Supreme Soviet. Many thousands of sailors will take off the naval uniform and transfer to peaceful, creative labor in the various branches of the national economy. The Party, Government, and the entire country are showing profound concern for the working and living arrangements of military personnel being discharged, each of whom will find an occupation to his liking. The Navy says good-bye to seamen, petty officers, officers and admirals going into the reserve, with praise and wishes for great success in their future work for the benefit of the Homeland." "Delo za vami, Komsomol'skie aktivisty!" (The Job is Yours, Komsomol Activists!), *Sovetskii Flot*, January 31, 1960.

[62] N. Galay, "The Numerical Strength of the Soviet Armed Forces," *Bulletin, Institute for the Study of the USSR*, May, 1962, p. 41.

[63] H. E. Horan, "The Navy of the Soviet Union," *Brassey's Annual, 1960* (New York: The Macmillan Company, 1960), p. 125.

[64] *Jane's Fighting Ships, 1966–1967*, p. 432, lists 500,000. An estimate of 465,000 is given in *The Military Balance 1966–1967*, p. 5.

[65] Two examples of this theoretical "discovery" of the dependence of arms development and production on economic strength are given: 1. "The sound basis for the possibility of significantly reducing our armed forces under present-day conditions which

nothing is gained by expending the time and treasure for developing new weapons unless enough of them are produced to achieve decisive results.[66] In traditional Tsarist as well as Soviet Russian military thought this could mean only the *mass* production of modern weapons. The implication seems clear that, in their typically oblique way, the dissenting Soviet theorists were justifying the cuts in conventional forces provided that greater amounts were spent on the production of new weapons. At any rate, it has been made unmistakably clear by a Soviet admiral that, to become effective, the Soviet Navy must be expanded greatly—which expansion depends on the success of the vast expansion of the Soviet economy called for by the Twenty-second Party Congress in 1961: "The further development of the Navy will be *entirely* determined by the capabilities of our economy. . . ."[67]

The Party line, frequently reiterated, has been that "the might of a navy is now determined, in the first place, not by the number of [com-

---

was given in the decisions and proceedings of the Fourth Session of the Supreme Soviet of the USSR has tremendous political and theoretical significance. The report of N. S. Khrushchev developed a number of important Marxist-Leninist precepts concerning war and the armed forces, primarily the dependence of military science and the national defense on the economic potential, the level of development of production forces, and the scientific and technological progress of the country. . . . Guided by Marxist-Leninist precepts, our military science is discovering the close interrelation between the economic potential of the state and the development of material, the emergence of new types of weapons, and the methods of conducting combat operations. This provides the cadres of the Army and the Navy with a thorough understanding of this important problem and enables them to consider it during their practical work toward strengthening of the combat power of the Soviet Armed Forces." (A. Lagovskii, "Ekonomika i sposoby vooruzhennoi bor'by" [Economics and Modes of Armed Conflict], *Sovetskii Flot,* February 6, 1960). 2. "Changes in military affairs, as the classics of Marxism-Leninism have scientifically proven, are conditioned by economic changes. . . . This precept of Marxism-Leninism has not lost its significance under modern conditions. The defense capability of a country and the combat might of its armed forces even in our time depends wholly on economic and moral-political factors which are closely interrelated and interdependent in function. These factors influence force levels, changes in tactics, operational art, and military strategy, as well as the organization of the armed forces." (Grundinin, *op. cit.*)

[66] "Economics has always had and continues to have a decisive influence on all aspects of military affairs, including the means of conducting armed conflict. 'Armaments, personnel, organization, tactics, and strategy,' wrote Engels, 'depend above all on the level of production attained at the time and on communications.' Experience in past and contemporary wars substantiates the correctness of this postulate." Lagovskii, *op. cit.*

[67] Italics added. "The further development of the Navy will be entirely determined by the capabilities of our economy and the achievements of science and technology. The fulfillment of the program for the gigantic development of productive forces in the country proposed by the Communist Party will create an ever more powerful material basis for the further perfection of the technical equipment of all branches of the Armed Forces, including the Navy. . . ." O. Chabanenko, "Na strazhe morskikh rubezhei Sovetskoi rodiny" (Guarding the Maritime Borders of the Soviet Homeland), *Ekonomicheskaia Gazeta,* July 30, 1961.

mission] pennants but by the quality of the warships and by their modern military equipment and weapons."[68] This statement by Admiral Gorshkov would appear to be an echo of a Party formula for rationalizing in acceptable theoretical terms the economic necessity of greatly limiting submarine production. It would seem to be the Party's intention to limit such production to the relatively small number required for lending added credibility to the overall Soviet nuclear deterrent rather than the very great number that would be required to give any substantial substance to a war-winning capability. This is particularly true of the highly expensive submarines having nuclear propulsion. The Navy leaders have a vested interest in the eventual success of the struggle of the military leaders in opposition to the Party proclivity, exemplified by Khrushchev, for limiting military spending to the already great amount required to develop and maintain an adequate deterrent posture. Consequently, the Navy Commander in Chief may be expected to be in sympathy with building the larger armed forces, including a great number of nuclear-powered submarines and other warships, that would provide a substantial war-fighting capability. And, indeed, it appears that Admiral Gorshkov has already begun to revise gradually his formulation of the subject just as he did in his successful campaign to restore large surface warships to practical acceptance. Only seven months after the Navy Commander in Chief had made the flat statement quoted above that it was only quality, not quantity, that counted, he significantly revised his position merely by adding a single, qualifying word which indicated that the number of ships in commission would, in fact, be a consideration: "The might of the Navy is determined by the combat capabilities of ships and aircraft, and not *just* by the numbers of commission pennants."[69] Perhaps in time, Gorshkov may again triumph, particularly if Soviet economic growth can be expanded beyond the high levels of the 1950's so that substantially more money might be provided the Navy to permit rapid construction of enough nuclear-powered submarines to replace the conventionally-powered diesel submarine force in a few years.

Actually, published estimates of nuclear submarine construction range from three to five per year, including both missile and torpedo attack

---

[68] "Although the large imperialist naval powers still continue to advertise the might of their fleet by various demonstrations of the numerica lstrength of their ships, times have changed. The might of a navy is now determined, in the first place, not by the number of pennants, but by the quality of the warships and by their modern military equipment and weapons. The Soviet Navy is at present more modern than the navy of any capitalist country." Gorshkov, "Vernye syny rodiny."

[69] Italics added. S. G. Gorshkov, "Velikye zadachy Sovetskogo Voenno-morskogo flota" (The Great Missions of the Soviet Navy), *Krasnaia Zvezda*, February 5, 1963.

types.[70] Although a senior Soviet Navy political officer has faithfully declaimed that an adequate number of Soviet submarines already have nuclear power plants,[71] his assertion has been challenged by a Soviet line officer: "Due to the use of nuclear power plants, submarines are becoming a class of ships the numbers of which will determine the combat might of the Navy as a whole."[72] As can be determined by adding up the estimates already given of the 28 missile and 12 torpedo attack submarines currently having nuclear propulsion, only 40 of the 400 total of operational submarines, or 10 per cent, have been built in the first 10 years of the USSR's nuclear submarine construction program. It can be readily seen that even should this rate be substantially increased, it would take several decades to provide nuclear propulsion for the large number of submarines needed solely to meet the defensive requirements created by NATO's strike carriers and Polaris submarines. Since the submarine has been repeatedly hailed as the main arm of the Soviet Navy under its neo-young school strategy, it seems that Soviet prestige alone would require that the USSR have several times as many of the latest type, that is with nuclear power, than the United States, whose main arm is considered to be aircraft carriers. The Soviet Navy's share of the military budget has been reliably stated to be only about 15 per cent.[73] In view of this fact, the pure envy in this statement by a senior Soviet naval aviation officer is obvious indeed:

> The Pentagon plans, in part, to construct by 1967 41 atomic missile submarines and have in the capacity of strike forces 15 strike and 10 heavy ASW carriers. On this is being spent colossal means. Suffice it to say, that the annual appropriations for the Navy comprise up to 35 per cent of the vast military budget of the U.S.A.[74]

---

[70] A nuclear submarine production rate of five per year was given in *Jane's Fighting Ships 1966–1967*, p. 433. Only a few additional estimates are available and they generally range from three to five per year. For example Capitaine Huan dates Soviet nuclear submarine construction from as early as 1956 with an initial program of three and with an annual production rate of three. He attributes this low rate to the fact that "the current financial allotment is as yet far too small for mass production, and the USSR still prefers to build the less costly non-nuclear ballistic missile submarines." Huan, *op. cit.*, p. 58. One semi-official British report was cited in the press as stating that "Russia has more than a dozen nuclear submarines operating from the Baltic to the Pacific. Five or six additional ones are expected to be added each year." Lord Kennet, *op. cit.*

[71] "Submarines, an adequate number of which are high-speed atomic submarines armed with very powerful missiles, comprise the main striking force of the Navy." V. Grishanov, "Povyshat' bditel'nost' i boevuiu gotovnost'" (To Increase Vigilance and Combat Readiness), *Krasnaia Zvezda*, July 29, 1961.

[72] A. Zheludev, "Atomnyi flot" (Atomic Navy), *Krasnaia Zvezda*, January 8, 1963.

[73] "Question: What portion of Soviet military expenditures goes to the Navy? Answer: Approximately 15 per cent of the Soviet defense budget goes to the Navy." *Answers to Questions Concerning the Soviet Navy*, p. G–2.

[74] Borzov, *op. cit.*

Major General Lagovskii of the Navy's supply service, in an article published just after the announcement of the third armed forces personnel reduction in January 1960, made an obvious and determined effort to give theoretical justification to the mass production of nuclear submarines. He started off by flatly contradicting the Party line on the subject by stating explicitly: "The influence of economics on the development of the means of armed conflict by way of new armaments is expressed *only* in their production on a mass scale."[75] To make absolutely certain that the intended practical application of this theoretical proposition to nuclear submarine production was not missed, Lagovskii went on directly to cite German submarine warfare in both World War I and World War II as two examples of failure to observe the law of mass production of armaments that he had postulated. This failure he ascribed to German industry's inability to produce adequate numbers of submarines. To clinch his argument against the Party's policy of limiting nuclear submarine production to the relatively modest number adequate for deterrent purposes, Lagovskii described Soviet submarine warfare (in obvious reference to the United States) as "this means of armed conflict which is so powerful, particularly against powers for whom sea communications are of tremendous importance."[76]

However, there has been a clear indication recently that the Soviet leaders may have made a final decision not to build nuclear-powered attack submarines in large numbers and are now engaged in reformulating their strategic theory to conform to economic necessity.[77] In the March 1965 issue of *Morskoi Sbornik* (*Naval Digest*), a long article by a senior Soviet naval officer purports to show that the importance of intercontinental sea communications has been diminishing since before World War I and would be of only secondary importance in a general nuclear war.[78]

---

[75] Lagovskii, *op. cit.,* italics added.

[76] *Ibid.*

[77] As Severyn Bialer has noted recently concerning Soviet decision-making: "For the past two years policies in most areas represented a 'middle road' between the views of the extremes. Sometimes this was achieved by support of aspects of opposing policies simultaneously." (Columbia University Seminar on International Communism, Minutes of the Second Meeting, October, 19, 1966, p. 2.) This writer believes this situation to obtain not only regarding Soviet policy formulation on how much to spend for nuclear submarines, but also concerning earlier Soviet decisions not to neglect large ship construction completely (even when the young school strategy was officially approved and should have ruled out any large ship construction).

[78] The potential significance of any such radical change in the major missions assigned to the Soviet Navy is attested to by the fact that the three leading U.S. specialists on Soviet military strategy, Thomas Wolfe, Raymond Garthoff, and Herbert Dinerstein, all list the cutting of U.S. sea lines of communications as a major Soviet mission. In fact, the latter lists it as the primary Soviet naval mission, making no mention of that of destroying the NATO naval forces, particularly the carrier striking forces and Polaris

The outcome of such a war would be largely decided during the initial period of strategic nuclear strikes. The destruction of the major ports would make it impossible to load or unload ships so shipping would be brought to an effective halt. The article concludes: "Consequently, even military operations for the disruption or protection of intercontinental transport can play only an auxiliary role among the missions to be carried out by naval forces."[79]

It is possible that this radical new conclusion does not represent the view of the Party leaders since even the highly authoritative *Morskoi Sbornik* occasionally publishes new views as trial balloons to test the general reaction at the various levels of the Soviet elite concerned with military policy recommendations and approval.[80] However, such a reformulation is wholly consistent with the general situation and would be a necessary preface to promulgating a Party decision that the Navy had been relieved of the requirement for a wartime campaign against NATO's sea lines of communications. Such a reformulation would provide a plausible rationalization for not building the huge fleet of nuclear-powered submarines that would be required to execute a successful campaign against Free World shipping, despite the very substantial antisubmarine warfare forces of NATO. Hence, it is entirely possible, if not probable, that the article in question is intended to constitute the theoretical justification for concentrating all of the nuclear submarines that the USSR finds it economically feasible to build on the imperative defensive mission of establishing a credible defense against strategic nuclear attack by Polaris submarines.

Since a number of years may pass before evidence is gained to clarify

---

submarines, which seem to the author to enjoy top priority in the Soviet scheme of things. Wolfe, *op. cit.*, p. 227; Garthoff, *op. cit.*, p. 203; Dinerstein *op. cit.*, p. 176.

[79] ". . . under contemporary conditions, oceanic communications in the first period of a general nuclear war will not have any essential significance and, consequently, even military operations for the disruption or protection of intercontinental transport can play only an auxiliary role in the system of other missions to be decided by naval forces.

"Regardless of the reduced role and lessened influence of the struggle for oceanic communications *on the general course and outcome of the war* . . . [a general nuclear] war will be short and its results, in general, will be decided already in the first period by operations of those forces and means which are had at the start of the war.

"From these considerations a conclusion is arrived at: in the first period of a worldwide nuclear missile war the major ports and naval bases most probably will be destroyed (put out of operation) by nuclear missile strikes." S. I. Filonov, "Vooruzhennaia bor'ba i okeanskie kommunikatsii" (Armed Conflict and Oceanic Communications), *Morskoi Sbornik,* March 1965, pp. 39–41.

[80] An indication that this may be the case is provided by a subsequent assertion by the Navy's Commander in Chief, also in the pages of *Morskoi Sbornik,* that cutting the enemy's "oceanic communications . . . continues to be one of the important tasks of the [Soviet] Navy." Gorshkov, "Razvitie sovetskogo voenno-morskogo iskusstva," p. 18.

this matter, one should at least keep in mind the possibility that the USSR has given up its previously declared intention of making a major effort at interdicting Free World shipping in the event of war. It may even be that the current Soviet strategic estimate finds that the USSR's ballistic missile submarines have made such a substantial contribution to the Soviet Union's missile deterrent that the increment of deterrence afforded by the threat of unrestricted submarine warfare against Free World shipping can be dispensed with and the large economies effected thereby can be of great help in meeting higher priority requirements.

Another alternate possibility, too, deserves mention in view of the fact that the author, a Captain S. I. Filonov, is neither of flag rank nor established as a writer on naval matters. It is conceivable that Filonov is a stalking horse for the numerous army marshals who dominate the Ministry of Defense and exploit that dominance in continuing efforts to reduce the role of the Navy and, hence, its slice of the defense budget pie. A discussion of just such efforts to downgrade the importance of the Navy to its former role as a mere seaward extension of the Army's coastal flank will follow.

In typical Soviet fashion, the struggle between the Army marshals and the Party leaders to establish the role and budget of the Navy is obscured for the uninitiate by the fact that the debate is conducted in vague, quasi-irrelevant terms. Just as the Sino-Soviet dispute was characterized in its early years by references to "dogmatists" or "revisionists" rather than to Mao or to Khrushchev and his successors, and just as the continuing efforts of the military to weaken the morale-corroding, efficiency-sapping Party control of the armed forces through a system of latter-day political commissars is couched in terms of a debate in which both sides are ostensibly arguing for the sacred Leninist principle of *edinonachalie* (one-man command), so the fight for control of naval policy and budget is couched in equally esoteric terms. In this case, the polemics revolve around the long-standing dispute about whether the Navy has, or should have, any missions "independent" of those required to support the Army's ground operations. Such a debate is inconceivable in a nation like the United States and the United Kingdom whose naval missions are primarily of a strategic offensive nature. The very fact of the existence of such a debate in the USSR strongly supports the thesis expressed in this book that Soviet naval strategy is primarily deterrent and defensive, despite the undeniable Soviet submarine capabilities for strategic nuclear strikes and interdiction of sea communications. Here the key question is much less one of Soviet capabilities than of intentions.

Be that as it may, the general outline of the debate and the categories of the participants are clear. On one side, the argument is that the Navy's main role should still be considered that of giving support to the Army's ground operations and protecting its coastal flanks from seaborne attack. Espousing this view are most of the Navy's incumbent flag officers, who generally give the impression from their writings of aiming at nothing higher than merely getting along with their Army seniors whose influence in the General Staff of the Army and Navy is paramount. Also to be found most strongly championing the pro-Army view, at least in periods that Party attitudes make it appear politically safe to do so, are the Army marshals. Taking the pro-Navy side in favor of acknowledging that the Navy not only should have, but obviously has to have, independent missions if any naval capabilities against aircraft carriers and Polaris submarines are to be developed, are retired admirals or those about to retire and relatively junior active-duty naval officers who, presumably, can be protected by their seniors for airing the privately shared views that those seniors find impolitic to express personally.

The postwar development of the pros and cons of the Navy having any "independent" missions is worth tracing briefly to afford an understanding of the current situation and to make comprehensible the developments yet to come before the issue is resolved. In 1946, Admiral G. Levchenko provided the first of the pro-Army statements of the Navy's postwar leaders by a sufficiently servile article with the embarrassing obvious title of "The Navy—Faithful Helper of the Red Army."[81] That article may have been occasioned by an Army demand for atonement for an article published two months before by the Navy's wartime Deputy Chief of the Main Naval Staff, Admiral V. A. Alafuzov. With an acid pen that for nearly two additional decades continued to castigate the Army leadership from the relatively safe retreat of retirement, Alafuzov asserted: "Naval operations can either be independent or in support of the Army."[82] As independent missions he listed defense of one's own sea communications and attacks on those of the enemy. Additionally, he listed as missions that could be either "independent" or "joint" with the Army, depending on the situation, operations for defense of one's own coastal objectives (especially bases) and attack on coastal targets in the enemy's country. The debate remained at a standoff until the end of the Stalinist era and the advent of Khrushchev and his choices for Defense Minister and Commander in Chief of the Navy, Marshal Zhukov and Admiral Gorshkov. The former maintained in a

---

[81] G. Levchenko, "Flot—vernyi pomoshchnik Krasnyi Armii (The Navy—Faithful Helper of the Red Army), *Krasnaia Zvezda,* July 28, 1946.

[82] V. A. Alafuzov, "O sushchnosti morskikh operatsii" (On the Fundamentals of Naval Operations), *Morskoi Sbornik,* April-May, 1946, p. 26.

speech at the Twentieth Party Congress in 1956 that the Navy was still "loyally" defending the seacoasts (with help from the Army and air forces).[83] The latter paid the required lip service to ground warfare as the controlling element, and merely dared hint that the appearance of new types of weapons might require some changes in naval science.[84]

The pro-Army position was stated in 1957 by a senior, active-duty naval officer, N. Nikolaev, in unmistakably clear and uncompromising terms: "The main mission of the Navy has been and will continue to be cooperation with the Soviet Army."[85] A possible rejoinder to this a month later by a rear admiral on active duty was careful to give the superficial appearance of acquiescing in the Navy's subordinate role but did so for the express reason that the Navy's capabilities at the moment were not great enough to permit it to carry out its assigned missions without outside assistance.[86] With the ouster of Marshal Zhukov in 1957 and the Party's subsequent strengthening of its control over the armed forces, the new Minister of Defense, Marshal Malinovskii, considered it expedient and, possibly, believed it to be objectively correct owing to the advent of missile submarines, to enunciate the following Party reformulation of the Navy's missions: "The Navy . . . is capable not only of defending our maritime borders but also of destroying enemy forces on the seas and oceans, as well as of delivering powerful blows against objectives located on other continents."[87] With the publication of *Military*

---

[83] Zhukov, *op. cit.* Marshal Zhukov was echoed by Marshal Vasilevskii: "Our Navy, together with the Army and air forces, reliably guards the maritime borders of our country." A. M. Vasilevskii, "Vooruzhennye sily Sovetskogo gosudarstva" (The Armed Forces of the Soviet State), *Izvestiia*, February 23, 1956.

[84] "The appearance of new types of naval weapons and combat equipment and, in connection with this, the changing character of ground warfare, require the further development of naval science as a component of Soviet military science which exerts a direct influence on the development of military science." S. G. Gorshkov, "Vernyi strazh morskikh granits" (Reliable Guard of the Maritime Borders), *Pravda*, July 24, 1955.

[85] N. Nikolaev, "Rol' voenno-morskogo flota v systema vooruzhennykh sil SSSR" (The Role of the Navy in the System of the Armed Forces of the USSR), *Sovetskii Flot*, May 29, 1957.

[86] "It is necessary to observe that, like the struggle for sea and ocean communications, fulfillment of the mission of repulsing enemy strikes from seaward or carrying out an invasion by one's own troops of enemy territory over the sea is not, *at present*, the prerogative of the Navy alone. Not one of these missions can the Navy accomplish by itself, but normally carries them out in mutual cooperation with the other branches of the armed forces. From this it is concluded that military operations at sea cannot be considered in isolation apart from relationships with the general conduct of war by all of the armed forces of the state." Iu. Ladinskii, "O teorii voenno-morskogo iskusstva" (On the Theory of Naval Art), *Voennaia Mysl'*, July, 1957, p. 31. Italics added.

[87] "Priem v Kremle v chest' sorokaletiia Sovetskoi Armii i Voenno-morskogo Flota" (Reception in the Kremlin in Honor of the Fortieth Anniversary of the Soviet Armed Forces), *Sovetskii Flot*, February 25, 1958. Writing in *Military Thought* the same month,

Strategy in 1962, the Party-dictated stand on the Navy's role in the nuclear age, as including independent missions, was formalized to a large degree: ". . . to the independent type of strategic operations should be attributed military operations in maritime theaters which are directed at the destruction of formations of the enemy fleet, disruption of his maritime communications, and defense of one's own maritime communications and coastal regions against nuclear strikes from the sea."[88] The most that Marshal Sokolovskii and his all-Army collaborators in the writing of *Military Strategy* could salvage from the situation was to list the various tasks that naval forces can fulfill in support of ground forces and adjure the Party and the Navy to remember that "although support of the Ground Forces will not be one of the main missions of the Navy, considerable effort must be expended in this direction."[89] This concession must have been widely welcomed in the Navy and, particularly, must have had for Admiral Alafuzov the sweetness of victory after a long and hard-fought campaign. He hastened into print to quote the concession verbatim and, for once, to agree with his Army opposite numbers: "The authors have made a correct prognosis of the future. . . ."[90] Despite the conformity to the Party line of Marshal Malinovskii's publicly-expressed views, the position that probably was much closer to his private views, and that still represent those of his successor in 1967, Marshal Andrei Grechko and of the other Army marshals, was expressed in late 1963 by a little known colonel in the pages of the Soviet Ministry of Defense's *Military-Historical Journal*. ". . . there is no independent naval doctrine or naval science. The Navy trains to perform its assigned missions in close cooperation with the other branches of the Armed Forces."[91] Marshal Sokolovskii and one of his coauthors of *Military Strategy* published an article in *Red Star* on 28 August 1964 that spelled out the Navy's shift to independent missions and the ostensible reason for it: ". . . equipping our Navy with atomic submarines with missiles, and with missile aviation

---

Marshal Rotmistrov amplified Marshal Malinovskii's view by indicating that two of the Navy's missions fell into the particularly important category of being "strategic": "Operations against oceanic and sea communications and to destroy strategic objectives in enemy territory occupy a special place in naval operations. These operations seek to undermine the military and military-economic power of the enemy, which determines their importance in armed conflict. Submarines and airplanes are the main forces conducting such operations." P. Rotmistrov, "O sovremennom Sovetskom voennom iskusstve i ego kharakternykh chertakh" (On Contemporary Soviet Military Art and Its Characteristic Features), *Voennaia Mysl'*, February, 1958, p. 89.

[88] Sokolovskii, *op. cit.*, 1st ed., p. 335; 2nd ed., p. 373.

[89] *Ibid.*, 1st ed., p. 356; 2nd ed., p. 400.

[90] V. A. Alafuzov, "K vykhodu v svet truda *Voennaia Strategiia*" (On the Appearance of the Work *Military Strategy*), *Morskoi Sbornik*, January, 1963, p. 94.

[91] I. Belousov, "Konferentsiia o Sovetskoi voennoi doktrine" (Conference on Soviet Military Doctrine), *Voenno-istoricheskii Zhurnal*, October, 1963, p. 123.

of long-range and nuclear weapons, permits a shift from carrying out wartime missions along the coast in cooperation with the Ground Troops to independent and decisive operations on the broad reaches of the oceans."[92] This seeming acceptance by the Army marshals of the Party's view of the nature of the Navy's missions may temporarily have silenced the pro-Army adherents, but it is unlikely to have terminated the dispute since the underlying reasons for the conflict remain unreconciled.

This latest move of the Army marshals to deprive the Navy of the "independent" wartime mission for interdicting NATO's sea communications,[93] if such it actually was, is reminiscent of the apparent reluctance shown in the first edition of *Military Strategy* to admit that the Navy had an obvious role in strategic nuclear strikes by virtue of its ballistic missile submarines. It may well be that the pro-Army opposition to present Party policy has shifted its tactics from generally opposing the assignment of *any* primary missions to the Navy beyond those involved in supporting the ground forces to the tactic of opposing the continued assignment to the Navy of the *individual* missions that have been declared by the Party to be independent naval missions. Plausible theoretical reasons for such opposition appear to be readily available. In the case of the mission to cut NATO sea communications the reason can be that the anticipated nature of nuclear war with its probable initial destruction of shipping terminals makes a submarine campaign against the shipping itself needlessly and expensively redundant. In the case of the strategic strike missions against NATO land targets by Soviet missile submarines, the tactic quite logically would be to show that the mission can be accomplished more effectively and economically by the Strategic Missile Forces. Whatever the truth may be, one can anticipate that this issue will continue to disturb the rest of the aging Army marshals and cause them to continue their efforts to find a way to change the Navy's role back to that of being the Army's "faithful helper."

---

[92] Sokolovskii and Cherednichenko, *op. cit.*

[93] See pp. 85–86 *supra*.

★ NATO Versus Soviet Missions

VIII

The Soviet Union, with a weak Navy, has been forced to adopt a strategically defensive maritime strategy, one designed primarily for deterrence, but failing that to ward off, as best it can, the seaborne attacks of a "NATO Navy" which can exercise command of the sea at the times and places of its own choosing.[1] The extensive writings on NATO naval matters in the Soviet literature make it unmistakably clear that Soviet strategists recognize the great threat of destruction to much of the USSR and to Soviet naval forces constituted by the overwhelmingly superior naval power of NATO.[2] Soviet concern is particularly evident with regard to NATO's capabilities for strategic nuclear attack on the USSR

---

[1] "In a future war, if the imperialists unleash one, the main mission of our Navy will be to combat the navy of the enemy." Alafuzov, "K vykhodu v svet truda *Voennaia Strategiia*" p. 92.

[2] The following quotations are typical of a great many that could be cited to illustrate what is undoubtedly a painfully accurate recognition of the preponderant naval superiority enjoyed by the NATO navies over the Soviet Navy and the consequent threat to Soviet security that is constituted by NATO's seaborne strategic striking power: "The imperialist powers are assigning a great place to naval forces in plans for a new war against the USSR and the countries of the socialist camp. They are intently building aircraft carriers, missile-carrying ships, and atomic submarines armed with missile weapons." (F. V. Zozulia, "Gordoe imia—moriak" [A Proud Name—Sailor], *Komsomol'skaia Pravda*, July 29, 1961). "In the U.S.A. an intensive, large naval construction program has been observed, especially of atomic missile submarines and strike carriers. The basic modernization of warships, especially of aircraft carriers, is also going on in England. All of the states which participate in NATO are greatly strengthening the missile weapons of their navies." (Sokolovskii, *op. cit.,* 2nd ed., p. 354). "Our fleets [based in the Black Sea, Baltic, Northern, and Pacific areas] . . . will be opposed by a strong enemy, one well-versed in naval operations. The Anglo-American command has devoted great attention to preparing for war against our Navy. . . ." (*Ibid.,* 1st ed., p. 357.)

from seaborne weapons systems, namely by Polaris missile-launching, nuclear-powered submarines and by fast carrier striking forces.[3]

Obvious reflections of this concern are the occasional forays into the Atlantic and Pacific in recent years by Soviet submarines and surface naval ships. So too is Soviet maintenance in the Mediterranean since early 1963 of a "standing naval force of five to six warships, plus several submarines with tenders and support ships."[4] A further evidence of such concern was apparent on 10 and 11 May 1967 when two different Soviet destroyers tried so hard to interfere with joint U.S.-Japanese antisubmarine exercises in the Sea of Japan, within two hundred miles of the Soviet coast and main Pacific Fleet naval base of Vladivostok, that they caused minor collisions with the destroyer USS *Walker*.[5]

---

[3] Only two illustrative quotations will be given at this juncture, one showing the Soviet view of the Polaris threat and another describing the threat posed by carrier strike forces. Additional support for this point may be found in the immediately following sections on the Polaris and carrier threats: "Great significance is attached [by NATO] to the use of nuclear-powered submarines for nuclear [missile] attacks deep within the territory of the socialist countries. By the start of a war, missile-carrying nuclear submarines can be deployed so as to launch missiles . . . mainly in the Arctic Ocean and the northern seas, in the Northeast Atlantic, and in the Western Pacific." (Sokolovskii, *op. cit.*, 2nd ed., p. 399.) "The enemy will attempt to deploy these units [carrier strike forces] in the most important theatres near the socialist countries and to deliver surprise nuclear attacks against important coastal objectives (naval bases, airfields, missile installations) and, possibly, against targets quite far in from the coast. For example, in the NATO exercise 'Fall—'60' a carrier-based striking force from the Norwegian Sea made 200 simulated nuclear attacks against targets deep within our territory. Most of the nuclear attacks were made within 21 hours. Such an attack represents a greater danger if the Navy cannot cut it off and destroy the carrier-based striking forces." (*Ibid.*, pp. 296–397.)

[4] Rear Admiral R. G. Colbert, U.S. Navy, Deputy Chief of Staff, Supreme Allied Command, Atlantic, in a speech at Norfolk, Virginia, on September 27, 1966. (*Reuter*, September 28, 1966.) Moreover, for years the USSR has maintained close electronic, acoustic and visual surveillance of U.S. Sixth Fleet operations in the Mediterranean, as well as of U.S. naval operations throughout the world, by means of specially-equipped fishing trawlers, hydrographic ships, and occasionally with Soviet warships. For example, the Commander in Chief U.S. Sixth Fleet, Vice Admiral William I. Martin, commented on the May 1967 joint U.S.-French naval exercises in the Mediterranean in which the Soviet intelligence collection trawler *Lotsman* "was a silent witness to the military cooperation between the United States and France . . . steaming along within a few miles of the [U.S.] flagship": "There have been times when Russian electronic intelligence ships have moved into the way seemingly to embarrass us; either we change course or [we would] ram them." (William Beecher, "French Join U.S. in Fleet Exercise," *New York Times*, May 6, 1967.)

[5] "In recent years there have been repeated incidents in which Soviet ships, by their maneuvers, have interfered with the operations of United States Navy units. The accident today, however, marks the first time that there has been a collision [between major combatant ships] according to the Navy." (John Finney, "Soviet Destroyer Scrapes U.S. Warship," *New York Times*, May 11, 1967). "The concern centered largely on the possible Soviet political motives which remain unclear to U.S. officials. They are convinced that the Soviet ships were engaged in deliberate harassment, but they tend to doubt

Soviet military doctrine holds that the initial period of a general war in which nuclear blows are exchanged is of incomparable importance, since it affords the opportunity to achieve at the very outset of the war at least some of the "military-strategic and politico-military objectives" that formerly could be gained only gradually during the course of a war as the cumulative effect of a series of tactical successes. Any such major successes made during the initial nuclear exchange would unquestionably affect the subsequent course of the war and, in the professed Soviet view, would be certain to predetermine its final outcome.[6] In view of the overwhelming importance of the initial nuclear exchange for the results of any future general war, it is not surprising that the Soviet leadership has devoted a significant, if relatively small, share of the USSR's gross national product in recent years to building a force of its own missile submarines to offset the deterrence gained for the West by the strategic nuclear strike capabilities of the Polaris submarines and strike carriers of the NATO powers.

Accordingly, it is the NATO naval forces' capabilities for strategic nuclear attack on the Soviet Union and the resultant assignment of defensive missions to the Soviet Navy that will be considered first. Next to be scrutinized will be the vulnerability of the NATO countries, especially the United States, to submarine-launched strategic nuclear attack. This vulnerability will be looked at in conjunction with the corresponding wartime mission of the Soviet Navy to conduct such attacks. Once these two important considerations of the initial nuclear exchange have been dealt with, our attention will then be directed toward a quasi-primary

---

that the incidents reflect a Soviet political strategy to increase East-West tension as a way to counter the widening American involvement in Vietnam. Rather, the incidents were generally believed to have been prompted by Soviet sensitivity to United States naval operations only a few hundred miles from Soviet territory." (John Finney, "U.S. Destroyer Scraped Again," *New York Times,* May 12, 1967). "It seems clear that in twice scraping the American destroyer *Walker* . . . the Soviet ships were systematically protesting the American presence in the area." (David K. Willis, "Washington Hopeful Ship Incidents Are Ended," *Christian Science Monitor,* May 13, 1967). Moscow Radio, in fact, commented: "It is impossible not to note that the incident in the Sea of Japan occurred at a place which is very far from the United States and very close to the USSR's state frontiers." (Moscow Radio, in Turkish to Turkey, 1730 hours, May 11, 1967.)

[6] "The peacetime stockpiles of nuclear weapons and their delivery systems—missiles and aircraft—may be completely used up by the contending sides in the very first minutes of the war for the destruction and devastation of the most important objectives of the enemy to the full depths of his territory in order to accomplish the main political and military-strategic missions in a short period right at the very outset of the war. Consequently, the initial period of a contemporary nuclear-missile war, obviously, will be a major and decisive period which predetermines the development and outcome of the entire war." (Sokolovskii, *op. cit.,* 2nd ed., p. 253.)

Soviet naval mission for protracted general war: to attack the vital but vulnerable oceanic lines of communications of NATO.[7] Following this, three other important missions will be considered as they derive from the corresponding NATO capabilities. The first of these will be the Soviet Navy's mission of protecting the USSR's own militarily important, indeed vital, coastal sea communications. Second will be the mission of defending the Soviet coasts against NATO amphibious invasions. The third and last mission to be considered will be Soviet capabilities to conduct amphibious operations. In view of the widespread misconceptions on this subject, care will be taken to show that the Soviet Navy could not possibly conduct transoceanic amphibious invasions in the face of NATO sea supremacy. Rather, it is shown that the Soviet naval mission in this regard is limited to short-haul amphibious landings in tactical support of the ground forces.

Soviet military leaders have publicly taken note of the announced U.S. goal of forty-one Polaris submarines by 1967.[8] Their writings observe that U.S. nuclear submarines with Polaris missiles are engaged in constant combat patrols in the Norwegian and Mediterranean seas. In the Norwegian Sea, "close to Soviet borders," where they constitute "a threat to peace" in the Soviet view, three to five Polaris submarines are said to be on constant patrol.[9] In the Mediterranean, there are reportedly three Polaris submarines making patrols.[10] Moreover, the Soviet press has noted the appearance of Polaris submarines in the Pacific as part of a planned, continuing buildup, initially, to one squadron of seven submarines and, eventually, to two squadrons that will total fourteen

---

[7] See the preceding chapter for discussion of the possibility that the interdiction of NATO Maritime communications may be in the process of elimination as a wartime mission for the Soviet Navy. Two examples of Soviet views on the vulnerability of NATO's sea lines of communications will suffice at this point: 1. "The most zealous advocates of military adventures in the West ought to stop and think of their . . . greatly extended communications lines. . . ." (S. G. Gorshkov, "Na strazhe morskikh rubezhei Sovetskoi derzhavy" [Guarding the Maritime Borders of the Soviet Power], *Pravda,* July 29, 1961). 2. "Thus the petroleum 'well-being' of the countries of the North Atlantic alliance is based almost entirely on the import of oil. From this comes the significance of their exceptionally extended maritime communications. The political and military leaders of NATO are giving great attention to the strengthening of the security of these [maritime communications lines] . . . Western strategies recognize that, in the event of war, the severing of these communications would be fraught with the most serious consequences for the countries of NATO." (A. Lagovskii, "Neft' i NATO" [Petroleum and NATO], *Krasnaia Zvezda,* February 26, 1965.)

[8] Borzov, *op. cit.*

[9] "Ugroza mira" (Threat to the Peace), *Krasnaia Zvezda,* November 19, 1961.

[10] Atomnaia lodka stolknulas' s sudnom" (Atomic Submarine Collides with a Merchant Ship), *Krasnaia Zvezda,* January 12, 1965.

units.[11] The Polaris submarines in the Pacific, it has been reported, are all slated to carry the A-3 Polaris missile with a 2,500 nautical mile range. This, according to the Soviet press, will make it possible "to strike the Asiatic regions of the Soviet Union from the waters of the Far East and Indian Ocean."[12] By early 1963, Soviet military writer V. P. Rogov acknowledged that Polaris submarines had come to be considered by Soviet strategists as "a greater threat to peace" than any other U.S. missile system, whether shipborne or land-based.[13] In the spring of 1964, the Soviet Navy's Commander in Chief informed readers of the Soviet military press that "the Navy plays a very important role in the plans of the imperialists. It is not accidental that the United States proposes a significant increase in the number of naval personnel, primarily for the atomic submarines armed with Polaris missiles."[14] Writing in the government newspaper *Izvestiia* six months earlier, the Soviet admiral, A. Chabanenko, had pointed out that the U.S. strategic nuclear missile force had two principal components—land-based Minuteman intercontinental ballistic missiles and *submarine striking forces* equipped with underwater launched Polaris missiles—and that because of the importance of the Polaris submarines in U.S. strategy a "green light" for their construction had been given.[15] Not surprisingly, in view of the great concern over the Polaris threat that has been evinced by Soviet leaders, countering that threat has been assigned at the Navy's most important mission. An unquestionably authoritative statement to this effect was published in August of 1964 in an article in *Red Star* by Marshal Sokolovskii and M. Cherednichenko, one of the other authors of *Military Strategy:* "The first priority mission of naval operations in the oceanic and sea theatres will be the destruction of atomic missile submarines."[16] In the next chapter the requisite tasks, weapons systems, tactics, and current capabilities of the Soviet Navy for fulfilling this "top priority" mission will be examined as closely as available information permits.

---

[11] V. Polianskii, " 'Polarisy' raspolzaiutsia po okeanam" (Polaris Submarines Are Deployed in the Oceans), *Krasnaia Zvezda,* December 27, 1964.

[12] *Ibid.*

[13] V. P. Rogov, "Imperialisty SShA delaiut stavku na Polaris" (The Imperialists of the U.S.A. Count on Polaris), *Morskoi Sbornik,* May, 1963, p. 85.

[14] S. G. Gorshkov, "Flot v bol'shom plavanii" (The Navy on the High Seas), *Krasnaia Zvezda,* March 21, 1964.

[15] "In the development of the United States' armed forces, the American military leaders are relying mainly on building a strategic nuclear missile force equipped with intercontinental ballistic missiles of the Minuteman type and nuclear-powered submarines equipped with Polaris missiles. This is why a green light has been given in the U.S. warship construction program for the construction of this type of submarine. A. Chabanenko, "Sovetskii admiral ob atomnoi flote SShA" (Soviet Admiral on the Atomic Navy of the U.S.A.), *Izvestiia,* November 30, 1963.

[16] Sokolovskii and Cherednichenko, *op. cit.*

In addition to taking note of the United States' 1967 force goal of Polaris submarines, the Soviet military leaders have called public attention to the corresponding U.S. goal for 1967 of fifteen strike carriers.[17] The 1962 edition of *Military Strategy* summarized as follows the strength and deployment as well as the strategic strike mission of U.S. and U.K. carrier task forces:

> The Anglo-American navy consists of seven attack carrier task forces, including two or three attack carriers and other warships [in each task force]. They are all deployed in military theatres; three attack carrier forces in the Atlantic, two in the Pacific, one in the Mediterranean, and one in the Indian Ocean. The Sixth Fleet in the Mediterranean and the Seventh Fleet in the Pacific are always in full combat readiness.
>
> The naval forces of the Anglo-American bloc have heavy attack aircraft capable of delivering nuclear strikes to great depths.[18]

This capability of attack carrier aircraft for making deep penetration strikes into the Russian heartland was concurred in and emphasized by Admiral Alafuzov in his otherwise often critical review of the first edition of *Military Strategy:*

> The Americans allot a completely vital role to strike carriers, even in unlimited war; these warships, according to their views, along with nuclear missile submarines, will conduct the mission of making nuclear strikes against targets deep inside the country of the enemy.[19]
>
> The authors stated the importance of the mission of combat against carrier strike forces with absolute correctness.[20]

In fact, both the 1962 and 1963 editions of *Military Strategy* stated that destruction of the enemy's *attack carrier striking forces* would be "the most important mission of our Navy from the very outset of a war."[21] Although the strike carrier threat yielded in importance to that of the Polaris missile submarines some time during the year from September 1963 to the same month in 1964,[22] destruction of the strike carriers still remained "an important wartime mission."[23] Unquestionably, the strike carriers do confront the Soviet Union with a threat that is responsible for the Soviet Navy's having been assigned a wartime mission of destroying

---

[17] Borzov, *op. cit.*

[18] Sokolovskii, *op. cit.*, 1st ed., p. 316.

[19] Alafuzov, "K vykhodu v svet truda *Voennaia Strategiia,*" p. 90.

[20] *Ibid.*, p. 95.

[21] Sokolovskii, *op. cit.*, 1st ed., p. 353; 2nd ed., p. 396.

[22] Obviously, the recognition of the Polaris threat as even greater than that of the attack carriers took place in the twelve months period between the time that the second edition of *Military Strategy* was sent to the printers on August 30, 1963 and the publication of the Sokolovskii-Cherednichenko article in *Red Star* on August 28, 1964.

[23] Sokolovskii and Cherednichenko, *op. cit.*

them that is a very close second in importance to the first priority one of combating Polaris submarines. Probably the distinction of first and second priority is based less on any essential difference in the seriousness of the two threats involved than on the fact that, although the USSR has developed and is producing weapons systems designed specifically for use against aircraft carriers, it still has to face up seriously to the problem of countering Polaris. Yet, the carrier threat clearly remains a very major one indeed in the view of Soviet leaders.

Soviet writers have frequently stressed the vulnerability of the continental United States and Western European members of NATO to attacks from Soviet missile submarines. A typical statement to this effect was made by Air Marshal Vershinen in 1957:

> The Submarine Force has become a formidable weapon which not only is capable of shelling coastal cities, but also can hit other targets with atomic and hydrogen weapons. . . . Many large U.S. cities and a number of Western nations, in the event of war, could be subjected to missile attack from submarines as well as from [intercontinental] missiles and bomber aircraft.[24]

Presumably to add to the credibility of their nuclear deterrent forces, the Soviet leaders frequently brandish their submarine missiles orally. On this count, the Soviet Navy's Commander in Chief, who is not normally given to blatantly propagandistic statements, is a gross offender in the Khrushchevian grand style of bombast:

> The Soviet Union has atomic submarines armed with the most powerful missiles . . . the most zealous advocates of military adventures in the West ought to stop and think of the fate of their shores . . . and of the fact that America's traditional invulnerability has been eliminated forever.[25]

That the Soviet Navy probably has been assigned at least some wartime missions for strategic nuclear missile strikes at U.S. and Western European targets, although quite likely only a relatively low priority *second strike* mission, is suggested by the very considerable number of Soviet statements to that effect.[26] Substantial support is lent to this proba-

---

[24] K. Vershinen, "Po povodu voinstvennykh zaiavlenii nekotorykh Amerikanskikh, Angliiskikh i Zapadnogermanskikh generalov i gosudarstvennykh deiatelei" (Apropos of the War-like Declarations of Some American, British, and West German Generals and Government Officials), *Krasnaia Zvezda,* September 10, 1957.

[25] Gorshkov, "Na strazhe morskikh rubezhei Sovetskoi derzhavy."

[26] Two quotations that indicate the assignment to the Navy of a strategic nuclear striking mission in any general war are cited: "Nuclear-missile strikes on objectives to

bility, of course, by the very fact that the USSR has built a force of ballistic missile submarines.[27]

Whatever the facts of the wartime mission assigned the USSR's ballistic missile submarine force, it would be well to keep in mind, in view of widespread misconceptions on this score, that the *Soviet Navy's basic wartime mission is definitely not submarine-launched strategic nuclear strikes at the United States.* Rather, it is the destruction of the submarine, surface ship, and naval air forces of those powers. As Admiral Alafuzov has emphatically stated: "In a future war . . . the basic mission of our Navy will be to combat the Navy of the enemy."[28] As this account undertakes to make clear, the available evidence supports the veracity of the Admiral's statement. This study also intends to show that the Soviet Navy has been given the unrealistic assignment of accomplishing the wartime destruction of NATO naval forces with only submarines supplemented within range of coastal air bases by naval aircraft and surface ships.

As early in the postwar period as 1946, Admiral Alafuzov, with carefully guarded words, noted that the "enemy" (clearly with the United States in mind), is "virtually dependent on its sea lines of communications." He went on to state his conviction that the postwar Soviet Navy should be assigned the appropriate wartime mission to exploit this NATO vulnerability: "to strike at the enemy's sea lines of communications and in this way significantly to influence the outcome of a war."[29] Recognition of the great vulnerability of NATO's sea communications has been a staple item in Soviet strategic writings and propaganda

the full depth of the enemy's territory, in the first place against nuclear weapons, will create favorable circumstances for the operations of other branches of the Armed Services. Together with the Missile Troops of Strategic Designation, Long Range Aviation and missile submarines will deliver strikes on strategic objectives and against the theatres of military operations . . ." (Sokolovskii, *op. cit.*, 2nd ed., p. 372). "The basic means for carrying out the retaliatory nuclear strike obviously will be the Missile Troops of Strategic Designation, and also missile submarines and Long Range Aviation." Sokolovskii and Cherednichenko, *op. cit.*

[27] The existence of a force of "Soviet ballistic missile submarines" was reliably reported by the U.S. Secretary of Defense in 1964. "Text of McNamara's Statement to Platform Group," *The New York Times*, August 18, 1964, p. 18.

[28] Alafuzov, "K vykhodu v svet truda *Voennaia Strategiia*," p. 94.

[29] "For a country little dependent upon sea communications, defense of sea lanes is a secondary, almost incidental, mission. If, however, the enemy of such a country is inaccessible, or nearly so, to invasion and at the same time is virtually dependent on its sea lines of communications, then that first country, if it is a naval power, is in a position to strike at the enemy's sea lines of communications and in this way to significantly influence the outcome of the war." Alafuzov, "O sushchnosti morskikh operatsii," p. 24.

broadsides since Admiral Alafuzov's opening gun in 1946.[30] The extensive propaganda suggests that not only has the Soviet submarine force's capability against merchant shipping become the greatest war fighting capability of the Soviet Navy but also is intended as a major deterrent factor to even limited NATO use of force against the USSR.

The potential wartime vulnerability of the United States' sea communications was made explicit in *Military Strategy:*

> We must consider that up to three-fourths of all the material and personnel of the probable enemy are across the ocean. According to the calculations of certain military theoreticians, in the event of war, eighty to one hundred large transports should arrive daily at European ports and 1,500 to 2,000 ships, not counting escorts, would be en route simultaneously.[31]

In 1960, A. Lagovskii, a leading Soviet military logistician, stated and illustrated the vulnerability of Western sea transport in the following way:

> The problem of sea communications for the Western countries even today is recognized as one of the most important problems in the conduct of war. The solution to the problem of supplying the NATO European armed forces with fuel, for example, depends almost entirely on the operation of a tanker fleet to effect the shipment of oil from the Middle East to Europe.[32]

Soviet military strategists, with the important exception noted in the preceding chapter, have drawn the logical conclusion from the vulnerability of NATO's maritime communications; both editions of the authoritative *Military Strategy* state unequivocally that "among the primary missions of the Navy in a future war will be the disruption of enemy ocean and sea shipping and the interdiction of his communications lines."[33] This mission, of course, the Soviet leaders would hope to accomplish with their unprecedently large peacetime submarine force. Soviet capabilities in this regard will be discussed in the next chapter.

The substantial postwar technical developments in antisubmarine warfare and the relatively large peacetime ASW forces that have been built and trained by the NATO powers have been recognized by Soviet strategists as a marked threat to any successful wartime submarine campaign against NATO shipping. In 1957, Soviet submariners were warned that

---

[30] See for example: A. Kruchenykh, "O vlianie reaktivnogo oruzhiia na taktiku flota" (The Influence of Missiles on Naval Tactics), *Sovetskii Flot,* November 15, 1957; Gorshkov, "Na strazhe morskikh rubezhei Sovetskoi derzhavy."

[31] Sokolovskii, *op. cit.,* 2nd ed., p. 399.

[32] Lagovskii, "Ekonomika i sposoby vooruzhennoi bor'by."

[33] Sokolovskii, *op. cit.,* 1st ed., p. 355; 2nd ed., p. 399.

NATO ASW forces were profiting from the continuous technological improvement in the state of the art: "Submarines must take into account the continuous development of antisubmarine warfare which has greatly complicated the nature of combat operations at sea."[34] The additional warning was sounded that "to get at the enemy, Soviet submarines must overcome the opposition of widespread antisubmarine forces.[35] The "opposition" was further delineated by public announcement that the United States had developed and installed a permanent system of long-range underwater sound detection for initial location and tracking of Soviet submarines.[36] The authors of *Military Strategy* asserted that of the "great" preparations the United States and United Kingdom were making for war against the Soviet Navy, the greatest were in ASW. They explained that NATO had prepared a large antisubmarine force and that the U.S. Navy alone had seven ASW groups built around "large antisubmarine aircraft carriers," of which four groups were operating in the Pacific and three in the Atlantic.[37] The collective authorship implicitly stated an important, although secondary, task of the Soviet Navy's primary mission for destroying the enemy's naval forces when they added that, in preparing for any future war, "this [situation] will have to be taken into account."[38] In November 1966, A. A. Kvitnitskii, a Soviet naval writer, called attention to what was asserted to be the American Naval Command's preference for submarines as the most effective ASW weapon, and U.S. plans to build up to a level of fifty nuclear-powered, torpedo-attack submarines by 1970 from the twenty-two built or building in September 1966.[39]

---

[34] "Nastoichivo izuchat', obraztsovo soderzhat' tekhniku podvodynkh lodok" (Persistently Study, Perfectly Maintain Submarine Equipment), *Sovetskii Flot,* October 19, 1957.

[35] F. Maslov, "Vnezapno i skrytno" (Suddenly and Covertly), *Krasnaia Zvezda,* October 12, 1963.

[36] V. Mikhailin, "Fizika i protivolodochnaia oborona" (Physics and Antisubmarine Defense), *Krasnaia Zvezda,* March 10, 1962.

[37] By early 1966, according to the U.S. Secretary of Defense, there were nine aircraft carriers committed chiefly to antisubmarine warfare. *The Baltimore Sun,* February 24, 1966.

[38] Sokolovskii, *op. cit.,* 2nd ed., p. 401. Despite the innumerable statements concerning the missions of the Soviet Navy to be found in the open literature, the writer could not find anything less vague than the statement quoted to reflect the obvious fact that the Soviet Navy has an objective requirement for the capability to destroy or neutralize the ASW forces of NATO. Otherwise the deterrent credibility of the Soviet submarine force in peacetime, as well as its "war-winning" capability in a general war, remains substantially undercut. One can readily appreciate the reluctance of Soviet leaders to discuss publicly objectively-required missions for which corresponding capabilities for their fulfillment are largely lacking.

[39] A. A. Kvitnitskii, "Napravlennost' razvitiia sil i sredstv PLO VMS SShA" (Direction of the Development of the ASW Forces and Equipment of the U.S. Navy), *Morskoi Sbornik,* November, 1966, p. 81.

In addition to United States and United Kingdom carrier task forces already described, the existing conventional submarine forces of NATO provide a serious threat to the USSR's sea lines of communications. Moreover, the Soviet press editorialized on the fact that the United States would have thirty-four nuclear-powered, torpedo-attack submarines by 1967.[40] In *Military Strategy* it was pointed out that these submarines would be used, at least in part, to interdict Soviet sea lines of communications.[41]

The Soviet merchant fleet has expanded very rapidly in recent years, and was programmed to double in tonnage between 1960 and 1965.[42] This expansion was accomplished so that at the beginning of 1967 the Soviet merchant fleet numbered 1,422 large merchant ships compared to 1,040 in the active U.S. fleet, and with plans to increase the Soviet fleet to 15 million tons by 1970 from the 9.8 million tons reached in early 1966, a further increase of over 50 per cent.[43] Considering this unprecedentedly rapid expansion in connection with the importance which maritime communications have come to play for the USSR, even back in 1941–45, as revealed in the following quotation from *Military Strategy,* one can readily appreciate the vital importance of those communications to the USSR in any protracted general war:

> The Navy carried out a variety of tasks . . . defending our own communication lines on the seas, lakes, and rivers. . . . The Great Patriotic War demonstrated that although the Soviet Union depended less on external communications than did other states, nevertheless, maritime communications were of extreme importance to us. More than 105 million tons of various types of cargo were transported during the course of the war. . . . 1,022 convoys with 3,233 transport ships were escorted in the Baltic Sea [alone].[44]

Admiral Alafuzov was so impressed with the importance of defending the USSR's maritime communications in any future war that shortly after the end of World War II he listed that mission as the first of seven he considered necessary in the postwar period, even placing it ahead of

[40] *Sovetskii Flot,* July 20, 1960.

[41] Sokolovskii, *op. cit.,* 2nd ed., p. 399

[42] U. S. Congress. Senate. Committee on the Judiciary. *Russia's Burgeoning Maritime Strength* (Washington: Government Printing Office, 1963), p. 2.

[43] Edwin M. Hood, Address to A.F.O.L.-C.I.O. Maritime Trades Department Seminar on Soviet Maritime Development, January 18, 1967. *The New York Times,* January 19, 1967. Mr. Hood, who is President of the Shipbuilders' Council of America, also pointed out that the USSR added 62 new ships to its merchant fleet in the second half of 1966 and that there is no reason to doubt that the 1970 plan goal of 15 million tons will be reached.

[44] Sokolovskii, *op. cit.,* 2nd ed., p. 205.

cutting the enemy's sea lines of communications.[45] Admiral Basistyi, a prominent Soviet naval writer, observed in 1956 that "the USSR's Navy plays an important role in the defense of the Soviet state. . . . We have many seas, lakes, and rivers which are of exceptionally great logistic importance."[46] The wartime admiral-turned-author, Fleet Admiral Isakov, admitted publicly in 1962, in *Izvestiia,* that although Soviet naval strategy in another war would have to remain strategically defensive, still "it will be necessary to make use of maritime communications."[47]

It can be appreciated, consequently, that the mission for "defense of Soviet maritime communications," as both editions of *Military Strategy* list it, is an important one, even if considered in that work and by other writers as secondary to the "primary" mission of destroying the enemy's naval forces.[48] Obviously, if the destruction of the NATO naval forces could be accomplished, the naval threat to Soviet shipping would automatically have been effectively nullified.

NATO capabilities for conducting large-scale transoceanic amphibious operations have not been lost from sight by Soviet military writers. Admiral Alafuzov has recently recalled in public print that the United States and England gained a great deal of experience in amphibious warfare, that the United States single-handedly had landed five divisions on the Normandy beaches two decades ago, and that the current U.S. capability along this line certainly was "significantly greater" than the two-division figure given in *Miltary Strategy*.[49] Both editions of that work gave the two-division figure for the U.S. Navy's amphibious lift capability and noted that those capabilities were being "further increased by the construction of new transport and landing ships" that would provide the United States with an increased capability "to transfer ground forces from America to Europe, the Far East, and to other areas."[50]

It was Admiral Alafuzov, again, who recognized as early as 1946 the need for the Soviet Navy to develop the naval forces that would be required for "defending against enemy efforts to invade from the sea."[51] In the report of the Minister of Defense to the Twentieth Party Congress in early 1956, Marshal Zhukov listed as the first of three areas receiving "primary attention" in making the U.S. Navy combat ready that of "cre-

---

[45] Alafuzov, "O sushchnosti morskikh operatsii," p. 11.
[46] Basistyi, "Na strazhe morskikh rubezhei.
[47] Isakov, "Problemy voiny na more."
[48] Sokolovskii, *op. cit.,* 1st ed., p. 353; 2nd ed., p. 396.
[49] Alafuzov, "K vykhodu v svet truda *Voennaia Strategiia*," p. 93.
[50] Sokolovskii, *op. cit.,* 1st ed., p. 104; 2nd ed., p. 120.
[51] Alafuzov, "O sushchnosti morskikh operatsii," p. 25.

ating the means for executing long-range naval transport and amphibious operations."[52] A book on the Soviet Navy by D. I. Kornienko, a professional Soviet writer on naval affairs, published by the Ministry of Defense in 1957, listed the countering of amphibious operations as one of the Soviet Navy's missions.[53] In 1961, an article in a Leningrad newspaper revealed that the Navy was not solely responsible for this mission, but that it was assigned to the Navy "together with other arms."[54] It would be logical to expect that the threat of an impending amphibious invasion would result in an "all hands" evolution to "repel boarders" so that other branches of the armed forces, including aviation and ground forces, could be expected to share the mission with the Navy. In 1962, in discussing naval missions in any future war, the first edition of *Military Strategy* stated that "although joint operations with the ground forces will not be a primary naval mission, considerable [naval] forces will be required for this." The first of several such missions subsequently listed was one to "annihilate enemy amphibious landing forces at embarkation points, at sea, and upon debarkation."[55] The Navy's critic of the first edition of *Military Strategy*, Admiral Alafuzov, accused the collective authorship of having minimized the importance of amphibious landing operations and reminded them that the ability to fulfill such missions in World War II had permitted the Allies to open new fronts in Africa, Italy, and France, and also permitted the United States ground forces to reach and occupy Japan.[56] Alafuzov's comment apparently agitated the Army authors of *Military Strategy* sufficiently to lead them to insert the following statement in the second edition in order to amplify the threat, and upgrade the importance of the mission of countering any attempted amphibious landing:

> The enemy may attempt to land large seaborne assaults, in which connection readiness to break up assault operations remains an important requirement of our naval, ground, and other types of armed forces.[57]

From the foregoing remarks it can be seen that Soviet military strategists do not by any means consider that the developments of the nuclear age have outmoded large-scale amphibious assaults. Quite the contrary, if not considered as important as the primary mission of destroying the

[52] Zhukov, *op. cit.*

[53] D. I. Kornienko, *Flot nashei rodiny* (Navy of Our Homeland), (Moscow: Voenizdat, 1957), p. 449.

[54] N. Kulakov, "Velikii flot velikoi derzhavy" (Great Navy of a Great Power), *Leningradskaia Pravda,* July 29, 1961.

[55] Sokolovskii, *op. cit.*, 1st ed., p. 356.

[56] Alafuzov, "K vykhodu v svet truda *Voennaia Strategiia,* p. 93.

[57] Sokolovskii, *op. cit.*, 2nd ed., p. 400.

enemy's naval forces, certainly the forestalling of any attempts at amphibious invasion of Soviet-held territory is now recognized as a mission of no mean importance.

Central to Soviet military doctrine is the tenet that final victory in a future war can only be achieved by actual occupation of the enemy's territory. As both editions of *Military Strategy* describe the requirements for bringing a war to a satisfactory conclusion from the Soviet point of view, there is no question but that Soviet military occupation of at least the key strategic areas of the United States would be considered necessary, as stated by Sokolovskii:

> For the achievement of those decisive political and military aims which a coalition of the socialist states would set for themselves in a future war, it would not go far enough to destroy the means for nuclear attack of the enemy and smash his main forces with nuclear missile strikes and also to disorganize his rear. For final victory in what is clearly a class war it will be absolutely essential to complete the total destruction of the armed forces of the enemy, take away his strategic staging areas, liquidate the military bases and occupy strategically important regions.[58]

Even should the USSR eventually build the veritable armada of troop transports that would be needed for a large-scale invasion of the North American continent, obviously it could not hope to carry out such an invasion across the Atlantic or Pacific in the face of opposition from the greatly superior naval forces of NATO. Admiral Alafuzov, in one of the most trenchant of his many criticisms of *Military Strategy*, pointed out, with unmistakable reference to NATO's command of the sea, that the weaker Soviet naval power would be defeated at sea in any transoceanic invasion attempt.[59] Since the USSR would find it hard to obtain the vast sums of money required to make a serious bid for sea supremacy, the

---

[58] Sokolovskii, *op. cit.*, 1st ed., p. 225, 2nd ed., pp. 345-346.

[59] "The authors must take into account the specific fact that a navy is capable of cutting off an amphibious landing while it is still at sea, before it even arrives off the coast. Worse than that, having a powerful navy in opposition, one cannot always take the risk of an amphibious landing." The Army authors of *Military Strategy* had aroused Alafuzov's ire by asserting that the Ground Forces would carry out all of the major missions in any future war; in venting his annoyance at this, the admiral provided a notable statement of the quasi-insoluble problem that lack of sea supremacy would create for any serious Soviet efforts to provide the armed forces, particularly the Navy, with truly war-winning capabilities: "The assertion that all first-priority missions can be fulfilled only by the Ground Forces is too categorical and unfounded. It belittles the significance of the other branches of the armed forces, particularly the Navy without which the Ground Forces would be wholly and completely handicapped, not to say worse, to carry out an invasion of the territory of an enemy across the sea." Alafuzov, "K vykhodu v svet truda *Voennaia Strategiia*," p. 92.

second edition of *Military Strategy* could only take note of Admiral Alafuzov's criticism to the extent of mentioning the need for the Navy to develop their capabilities for amphibious landings. Even this was stated in a context that avoided any implications that the Soviet Navy should develop a transoceanic amphibious capability.[60] Nor is a requirement for such a capability included in the innumerable statements of Soviet naval missions available in the open literature.

Leading U.S. specialists on Soviet military affairs such as Thomas Wolfe and Raymond Garthoff have correctly understood and expressed the USSR's objective need for transoceanic amphibious capabilities to support the aim of eventual war against the United States which they posit, but it appears that, aside from the questionable assumption as to the USSR's aims, they have failed to appreciate the immensity of the undertaking that would be involved in building the naval forces that would be required to enable the USSR realistically to contest for command of the sea. Otherwise Colonel Wolfe certainly would not have stated that "it *still remains to be seen* whether they [Soviet combined-arms advocates] establish a claim on the Soviet budget for the resources necessary to develop naval and amphibious capabilities on the formidable scale required for invasion of an overseas opponent like the United States."[61] There is not the slightest likelihood of the USSR's undertaking such a course in the foreseeable future. Certainly, Dr. Garthoff's marked caution in suggesting that "large scale amphibious operations over long ranges . . . seem to loom large as a likely area of increased future naval interest" was well placed.[62] It is a well-justified prognostication that budgetary limitations in addition to Party and Army dominance over military strategy will combine to insure that the Soviet Navy's logical interest in developing *long-range* amphibious capabilities for a protracted general war will remain purely an academic interest.

Yet, as certain as it appears that the USSR will not undertake the development of transoceanic capabilities for amphibious invasion, it appears equally certain that they have now and intend further to develop significant, if not large, capabilities for short-haul amphibious landings in support of Army operations. A consensus apparently has been reached among Soviet naval writers that amphibious operations are still feasible

---

[60] "Account must also be taken, in the development and organization of the Navy, of the problem of assuring joint operations with the ground forces and, primarily, the mission of bringing ashore amphibious landing forces." Sokolovskii, *op. cit.*, 2nd ed., p. 313.

[61] T. W. Wolfe, "Shifts in Soviet Strategic Thought," *Foreign Affairs*, April, 1964, pp. 475–486. Italics added.

[62] Garthoff, *op. cit.*, p. 199.

in the nuclear age.[63] Marshal Rotmistrov has stated unequivocally that amphibious landings will be employed on the coastal flanks of what he terms the "assaults in depth" that characterize contemporary Soviet military tactics.[64] Recently the authoritative political-military journal *Communist of the Armed Forces* listed as one of the Soviet Navy's tasks in fulfilling its mission for supporting the ground forces that of amphibious operations in sea and coastal areas.[65]

---

[63] "A detailed analysis of the present situation and of views on the development of weapons, equipment, and means for the transport and landing of troops supports the conclusion that it is feasible to carry out landing operations under contemporary conditions." N. P. V'iunenko, "Sovremennye morskie desanty" (Contemporary Naval Landings), *Morskoi Sbornik,* September, 1963, p. 21. See also: A. G. Svetlov and L. A. Shimkevich, "Osobennosti vysadki morskikh desantov v sovremennykh usloviiakh" (Characteristics of Amphibious Landings in Contemporary Circumstances), *Morskoi Sbornik,* March, 1964, p. 27; and E. Ivanitskii, "Morskie desanty" (Naval Landings), *Voennye Znanie,* February, 1958, p. 25.

[64] Rotmistrov, *op. cit.,* p. 89.

[65] G. Glazov, "O nekotorykh osobennostiakh vedeniia boevykh deistvii v iadernoi voine" (On Several Features of the Conduct of Combat Operations in Nuclear War), *Kommunist Vooruzhennykh Sil,* No. 3, February, 1964, p. 45.

★ *Major Tasks and Capabilities*

Having examined the correlation of Soviet naval missions with corresponding NATO naval and maritime capabilities and vulnerabilities, it is in order next to consider the various requirements noted by Soviet naval and military writers as necessary for carrying out the Soviet Navy's general war missions. In the process, attention will be given to the variety of tasks, weapons systems, tactics, and capabilities that have been developed by the USSR. This treatment will include, as appropriate, but often only implicitly, the effect had on the weapons systems and tactics employed for fulfilling each mission by "the revolution in military affairs."[1] This is the term Soviet writers customarily use to refer to the changes that have been brought about by technological advancements in missiles, atomic and hydrogen weapons, nuclear propulsion, electronics, cybernetics, and so on.

Generally speaking, a Party propaganda line has been adopted concerning the effect on the armed forces of the technological revolution. Typical of the numerous Soviet statements of the changes allegedly wrought in naval science and on the Soviet Navy is the following:

> The revolution in military affairs has fundamentally changed our Navy. Submarines of various types, which under the circumstances attending a nuclear-missile war are incomparably more effective than surface ships, are now considered its main force. In addition, the foundation of the submarine fleet is atomic submarines armed with nuclear-missile weapons. Modern submarines have the capability of directing fire against, and

---

[1] For a fuller statement of the author's views on the effect of the technological revolution on Soviet naval strategy, see his chapter, especially pages 159–169, in *The Military-Technical Revolution; Its Impact on Strategy and Foreign Policy,* John Ericson (ed.), (New York: Praeger, 1966), pp. 148–169.

destroying with ballistic and homing missiles [respectively], important strategic targets and aggressor warships. Naval missile-carrying aviation can successfully conduct combat operations in coordination with submarines.[2]

Understandably, the strictures of Soviet military security greatly limit the amount of technical detail available in the open literature on the sensitive subjects under discussion. Yet, a considerable amount of rather informative general information is available and has been set forth in the remainder of this chapter in the same order as the corresponding Soviet naval missions were treated in the preceding chapter.

Soviet writings have noted several factors that adversely affect the Soviet Navy's wartime prospects for being able to fulfill its highest priority task of combating Polaris submarines. One is the general state-of-the-art factor that ASW weapons being developed "are still lagging far behind requirements placed on them due to the much greater leap forward in the development of submarines."[3] It is evident that the USSR is hoping that its military research and development will result in one or more technological breakthroughs that will enable it to offset the substantial military superiority that the United States has gained over the USSR.[4] However, in the ASW field, as "expert" a witness as Vice Admiral Charles N. Martell, the U.S. Navy's director of ASW programs, has recently testified before the House Armed Services Committee that in the greatest problem area, that of initial detection, no breakthrough is to be expected.[5] In a statement of rare frankness in matters touching on so important and sensitive a subject as the USSR's weakness against NATO's

---

[2] N. Sbytov, "Revoliutsiia v voennom dele i ee resul'taty" (The Revolution in Military Affairs and Its Consequences), *Krasnaia Zvezda,* February 15, 1963.

[3] D. Kulinich, "Raket ischchet podvodnuiu lodku" (The Missile Seeks the Submarine), *Krasnaia Zvezda,* February 2, 1962.

[4] The most significant and authoritative recent article on overall Soviet military strategy concluded on the theme that since revolutionary changes had already taken place in all of the most important areas of military affairs and since the possibility of a thermonuclear war cannot be excluded, it is necessary to develop and utilize new means for conducting such a war. (Sokolovskii and Cherednichenko, *op. cit.*) Marshal Malinovskii is quoted as having made an even more specific comment looking forward to technological breakthroughs: "Science does not exclude the possibility of creating fundamentally new weapons for the destruction of various targets. Ever new problems in developing and equipping the Armed Forces with more efficient types of armaments . . . will be raised and solved in the future." (Sbytov, *op. cit.*)

[5] "Soviet Submarines Pose Threat, U.S. Admiral Says," *op. cit.* Based on a December 1966 interview with Vice Admiral Martell, a *Washington Post* correspondent set out the rationale for this conclusion: ". . . U.S. specialists, after their multi-billion dollar search, have not come up with any technological breakthrough to doom missile-carrying submarines. They assume their Soviet counterparts, with a lesser effort, have not done so either." George C. Wilson, "U.S. Sub Lore Said to Have 20-year Lead." *Washington Post,* December 22, 1966.

maritime capabilities, a Soviet naval writer has recently admitted that initial detection of submarines remains an unsolved problem in Soviet ASW.[6] It is well to keep in mind such admissions as this when evaluating propagandistic claims like the Soviet Defense Minister's that "antisubmarine aviation has become a very important force in our Navy [because] it is capable of locating and destroying the submarines of the enemy."[7]

The key ASW problem—initial detection of enemy submarines—is particularly acute in the case of Polaris submarines owing to the great distances from Soviet coasts at which Polaris missiles may be fired. *Military Strategy* took specific note of the fact that these ranges are as much as 2,500 miles for the Polaris A-3 and, in any event, are no less than 1,500 miles for the A-2.[8] This means that with just the A-2 the major industrial, military, and political centers of European Russia could be hit from such unfeasible areas for the USSR to conduct continuing ASW searches in as the Arctic Ocean, the Irish Sea, the Bay of Biscay, or the Mediterranean. With the A-3 those same cities could be attacked from far north of Spitsbergen, west of Iceland, from off either coast of sub-Saharan Africa, or the Arabian Sea. Small wonder that a leading Soviet military strategist, N. Lomov, has written: "The main actions of the enemy navies in a contemporary global war will be conducted not in the internal seas, but in the ocean theaters. This is instructive of the tasks for construction of our Navy."[9] Nor is it surprising, except perhaps as a matter of doubtful discretion in admitting even such an obvious weakness, that another Soviet naval officer (D. Kulinich), acknowledged that "the antisubmarine warfare zone must now embrace tremendous areas of the seas and oceans. Our Navy is not capable of fulfilling this task with the old weapons that are currently available."[10]

---

[6] "The [Soviet] Navy has developed a capability to throw light on the situation over great [ocean] areas in a comparatively short time that facilitates search for the enemy and tracking him. Only the [initial] detection of submarines constitutes an admitted difficulty." B. F. Petrov, "Soderzhanie i kharakter sovremennykh boevykh deistvii na more" (The Content and Character of Contemporary Naval Operations), *Morskoi Sbornik,* January, 1965, p. 9.

[7] R. Ia. Malinovskii, "45 let na strazhe sotsialisticheskoi rodiny; Doklad Ministra Oborony SSSR Marshala Sovetskogo Soiuza R. Ia. Malinovskogo" (45 Years of Guarding the Socialist Homeland; Report of the Minister of Defense Marshal of the Soviet Union R. Ia. Malinovskii), *Kransnaia Zvezda,* February 23, 1963.

[8] Sokolovskii, *op. cit.,* 2nd ed., p. 104.

[9] N. Lomov, "Osnovnye polozheniia Sovetskoi voennoi doktriny; revolutsiia v voennom dele, ee znachenie i posledstviia" (Fundamental Tenets of Soviet Military Doctrine; the Revolution in Military Affairs, its Significance and Consequences), *Krasnaia Zvezda,* January 10, 1964.

[10] Kulinich, *op. cit.* Even *Military Strategy* cautiously admits that "equipping nuclear submarines with the Polaris A-3 missile . . . makes them less vulnerable to the [USSR's]

As mentioned previously, the USSR believes the United States to have a system of long-range underwater sound detection for use in making initial detection and for tracking. Accordingly, it may be assumed that the Soviet naval planners would give the utmost consideration to the feasibility of establishing such a system for the USSR.[11] However, bearing in mind the remote areas from which Polaris missiles could be fired against European Russia, a glance at a map will reveal the utter infeasibility, politically or militarily, of the USSR ever obtaining the waterfront real estate, through purchase, lease, or limited wars, that would be required to establish such a system over meaningfully large parts of the Polaris firing areas.

Nor is lack of ocean frontage the only geographic handicap confronting Soviet planners who wrestle with the immensely difficulty it not impossible problem of ASW against Polaris submarines. There is also a critical lack of unrestricted access to the open oceans from Soviet bases for the Baltic, Northern, Pacific, and Black Sea fleets. As the authors of *Military Strategy* gave as their main criticism of Stalin's efforts to build up large, balanced fleets to challenge the West's sea supremacy, "no consideration was given to the fact that two of our fleets were based in closed seas [the Baltic and Black seas], while the Northern and Pacific fleets faced great difficulties in reaching the open seas."[12] The Soviet authors are referring here to the fact that the Danish and Turkish straits could be sealed off in wartime against Soviet submarine transit, while even across the relatively large stretches of water in the Greenland–Iceland–United Kingdom line or along the Kurile Islands chain and the three exits from the Sea of Japan, effective submarine-surface-air barriers could bar passage of Soviet submarines.

This severely restricted access to the open oceans for the naval forces of the four Soviet fleets greatly simplifies the wartime tasks of the NATO navies for preventing Soviet use of surface warships (even those with antiaircraft missiles) beyond the range of effective shore-based air cover. Since the maximum combat radius of that air cover is presently less

---

shore-based antisubmarine weapons." Sokolovskii, *op. cit.*, 2nd ed., p. 104. The "shore-based" weapons referred to are obviously naval aircraft.

[11] The author of the book *The Soviet Air Force,* which has an informative chapter on the Soviet Naval Air Force, has recently written the following perceptive comment on the vital significance for Soviet ASW efforts of Soviet lack of a long-range underwater detection system: "But as long as there is no method of long-range underwater detection the Polaris submarine weapons system is the key factor in contemporary missile strategy and the number and range of Polaris missiles will increase in the next year or so and so increase Soviet defence problems short of a breakthrough in long-range underwater detection of submarines by Soviet scientists and engineers." Asher Lee, "Some Problems of Soviet Strategy," *Brassey's Annual 1964* (New York: Praeger, 1964), p. 248.

[12] Sokolovskii, *op. cit.*, 2nd ed., p. 170.

than 2,000 miles,[13] generally speaking, the effective air cover radius, allowing some time to patrol at the end of the outward leg, would be considerably less. Consequently, this would permit the Polaris submarines, particularly those with the A-3 missile and later the Poseidon, a very large range margin in which to select firing positions. This accounts for the fact that a Soviet authority has stated that, "Only nuclear-powered, specially-equipped, antisubmarine submarines will constitute an effective means of antisubmarine defense in the future."[14] However, other highly reputable naval authorities, such as Fleet Admiral Isakov, no doubt considering the enormous areas to be covered in search of Polaris submarines, have stoutly maintained that "antisubmarine defense is generally impossible without aviation."[15] Other Soviet officers have argued the potential effectiveness of ASW aircraft even against nuclear-powered submarines.[16] In effect, the authors of *Military Strategy* acknowledged that the USSR has a requirement to develop and produce antisubmarine aircraft that could detect NATO submarines before they get within firing range of the USSR—that is, aircraft able to conduct patrols more than 2,500 miles from Soviet coasts.[17] The Soviet Air Day Show in 1961 had a few new jet seaplanes in the flyby, but even they apparently have not been produced in any quantity and provided to the fleets.[18]

---

[13] *Jane's All the World's Aircraft, 1966–1967,* ed. R. V. P. Blackman (New York: McGraw-Hill, 1966), p. 346.

[14] Zheludev, *op. cit.*

[15] Isakov, *op. cit.*

[16] Borzov, *op. cit.* These Soviet authors fail to point out that ASW aircraft, because they must carry a heavy load of electronic equipment and operate in the denser, more fuel-consuming atmosphere at just above sea level, have an even shorter range than the Soviet reconnaissance aircraft that can operate at high altitude. The only answer, as has been conclusively proven by the experience of the Western naval powers, is to operate ASW aircraft, both fixed and rotary-winged, from aircraft carriers. Singularly, the total inadequacy of Soviet shore-based aviation for operating far out at sea on a sustained basis to search for Polaris submarines has been overlooked in the writings of the present and former Rand analysts who have monopolized the field of Soviet military strategy in the United States. Thus, Dr. Garthoff cites with implied approval the claim of a Soviet naval writer who, with obvious reference to the Soviet Naval Air Force, asserts that: "The air force is the most universal type of force of the fleet." (Garthoff, *Soviet Military Doctrine,* p. 368.) Similarly, Colonel Thomas Wolfe, U.S. Air Force (Retired), implies that the Soviet Navy's lack of aircraft carriers is compensated for by a "substantial land-based air arm" that is one of the "factors which have given the naval forces greater weight in the Soviet scheme of things than was formerly the case." (Wolfe, *Soviet Strategy at the Cross-roads,* p. 228.) Although this may be literally true, it is misleading in the context in which it is presented of a complete failure to recognize the critically limited capabilities of any land-based air force for extensive, continuous operations far at sea.

[17] "Naval aircraft must be able to hit enemy warships at sea before the ships' . . . missiles are close enough to deal blows against targets in the socialist states." Sokolovskii, *op. cit.,* 2nd ed., p. 313.

[18] In recent years, obviously for the deterrent effect obtained, the USSR has made a

It now appears to be accepted Soviet doctrine that submarines, aircraft, and surface ASW ships will all play a role in Soviet efforts to counter Polaris submarines, although the necessarily diminished role of surface ships under existing conditions of limited range air cover is reflected in a correspondingly lighter emphasis on surface ships as compared to submarines and aircraft.[19]

Soviet tactics for ASW make allowance for the varying effective patrol ranges of submarines, airplanes, and surface ships. It is done by establishing a series of several different ASW defense zones extending concentrically outward from the Soviet coastline.[20] Logically, the effective patrol radius of land-based aircraft would be the outer limit of an ASW zone in which surface ships and aircraft could be used, while the area beyond that out to the maximum Polaris range would constitute another zone in which only Soviet submarines could patrol. Even a superficial consideration of the vast areas of the oceans involved in the outer submarine patrol zone makes it obvious that many times more submarines than any country could afford to build would be required to ensure locating and destroying a high percentage of the forty-one Polaris submarines scheduled for completion in 1967.[21]

Out of the total of 385 "modern" submarines, it can be seen that the USSR has no more than 97 effective ASW submarines, of which only a dozen are nuclear-powered.[22] Consequently, it is easy to appreciate why

---

practice of showing their operational weapons systems in published photographs, particularly in *Red Star*. However, no photos of the jet seaplane, nor the usual accompanying articles, have appeared. Moreover, the assiduous naval annuals such as *Jane's, Brassey's Marine-kalendar, Flottes de Combat,* etc. have failed to obtain any indication that the Soviet fleets have any *operational* seaplane other than the old, slow Beriev-6 "Madge" which has a maximum radius of only 1,500 miles. (Asher Lee, *The Soviet Air Force,* [New York: John Day Co., 1963], p. 154.) The 3,900 mile range Tupolev-95 "Bear" bomber might conceivably be utilized in an ASW role if fitted with ASW equipment, but it seems more likely that the USSR will find a less expensive aircraft to use in an ASW role. (*Jane's All the World's Aircraft 1965–1966,* pp. 335–336.)

[19] Sokolovskii, *op. cit.,* 2nd ed., pp. 313 and 381.

[20] As early as 1946, postwar Soviet military doctrine called for "several echelons of defense in depth" as well as for "constantly active defense" as general principles to be observed in all military, economic, and scientific areas. (F. Isaev, "Strategicheskoe iskusstvo Krasnoi Armii v velikoi otechestvennoi voine" [Strategic Art of the Red Army in the Great Patriotic War], *Krasnaia Zvezda,* February 20, 1946). A more recent writer has observed that ". . . a missile-launching submarine which has as its target an industrial center . . . does not need to be in position close to its target. Due to this, the ASW zones must now embrace tremendous areas in our seas and oceans." (Kulinich, *op. cit.*)

[21] "Soviet Submarines Pose Threat, U.S. Admiral Says," *op. cit.*

[22] *Jane's Fighting Ships 1966–1967* indicates, on page 433, that only twelve Soviet nuclear submarines are of the torpedo-attack type, which, of course, is the type that would be used in the ASW role as submarine hunter-killers. In addition, the same issue of *Jane's* lists 85 diesel submarines with modern or improved sonar that would fit them for ASW work, this includes 40 of the F-Class, 25 Z-Class, and 20 R-Class. It should be kept in mind also that any modern submarine possesses considerable ASW capabilities.

a Soviet marshal, even a tank officer, would understand the problem well enough to call for the "mass use" of submarines by Soviet ASW.[23] However, as discussed earlier, all evidence available to date indicates that the USSR is not undertaking any large scale production of the very costly nuclear-powered submarines, whether missile or torpedo-attack types.

In view of the vast ocean areas involved, normal large-area search methods, even for aircraft, would seem infeasible. In fact, one Soviet statement suggests that the use of air barriers is the tactic currently favored as Soviet tacticians endeavor to work out some practical methods of countering Polaris.[24] Submarine tactics against Polaris are apparently still in the development stage, with Soviet claims, for once, reasonable and modest—merely that Soviet submarines are making progress in learning ways of conducting warfare in the ocean depths.[25]

The Soviet press, however, has made an improbable claim of closely-related interest. It has stated that Soviet nuclear-powered submarines were first to operate in the Arctic Ocean and described a training exercise of one of them in which "the main mission of the ship lay in quickly reaching the North Pole and there barring the path of the 'enemy' missile-carrying submarines which have been penetrating the Barents Sea."[26] The Soviet press has also repeatedly stated that the USSR has solved the problems of under-ice travel and of accurate navigation at high latitudes.[27] Moreover, claims have been made that Soviet nuclear-powered submarines "are capable of cruising for weeks and months under the ice and of carrying out a cruise of many thousands of miles at high speed, without surfacing, without visiting a base, and without re-

---

[23] "Owing to the use of new weapons of war, operations at sea are characterized by the conduct of combat operations over great distances with selected targets and, especially important, with the mass participation of submarine forces and aviation." Rotmistrov, op. cit.

[24] "Yes, the enemy can move at great depths and speeds, but if the whole force of ASW aviation is opposing him, he will not cross forbidden boundaries." S. Ruban and N. Antonov, "Nad okeanskimi glubinamii" (Over the Ocean Depths), Krasnaia Zvezda, June 5, 1963.

[25] "Soviet submarines are learning successfully to achieve victory in the depths of the sea." ("Udarnaia sila flota" [Striking Power of the Navy], Sovetskii Flot, January 31, 1960). Another article stated: "Our antisubmarine forces are equipped with modern search apparatus and weapons for destroying submarines, including atomic [submarines], and each day they are acquiring knowledge and perfecting their skills. . . ." (Mamaev, op. cit.)

[26] V. Gol'tsev, "Lednyi pokhod" (Ice Cruise), Izvestiia, January 21, 1963.

[27] "It is appropriate to note that navigation in the Arctic by our surface ships and submarines has been a more or less routine matter for a long time and the mastering of the Northern Sea Route goes back to prewar times. With the advent of atomic power, capabilities and practical application in this field have expanded immeasurably. At the XXIInd Party Congress [1961] it was correctly noted that our submarines had learned well how to cruise under the Arctic ice and how to find positions at high latitudes with precision." Gorshkov, "Velikie zadachy Sovetskogo voenno-morskogo flota."

fueling."[28] One Soviet nuclear-powered attack submarine commanding officer has been quoted in the press to the effect that his submarine attained an underwater speed in excess of 60 kilometers per hour (over 32.5 knots).[29] The most recently published authoritative Western commentary on Soviet claims to have achieved a nuclear submarine capability for under-ice navigation to the North Pole stated that U.S. Navy authorities doubted the Soviet claims.[30] However, that was in 1963 and it must be assumed that if the Soviet has not yet developed such a capability, it can only be a matter of a relatively short time until they do.

In view of the inherent geographical and technical (i.e. "state-of-the-art") limitations on the Soviet Navy's present and foreseeable capabilities for developing any substantial ASW capabilities against the Polaris weapon system, the well-informed Soviet or foreign reader will discount heavily the frequent propaganda assertions regarding the unlimited anti-Polaris capabilities of the Soviet Navy. The following is a typical propaganda claim regarding Polaris submarines: ". . . these pirate ships . . . will be good targets . . . and will be detected and sunk . . ."[31] Such panegyrics are a regular feature of the speeches made by leading Soviet personages on the occasion of the numerous Soviet holidays. When the Navy Commander in Chief blathers blandly that "the Soviet Navy . . . is able to fulfill *any* operational mission"[32] or the Minister of Defense bellows that the Navy is completely capable "not only of defending our maritime borders but also of annihilating the enemy's naval forces on the seas and oceans,"[33] the sophisticated reader may reasonably make some major mental reservations about the literal accuracy of such statements.[34]

On the other side of the propaganda coin of Soviet slogans of military invincibility are corresponding word pictures of Western military vulner-

---

[28] Ivanov, *op. cit.*

[29] Gol'tsev, *op. cit.*

[30] "Moscow has said that a Soviet nuclear submarine cruised under the Arctic ice to the North Pole, but [U.S.] Navy authorities doubt this claim." Hanson Baldwin, "Soviet Submarine Lag," *The New York Times,* April 18, 1963, p. 6.

[31] Mamaev, *op. cit.*

[32] Gorshkov, "Na strazhe morskikh rubezhei Sovetskogo derzhavy," Italics added.

[33] "Priem v kremle v chest' sorokaletiia Sovetskoi Armii i Voenno-Morskogo Flota," *op. cit.*

[34] For his part, this writer tentatively concludes that such statements are deliberate misrepresentations motivated by domestic requirements for sustaining morale and production as well as by a complex of foreign propaganda objectives. Among these latter logically might be that of enhancing the credibility of the USSR's nuclear capabilities. Another aim could well be to sustain, in undiminished form as a support to Soviet foreign policy, the great military prestige that the USSR enjoys in Free World capitals, especially those of the under-developed and uncommitted nations. As this study undertakes to make clear, the prestige the USSR enjoys as far as it derives from the Soviet Navy, has been greatly exaggerated in the public media.

abilities. In the case of Polaris, this propaganda attempts to discredit the deterrent capabilities of Polaris by alleging that the Polaris system is highly vulnerable to Soviet military capabilities. Thus, the reader of Soviet military newspapers and journals learns variously that "such advanced bases of aggression as those for atomic missile submarines at Holy Loch, Scotland, and Rota, Spain" are the Achilles heel of the Polaris system,[35] that the communications stations broadcasting to Polaris submarines are in fact the really vulnerable point because they provide essential *command and control*,[36] as well as that the Polaris submarines themselves are vulnerable or ineffective because they are too noisy,[37] at great disadvantage against aircraft,[38] "very sensitive to underwater nuclear explosion,"[39] so inaccurate that they can only be used against large population centers,[40] have nuclear warheads of little force,[41] and in *Military Strategy* it was asserted that Polaris submarines are even vulnerable to cruise missile attack![42] This last claim was too much for Admiral Alafuzov's obviously limited patience with *Military Strategy's* Army officers-cum-naval strategists, and he retorted bluntly and with scarifying sarcasm:

> . . . without any basis whatever they state categorically that the missile-carrying nuclear submarine is in reality vulnerable and that an effective means against it "is the homing missile launched from a submarine or surface ship." Such an unproven conclusion seems brash and unconvincing. Apparently, the indisputable fact that nuclear submarines will operate only when submerged was not taken into consideration.[43]

---

[35] T. Belashchenko, "Amerikanskie bazy—forposty agressii i provokatsii" (American Bases—Advance Posts of Aggression and Provocation), *Krasnaia Zvezda,* January 22, 1965.

[36] "U.S. Polaris submarines . . . are by no means an isolated, autarchic system . . . On the contrary, their efficiency depends entirely on the work of surface bases and installations. In addition to logistics, intermediate and advanced bases, the U.S. Navy in general, and its missile-carrying submarines in particular, need an extensive communication system and control and navigation systems . . . the radio stations which guide atomic submarines and help them train their missiles on the target constitute one of the weakest points of the entire system." Y. Shvedkov, "Bases in Pentagon Strategy," *International Affairs,* May, 1964, p. 57.

[37] Chabanenko, *op. cit.*

[38] Borzov, *op. cit.*

[39] Polianskii, *op. cit.*

[40] Rogov, *op. cit.,* p. 84. Sokolovskii, *op. cit.,* 2nd ed., pp. 86–87.

[41] Sokolovskii and Cherednichenko, *op cit.*

[42] The first edition of 1962, which drew down Alafuzov's wrath, stated on page 340: "Effective weapons against missile-carrying nuclear submarines are homing missiles from submarines and surface ships." The revised edition of 1963, in what the writer construes as an effort, although completely inept and unsuccessful, to correct the offending statement, repeated a different version of the same error: "Effective weapons against missile-carrying nuclear submarines are hunter-killer submarines with homing missiles and torpedoes, also surface ships." (Page 381.) One suspects that the intended correction was "homing torpedoes" without any mention of missiles.

[43] Alafuzov, "K vykhodu v svet truda *Voennaia Strategiia,* p. 94.

Judging from the widely-varying and generally unpersuasive reasons alleged for the Polaris system being so vulnerable and ineffective, the Communist Party line on this important propaganda subject is in a surprisingly arrested and inchoate form. Happily for them, the Soviet leaders are not troubled by their wholly expedient practice of making related statements that non-Marxists would consider inconsistent with the propaganda portrayal of Polaris. An example is the Soviet Party's assignment of countering Polaris as the Navy's top mission. Most inconsistent of all, since the Soviet Navy's vaunted strength lies mainly in its nuclear-missile submarine force, the Soviet leaders are caught in the wholly untenable position of having to establish the deterrent credibility of its own missile submarines while attempting to weaken the credibility of its opponent's. Consequently, statements in direct contradiction to the derogatory remarks about Polaris are made in favor of the Soviet nuclear missile submarines. Thus, one finds the Soviet Navy's Commander in Chief giving Soviet missile submarines plaudits such as the following:

> Our Navy has also changed in a radical manner. The basis of its striking power is now atomic submarines equipped with long-range missiles for various purposes. They are absolutely new and not comparable to any other ships which are carriers of missile weapons. Owing to their unlimited power supply, the new submarines are able to develop high speed and to remain submerged for a long time. They are *essentially invulnerable;* they can persistently search for and track enemy ships, and utilize their missiles against them in any, even the most remote, areas of the world's oceans without coming to the surface.[44]

From the foregoing, it should be clear that the Soviet leaders are caught on the proverbial horns in their dilemma of needing to establish the credibility of their missile submarine deterrent while weakening the credibility of Polaris. Obvious, too, is the fact that the capabilities which would be required to counter substantially the Polaris submarine threat are so extensive that they would take years to develop, even should the Soviet leaders decide they could afford to undertake such an enormously expensive program.

Early in the postwar period the fact was recognized in the USSR that aircraft carriers continued to constitute the "cornerstone" of the U.S. Navy.[45] With the introduction of nuclear bombs as the primary general

---

[44] S. G. Gorshkov, "Sovetskim vooruzhennym silam" (To the Soviet Armed Forces), *Trud,* February 22, 1963. Italics added.

[45] "Aircraft carriers constituted weapons of decisive significance in the war in the Pacific and remain the cornerstone of the postwar U.S. Navy." I. A. Razumnyi, "Avianosnie soedineniia flota SShA v voine na Tikhom okeane" (Aircraft Carrier Task Forces of the U.S. Navy in the War in the Pacific), *Morskoi Sbornik,* July, 1946, p. 81.

war weapon of NATO carrier striking forces, Soviet strategists were faced with the imperative defensive task of developing a capability for destroying those forces before they could launch their strike aircraft. The unacceptable alternative was to accept the risk of successful penetration of Soviet air defenses by those strike aircraft. The extreme difficulties posed by this task are nicely reflected by the unusually uncertain wording in which they were described in both editions of *Military Strategy:* "It is essential to *attempt* to destroy the attack carriers before they reach aircraft launch positions. . . ."[46] Recognition was granted to the fact that weapons systems and tactics for countering strike carriers would have to overcome the concentration of antisubmarine, antisurface ship, and antiair firepower that is organic to each carrier striking force.[47] It was further recognized by the Soviet leaders that their defenses would have to be prepared to deal with the relatively hard-to-detect radar return of a single aircraft carrier, including those with nuclear propulsion, which would be moving into launch position unaccompanied by any screening forces.[48] In addition, cognizance was taken of the apparent intent of the U.S. Navy to employ an increasing number of nuclear-powered destroyers primarily for antiaircraft and antisubmarine warfare protection of carrier task forces—an employment that would, in particular, provide a surface ASW ship with the speed and endurance required to contest against nuclear-powered submarines.[49]

The guided missile submarine, particularly with nuclear propulsion, has been the primary weapons system designed by the Soviet Union in her efforts to find an adequate defense against NATO's strategic nuclear strike carrier forces. That this is the case was affirmed openly in 1961 by Khrushchev himself.[50]

However, aircraft armed with air-to-surface missiles have been acknowledged to share substantially in combating carrier forces.[51] Not only the

---

[46] Sokolovskii, *op. cit.,* 1st ed., p. 354; 2nd ed., 1963, p. 397. Italics added.

[47] *Ibid.,* 2nd ed., p. 396.

[48] "Attack carrier groups can break up into smaller groups. Such groups can include one attack carrier and covering forces. The American press expresses the idea that attack carriers, especially with atomic power plants, can operate without protection. All this must be considered in organizing combat against aircraft carriers." *Ibid.,* p. 397.

[49] Zheludev, *op. cit.*

[50] "As Khrushchev pointed out at the XXIInd Congress of the Communist Party of the Soviet Union [in 1961], the Soviet submarine force with atomic engines and armed with ballistic and homing missiles, vigilantly stands watch over our socialist achievements. It will return shattering blows against aggressors, including their aircraft carriers, which will constitute a rather good target for our missiles in case of war." Argunov, Zheltikov, and Larionov, *op. cit.*

[51] "Together with submarines, naval missile-carrying . . . aviation has become a very important force in our Navy. It is capable of locating and destroying . . . the surface ships . . . of the enemy." Malinovskii, "Rech' tov. Malinovskogo."

medium-range bombers of Soviet naval aviation but, according to Marshal Malinovskii while he was Defense Minister, the heavy bombers of Soviet long-range aviation have been assigned to contribute to the anti-carrier defense.[52] Surface striking forces armed with surface-to-surface guided missiles have allegedly been earmarked to participate in this all-out effort.[53] The Soviet Navy's coastal missile units are also integrated into the same effort.[54] Even conventionally-powered, as well as nuclear-powered, torpedo attack submarines have been assigned a role.[55] Furthermore, part of this defense system are the antiaircraft weapons of the surface naval forces and of the USSR's national air defense organization, the PVO Strany.[56]

The tactics to be used by these forces have been carefully planned to take advantage of the characteristics and relatively weak points of carrier striking forces. Notice was taken of the fact that, in 1963 at least, carrier launching areas were contained by rather limited sea areas, such as the Norwegian Sea, the Mediterranean, or the East China Sea.[57] The total vulnerability of carriers, once their radar screening ships have been sunk, has been alleged.[58] The restraints on the maneuverability of carriers when refueling and while heading into the wind to launch or recover aircraft have been noted.[59] As concerns their utility in a protracted war, the

---

[52] "Carrier strike forces can be successfully combated by both aircraft of naval aviation and of long-range aviation. Armed with air-to-ship missiles with nuclear warheads, these planes can strike without coming within range of the air defense weapons of the carrier force." Sokolovskii, *op. cit.,* 2nd ed., p. 398.

[53] "Armed with homing missiles, Soviet surface warships have the capability of destroying at sea, from hundreds of kilometers away, the merchant ships and warships of the enemy, in particular his aircraft carriers which, as Nikita Sergeevich Khrushchev correctly observed at the XXIInd Congress of the KPSS, make good targets for our homing missiles." Isachenkov, *op. cit.*

[54] "Yet other forces [in addition to 'modern submarines and missile-carrying aviation'] are needed for active combat against an enemy within the limits of the defense zone of a naval theatre and to support the combat and operational activities of the main striking forces of the Navy. Among such forces are surface missile ships and craft . . . coastal missile units, etc." (Gorshkov, "Zabota partii o flote," *op. cit.,* p. 16). "Coastal missile installations can also be used to destroy enemy naval forces." (Sokolovskii, *op. cit.,* 2nd ed., p. 399).

[55] Sokolovskii and Cherednichenko, *op. cit.*

[56] Sokolovskii, *op. cit.,* 2nd ed., p. 395.

[57] *Ibid.,* p. 397.

[58] "The radar picket forces need only be penetrated or neutralized to make the carriers and other units of the force defenseless against missile strikes from submarines and naval aircraft." (*Ibid.,* 1st ed., p. 354). The revised edition is not even specific about the requirement for penetrating the radar picket forces, but asserts, instead, that submarines and aircraft can attack carrier task forces without coming within the defense zone of the carrier screen: ". . . radar picket forces will be located on the perimeter of the area. But these forces and weapons can no longer reliably protect the attack carriers and other elements of the force from missile strikes from submarines and naval aircraft." (*Ibid.,* 2nd ed., p. 397.)

[59] *Ibid.,* p. 397.

dependence of carrier forces on bases and mobile logistic support forces has been mentioned to point up their vulnerability.[60] Soviet tactics clearly envisage exploiting the large radar returns that result from the widely spread ships of a carrier task force, as well as employing the ubiquitous Soviet fishing trawlers to gain initial detection of the approach of such forces.[61] Then the primary tactic for attacking such forces, professedly, is to launch missiles, from submarines, aircraft, surface ships, or coastal missile installations, while the missile-launching platform is still outside the "zone of antisubmarine and antiaircraft defense of the attack carrier force."[62] However, as applied to missiles launched by submarines, surface ships, or coastal missile batteries, this tactic has one major handicap: the requirement for another aircraft or submarine near the target to provide forward guidance to the missile.[63]

Repeated claims have been made in Soviet military literature that their submarines are equipped with torpedoes with nuclear warheads.[64] Some Soviet nuclear-powered submarines are alleged to be armed with antiship missiles that can be fired from underwater.[65] In view of Soviet practice in recent years, it seems likely that they would publicly parade such important new weapons if they actually had developed them in order to increase the USSR's nuclear deterrent credibility; however, no evidence to support the Soviet claims has come to light.[66]

---

[60] *Ibid.*

[61] Isakov, *op. cit.* On the role of trawlers as an early warning screen covering the Atlantic approaches to the Soviet Union, see W. V. Kennedy, "The Soviet Fleet," *Ordnance,* May-June, 1958, p. 976.

[62] "The presence in our Navy of missile-carrying submarines and missile-carrying aircraft permit approaching the aircraft carrier to the distance of missile launch, without entering the zone of antisubmarine and antiaircraft defense of the attack carrier forces." Sokolovskii, *op. cit.,* 2nd ed., p. 397.

[63] Kruchenykh, *op. cit.*

[64] "In the Navy, atomic-powered submarines armed with missiles and torpedoes with nuclear warheads have become the main arm." ("Vooruzhennye sily," *Ezhegodnik 1963g, Bol'shaia Sovetskaia Entsiklopediia* [Yearbook 1963, Great Soviet Encyclopedia] [Moscow: Great Soviet Encyclopedia Press, 1963], p. 75.) ". . . our Navy . . . is primarily a submarine navy, the basis for which are atomic submarines armed with missiles and torpedoes with nuclear charges." (Kasatonov, "Boevaia vakhta Sovetskikh moriakov.")

[65] "An effective means of combating strike carriers and other surface forces is by the use of missile-carrying nuclear submarines. The old-style submarines destroy ships by direct hits below the waterline with torpedoes; these submarines are close to the target and close to the surface, which makes them easy targets. Nuclear submarines carrying homing missiles have become a great threat to surface ships. They are highly autonomous, have great underwater cruising speed, and can strike with their missiles from great distances, *even from under the water.* Therefore, the nuclear submarine is less vulnerable, highly maneuverable, and can successfully conduct battles against aircraft carriers and other surface ships." Sokolovskii, *op. cit.,* 1st ed., p. 354. Italics added.

[66] It has been impossible so far to determine with certainty whether or not such seemingly unlikely claims to having in operational use torpedoes with nuclear warheads and sub-

Soviet propaganda has made an intense effort to discredit the aircraft carrier. This sustained propaganda campaign has had three noteworthy aspects. First, the carrier is claimed to have been outmoded by the revolution in military affairs.[67] As one Soviet writer alleged, the carrier has an "organic defect—great vulnerability to nuclear-tipped missiles."[68] Secondly, Soviet propaganda claims a complete and infallible capability for sinking aircraft carriers,[69] even though *Military Strategy,* probably inad-

---

marine-launchable cruise missiles are anything more than propaganda. That such claims are unfounded and made solely for propaganda might well be the case is suggested not only by the USSR's failure to demonstrate their possession of such weapons but also by the strong motivation that the USSR currently has to enhance the deterrent image of their Navy to attempt to overcome somewhat the public knowledge of the overwhelming nuclear strike capabilities of NATO naval forces. This would be a relatively difficult ploy to disprove since the weapons claimed are within the state of the art and weapons are not as readily observable as are weapons platforms such as a ship or aircraft.

[67] Anti-carrier propaganda runs the gamut from superficially rational assertions such as those of Admiral Gorshkov and Marshal Eremenko, quoted first below, to the attempt to completely belittle carriers or to apply the "devil theory" of international relations to U.S. industrialists as subsequently cited: "In World War II, aircraft carriers represented the striking nucleus of the U.S. and British navies, and were widely employed in combat operations in the Atlantic and, particularly, in the Pacific. Now the foundation of the Navy consists of nuclear-missile weapons, electronic systems, and atomic energy, and the significance of aircraft carriers has fallen sharply. They, as battleships, have already had their day and are inevitably moving into the past. In their place are new ships—missile-carriers." (Gorshkov, "Vernye syny rodiny.") ". . . the Navy . . . in its past form has become irrevocably obsolete. Military bases are also losing their previous importance from the standpoint of the Navy. . . . But the conditions for basing submarines differ sharply from the conditions for basing the big warships of the recent past. The transition of submarines to atomic power poses this question in an entirely new light. And now a point has been reached when, with the emergence of the missile and nuclear weapons, even aircraft carriers have become so vulnerable that their use appears to be inexpedient." (A. Eremenko, "Strategicheskoe i politicheskoe znachenie voennykh baz" [Strategic and Political Significance of Military Bases], *Mezhdunarodnaia Zhizn'*, November, 1960, p. 85); "My opinion is that these colossal aircraft carriers would be floating corpses should they be used against a powerful opponent who has modern means of conducting war. In spite of the fact that the latest types are equipped with atomic propulsion plants and possess great speed, they are ships of the past, just like the battleships." (Isakov, *op. cit.*); "Vital influence on the establishment of the warship building program and the path of the development of the [United States'] Navy is exerted by the monopolies receiving vast incomes from the construction of carriers and airplanes. Yet, as the foreign press, particularly the American, writes, the continued construction of new aircraft carriers is not at all in conformity with the views which are firmly established in the U.S. on the role and significance of this class of warship in the future." (Ya. Nikonov, "Viazvimost' avianostsev v atomnoi voine" (Vulnerability of Aircraft Carriers in Atomic War), *Sovetskii Flot,* August 2, 1958.

[68] "The installation of nuclear propulsion plants in strike carriers does not eliminate the primary defect of this class of ships which has become, one might say, their organic defect —great vulnerability to nuclear-tipped missiles. The utilization of carrier-based aircraft as carriers of nuclear weapons, the primary weapon of aircraft carriers, has also little prospect for the future. Leading naval circles in the USA must face up to this situation. . . ." A. Zheludev, "Atomnyi flot" (Atomic Navy), *Krasnaia Zvezda,* January 9, 1962.

[69] "Our atomic submarines, equipped with long-range missiles and torpedoes with power-

vertently, implied strong doubt about Soviet capabilities for preventing NATO's carriers from launching initial strikes at the outbreak of war.[70] Thirdly, the USSR has overflown U.S. aircraft carriers at sea on numerous occasions in an obvious effort to lend credence to Soviet propaganda claims about the great vulnerability of carriers and Soviet capabilities to destroy them.[71] One is reminded of Admiral Arleigh Burke's apt comment on such Soviet propaganda that he made in an address to the Coast Guard Academy in 1958:

> Mr. Khrushchev has frequently expressed himself publicly and officially concerning our naval forces. He has, of course, drawn upon the old Communist tactic of trying to frighten us away from relying on naval forces. He calls them useless, good only for ceremonial visits, vulnerable to being reduced to bolts and molten metal. He has good reason for not liking American naval forces. He doesn't like them because he can't do anything about them. Hence, he resorts to the only device left to him short of armed action against us. He threatens and ridicules in the hope that somebody will believe him.[72]

Since the NATO lead in naval development and greater resources afford the Soviet successors to Khrushchev little hope for reducing their naval inferiority significantly, it is unlikely that they will feel able to dispense with his propaganda tactics against Western naval forces, in general, and the aircraft carrier in particular.[73]

---

ful nuclear warheads, can successfully conduct combat operations, either independently or in coordination with aviation and other naval forces, against aircraft carrier forces . . . destroying them in any part of the World Ocean." (Mamaev, *op. cit.*) Despite its egregious slip, from a propaganda viewpoint, regarding the uncertain Soviet capability for sinking carriers to prevent their launching their initial strikes, *Military Strategy* does conclude on an unwarrantedly optimistic note as follows: "Our naval strength has grown considerably because it has been equipped with new weapons. . . . It has become capable of carrying out the tasks assigned it far from Soviet waters. Modern [Soviet] submarines, armed with ballistic and homing missiles, have the capability to strike population centers and destroy the warships of any aggressor." (Sokolovskii, *op. cit.*, 2nd ed., p. 248.)

[70] See footnote 46, p. 118.

[71] W. C. Chapman, "The Soviet Air Forces," *Naval Review 1965* (Annapolis: United States Naval Institute, 1964), p. 177. The facts that have largely escaped public attention are that the first such flights coincided with Congressional hearings on the carrier construction program and that carriers are easily located in peacetime when their movements are reported in the press and no restrictions are imposed on radio transmissions that can be easily used for radio direction finding.

[72] Quoted in *Baltimore Sun,* October 13, 1958.

[73] Writing a decade ago Raymond Garthoff, perhaps understandably, took at face value the Soviet propaganda assertion that the aircraft carrier was too vulnerable to be of value: "But the Soviets have definitely concluded that because of its vulnerability to modern weapons systems the aircraft carrier is an unacceptable weapons system." (Garthoff, *Soviet Strategy in the Nuclear Age*, p. 201.) Writing in February 1967, the Soviet Navy's Commander in Chief repeated the earlier admission made in *Voennaia Strategiia* in 1962 that the aircraft carrier continues to be an important weapons system: "True, in the West now

As mentioned earlier, the Soviet Navy's guided missile submarines could, if unanticipated circumstances required it, be used against land targets, but with poorer accuracy than against the more sharply defined ship targets for which their terminal homing guidance system was designed.[74] However, in the words of a Soviet engineer, Admiral N. V. Isachenkov, it is "ballistic missiles [that] are basically designed for the destruction of land targets such as naval bases and industrial complexes."[75] As also noted earlier, the most recent estimate available indicates that the USSR now has a force of about fifty-three ballistic missile submarines.[76] Ten of these are former Z-class torpedo-attack, diesel-powered submarines that apparently were converted in a few months' time to provide an initial missile submarine deterrent capability.[77] Thirty more, also diesel-powered, are of the G-class which appear to have been designed from the keel up as ballistic missile submarines.[78] Only thirteen of the fifty-three have the great advantages of nuclear propulsion that characterize all of the Polaris missile submarines.[79] Moreover, the rate of production of the Soviet ballistic missile, nuclear-powered submarines, which are all of the H-class, can be seen from comparing the figures given in successive recent issues of *Jane's* to be only one, or possibly

---

as before aircraft carriers are charged with important tasks even in nuclear missile war." (Gorshkov, "Razvitie Sovetskogo voenno-morskogo iskusstva," p. 19.)

Another of the leading U.S. specialists on Soviet military strategy, all of whom seem to have been employees of the U.S. Air Force's Rand Corporation at the time their major works were written, quotes with that implied approval which lack of dissenting comment indicates that Soviet leaders are "convinced that, in the nuclear age particularly, large surface ships are an unnecessary luxury," that "much smaller vessels can execute naval tasks as well or better than the larger ships," and that "the American fleet, with its many large surface vessels, is to a great extent obsolescent." (Dinerstein, *War and the Soviet Union*, p. 248). It should not be difficult to appreciate that while naval ships and craft as small as destroyers, submarines, and even torpedo boats can carry surface-to-surface missiles, it is not solely this criterion of being able to carry the latest weapon of the military-technical revolution which is at issue. Rather, the question is one of providing absolutely essential air coverage for surface naval forces operating outside the range of shore-based air cover. For this, the missile, whether conventional or nuclear-tipped or whether carried in a submarine, ship, or aircraft, has no solution and so cannot replace the aircraft carrier. No amount of propaganda should be allowed to obscure this salient fact.

[74] Interestingly, none of the leading U.S. specialists on Soviet military strategy have noted in their writings, even at junctures where such notice would have been relevant, either that Soviet nuclear-powered missible submarines are of two types, the most numerous one of which (the guided missile submarine) is designed for use against ships rather than against shore targets.

[75] Isachenkov, *op. cit.*

[76] *Jane's Fighting Ships 1966–1967*, pp. 433–434.

[77] *Ibid.*, p. 434.

[78] *Ibid.*

[79] *Ibid.*, p. 433.

two, per year.[80] From this it is obvious that the USSR is not undertaking to match the U.S. nuclear-powered, ballistic missile force goal for 1967 of having operational forty-one Polaris submarines. Despite the particularly advantageous characteristic of nuclear propulsion for a ballistic missile submarine of affording much greater underwater endurance for longer on-station time, the production of the new but diesel-powered G-class and the minimal production of nuclear-powered units of this type strongly indicate that a large share of the USSR's ballistic missile submarine force will continue to have recourse to diesel propulsion for many years to come. In fact, the USSR has made an authoritative admission to this effect.[81]

Both the Navy Commander in Chief and his deputy have stated a military requirement for being able to hit any land target in the "World Ocean" with submarine-launched missiles.[82] The most recent specific estimate available, published in December 1963, gave the range of Soviet submarine missiles as 350 miles.[83] Even should this range eventually be doubled or tripled (in the way that the range of Polaris missiles has been increased in the second and third versions of the original 1,500-mile missile), great problems would still remain. The lack of nuclear propulsion in over three-fourths of Soviet ballistic missile submarines and the unavailability of any forward bases such as the U.S. possesses at Holy Loch, Scotland, at Rota, Spain, and at Apra Harbor on Guam, means a long, slow, and hazardous journey from Soviet Northern Fleet and Pacific Fleet bases through the Greenland–Iceland–U.K. line and through the Sea of Japan and the Kurile Islands, to reach stations within range of the continental United States. Of equal seriousness, by the time that the diesel-powered units have finally arrived on station, it can be only a relatively short time before they have to begin the long trek back. The inescapable consequence of this, of course, is that the number of submarines that can be maintained on station is very greatly reduced. The long trip

---

[80] For the author's estimate of the USSR's construction rate for nuclear submarines, see p. 84, footnote 70.

[81] See quote associated with footnote 119, p. 134 *infra.*

[82] ". . . considering the intentions of the aggressors and the role given to their navies in the plan for a nuclear attack on the socialist countries, the Soviet Union must be prepared to reply with crushing blows on naval and land objectives over the entire area of the world's seas." (Gorshkov, "Velikye zadachy Sovetskogo Voenno-morskogo flota.") "The main striking force of the Navy today is submarines which have excellent missile-firing atomic-powered units capable of delivering irresistible and devastating strikes on sea and land targets in any part of the World Ocean." (V. A. Kasatonov, "Tridtsat' slavnikh let" [Thirty Glorious Years], *Krasnaia Zvezda,* July 27, 1963.)

[83] Lord Kennet, *op. cit.,* p. 153. In December 1966, Vice Admiral C. B. Martell, the U.S. Navy's director of antisubmarine warfare programs, described Soviet submarine missiles as having a range of only "a few hundred miles." U.S. Admiral on Soviet Missiles, *United Press International,* December 21, 1966.

involved, combined particularly with the fear of detection and consequent loss of credibility as part of the USSR's strategic nuclear deterrent, may well account for the Soviet failure to conduct such patrols regularly.[84] It is assumed that the United States would have detected such patrols and that news of them normally would have been leaked to the press.

In this regard, Khruschchev, while still enjoying the plenitude of power as Party chairman and premier, posed a rhetorical question which may reveal much more than he intended. After characterizing "the Pentagon's policy of sending missile-carrying submarines cruising off the coasts of the USSR" as "another criminal manifestation of the brink-of-war policy" of the United States, Khruschchev added: "Our country also has atomic-powered submarines armed with missiles, but what would happen if we sent our submarines cruising off the coasts of America?"[85] A factual answer to this question might well have been that many of them would have been detected and given sensational treatment in the U.S. press, with the result that the credibility of the USSR's submarine component of its national nuclear deterrent would have been much reduced. Soviet leaders may have been trying to support their foreign policy of "peaceful coexistence" with a show of nonaggression or, alternatively or additionally, they quite possibly were further inciting the left-wing hue and cry against foreign governments willing to permit use of their ports by Polaris submarines. At any rate, the question tacitly admitted either the USSR's technical inability to maintain patrols of nuclear submarines off the U.S. coasts at all or to do so undetected.

Although Khrushchev's revealing question was posed back in 1960, even by early 1967 we are reliably informed by U.S. authorities that Soviet missile submarines are not maintained on patrols within missile range of the continental United States.[86] Consequently, it seems a fair presumption that the political and technical reasons that prevented the Soviet missile submarines from operating undetected off our coasts in 1960 continue to be unresolved. It seems improbable that any Communist leaders would willingly pass up the great increase in credibility of their strategic nuclear deterrent that would accrue from having their missile submarines known to be on station and ready to participate in the

---

[84] In his 20 December 1966 press conference, the U.S. Navy's director of antisubmarine warfare programs stated that, although the USSR's submarines have begun to operate more freely in distant waters than they have in the past when they remained in Soviet coastal waters, they "avoid sensitive areas" and have not been sighted off U.S. coasts [i.e. within missile-launching range] or near Vietnam. "U.S. Admiral on Soviet Missiles."

[85] Quoted in V. Shiltov, "Raketa startuet iz-pod vody" (The Missile is Launched from Underwater), *Krasnaia Zvezda*, November 1, 1960.

[86] "U.S. Admiral on Soviet Missiles."

possibly decisive initial nuclear exchange.[87] Considering the fact that Soviet ballistic missile submarines are not being deployed on regular Polaris-type patrols and so could not be counted on to deliver part of an initial nuclear strike, it would be logical to assume that present Soviet strategy can only plan on their employment in a second-strike role. Such a decision might have been made on the basis of a decision that the USSR's intercontinental ballistic missiles and nuclear bombers provided adequate deterrent credibility without the operational difficulties, risk, and expense of maintaining missile submarines on station within striking distance of the United States. Particularly after the United States' strong reaction in October 1962 to Soviet shipment of strategic missiles and aircraft into Cuba, disinclination of the Soviet leaders to take any further move that might be interpreted in the United States as brandishing their missiles may constitute a major factor.

At any rate, if the mission of the USSR's ballistic missile submarines has been restricted to a second strike role, that fact would explain to a considerable degree both why slightly less than one-third (thirteen out of forty) of the nuclear submarines carry ballistic missiles and why the first edition of *Military Strategy* was worded so as to leave strong doubt that missile submarines were intended to take part in an initial nuclear strike.[88] It would, furthermore, partly account for the fact that the submarine-launched strategic strike mission is given reduced prominence in statements of the Soviet Navy's assigned missions for general nuclear

---

[87] Of related interest is the fact that Khrushchev reported to the Supreme Soviet 17 December 1962 shortly after the Cuban missile crisis that the situation had caused a full combat alert in the Warsaw Pact forces and in the Soviet Army and Navy. In this report Khrushchev mentioned that "our submarine fleet, including atomic submarines, occupied assigned stations." Note that no mention of *missile* submarines was made, although that conceivably might have been out of deference to the sensitivity of an aroused U.S. public opinion. Khrushchev, "Sovremennoe mezhdunarodnoe polozhenie."

[88] "The main aim of military operations in naval theatres will be the defeat of the enemy fleet and the disruption of his oceanic and sea lines of communication. In addition, there *may* be the mission of delivering nuclear-missile strikes against shore targets. . . ." (Sokolovskii, *op. cit.,* 1st ed., p. 353.) Italics added. Similarly, statements on missile submarines were conspicuously absent in the first edition listing of the strategic nuclear strike forces: "Now the main role will belong to the Strategic Missile Troops and, partly, to Long Range Aviation employing nuclear weapons." (*Ibid.,* p. 333.) The second edition changed this listing to include "missile-carrying submarines" but the comparable passage to the first-quoted above still was indefinite, although it at least expanded the approved area for the Navy's operations beyond the defensive "naval theatres" limit stated in the first edition to include "oceans" in the second: "The main goal of military operations for naval forces on the oceans and in naval theatres is the defeat of the enemy's naval forces and the severance of his oceanic and sea communications. Along with this, the Navy *may* accomplish missions of launching nuclear missile strikes." (*Ibid.,* 2nd ed., pp. 337 and 396.) Italics added. Even assuming editorial oversight, it seems clear that there has been some uncertainty as to the wartime nuclear strike role of the Soviet ballistic missile submarine force.

war. In such standardized statements, the submarine-launched nuclear strike mission normally is mentioned last in an "also" clause that comes after the missions for destroying the enemy's naval forces and for interdicting his sea communications.[89]

Scrutiny of Soviet statements also discloses that, in mentioning the types of targets for ballistic missile submarines, naval bases are either mentioned specifically or referred to by implication among the few types of targets specified.[90] This detail becomes significant when considered in connection with the ballistic missile submarines' nondeployment on regular patrols, the low priority awarded to the construction of nuclear-powered ballistic missile submarines, and the fact that, unlike strategic air bases and missile sites, NATO naval bases constitute no immediate threat to the USSR, and only become a significant factor when and if a general war should extend beyond the initial nuclear exchange stage into one of protracted war. Based on these facts it seems reasonable to hypothesize that naval bases and other naval shore complexes constitute the most important, if not all, of the targets assigned for submarine-launched missile strikes.

From all that has been discussed, one may form a fairly definite conclusion concerning the strategic aim underlying the construction of the Soviet ballistic missile submarine force. This conclusion is that the force was primarily constructed for its deterrent "fleet-in-being" effect and not for any contribution to fighting a short war that would begin and end with an initial nuclear exchange. Unquestionably, the destruction of U.S. naval bases would be important in any protracted war. Yet, considering the pressing restrictions on Soviet military spending and in view of the essentially deterrent nature of the other elements of the USSR's strategic nuclear strike forces, it cannot be assumed lightly that the USSR would have expended the money for the force primarily for its use as a counterblow in a second strike situation that quite possibly might never have the

---

[89] "[By employing submarines armed with missiles having atomic warheads, the Soviet Navy now can] carry out its traditional war activity against communications lines and can also attack targets along the enemy coast." (Vladimirskii, *op. cit.*) "The Navy . . . is able not only to defend our maritime borders but also to destroy enemy forces on the seas and oceans, as well as to deliver powerful blows against objectives located on other continents." ("Priem v kremle v chest' sorokaletiia Sovetskoi Armii i Voenno-Morskogo Flota.") "The Navy . . . will strike powerful nuclear-missile blows at the naval formations of the enemy and also at important targets in the land theatres of operations." (I. Glebov, "Razvitie operativnogo iskusstva" [Development of Operational Art], *Krasnaia Zvezda,* April 2, 1964.)

[90] "One must realize that a submarine equipped with missile weapons can be extremely dangerous for naval bases and other enemy targets." (Vladimirskii, *op. cit.*) "Ballistic missiles are mainly assigned to the destruction of land targets such as naval bases and industrial complexes." (Isachenkov, *op. cit.*) "Our missile submarines can also use their weapons with great effectiveness against coastal military targets." (Mamaev, *op. cit.*)

chance to develop. On the other hand, credible initial deterrence is a basic requirement for continued activity by a militarily weaker state, such as the USSR, that has declared its unswerving intention to vanquish its stronger protagonist, the United States, by means of *economic action* and by political, *psychological,* and *unconventional warfare* aided, when feasible and promising, by "small" (limited) wars. After all, if even with their entire submarine fleet the Soviet leaders can balance off (in the sense of deterrence) the vastly more expensive and more powerful carrier and Polaris striking forces of NATO, then they have achieved a highly desirable application of the "principle of disproportionate cost." This principle holds that a weaker power may deter attack by a stronger power merely by developing and publicizing a capability for wreaking an unacceptably great amount of damage on an aggressor. Obviously, this principle operates to the potentially great advantage of the weaker power in a deterrent situation.[91]

Little can be gleaned from the open literature on tactics the USSR would employ if the decision were made for prosecuting a submarine-launched nuclear missile strike against U.S. targets. This uncertainty might conceivably be due to the fact that many more pressing matters of naval tactics remain to be worked out for employment and coordination of the various missile-equipped weapons platforms.[92] At any rate, the only pertinent item of potential significance uncovered by the research for this study was the statement that submarine-launched missile strikes against land targets could be launched from unexpected directions.[93]

---

[91] "The third type of deterrent is that of 'disproportionate cost' and is of great antiquity. Here the presumptive aggressor is deterred because he decides that the game is not worth the candle. A potential aggressor is persuaded not to initiate a war because the cost of victory seems likely to exceed its value. As one might expect, this type of deterrent has often been used by the weak against the strong. . . . While overwhelming military superiority (the first type) will deter relatively weak powers from aggression, the latter may protect themselves from stronger powers by possessing and publicizing their ability to inflict an unacceptable level of damage on the attacker." Dinerstein, *War and the Soviet Union,* p. 20.

[92] "In the postwar period, Soviet military science received further creative development. In this regard, much work has been accomplished. We have elaborated the fundamental principles for the conduct of modern warfare. However, it must be noted that, in the elaboration of the military-technical part of the doctrine, as it was called by M. V. Frunze, there are still many disputable and vague propositions." (P. Zhilin, "Diskussii o edinoi voennoi doktrine" [Discussions on a Unified Military Doctrine], *Voenno-istoricheskii Zhurnal,* May, 1961, p. 74.) "Missiles and other armaments of the modern navy are continually being perfected. This naturally gives rise to continual changes in views on the character and methods of naval combat operations." (Argunov, *op. cit.*)

[93] "Completely new possibilities for utilizing nuclear missile weapons were opened with the equipping of submarines with missiles. By launching missiles from them it is possible to deliver blows against continental targets from different, and sometimes the most unexpected, directions." *Ibid.*

8

8

This suggests that the United States should pay particular attention to its ASW defenses in such close-in but out-of-the-way areas as the Gulf of Mexico and Hudson Bay.

Although the 350-mile range mentioned would have to be multiplied about sevenfold to reach the United States from the North Pole, the range could be sufficiently shortened by deep penetration of Hudson Bay. Two Soviet writers have taken the typically oblique Soviets means for claiming a new capability by citing U.S. writers to the effect that "Soviet submarines can pass under the Arctic ice, penetrate, for example, into Hudson Bay, and 'launch missiles against Detroit and other industrial targets of the Great Lakes.' "[94] Similarly, Hanson Baldwin, the military editor of *The New York Times,* has been cited to establish the credibility of Soviet strategic nuclear strike capabilities from submarines in the Arctic: "Baldwin further observes that the creation of an atomic submarine fleet equipped with missiles opens for the USSR a new ocean, the Arctic, and makes the North American continent vulnerable to attack from short distances."[95] Again, Soviet writings regarding their submarine nuclear-strike capabilities from the Arctic, as from elsewhere, are polemical in nature and appear to be primarily designed to enhance the credibility of Soviet strategic nuclear-strike capabilities. The Soviet retort to a British general in 1958 is typical in this regard:

> General Gale stresses that the passage of the U.S. submarine Nautilus under the Arctic ice has opened up a "new field in military strategy" and that now "Soviet Russia is vulnerable to nuclear attack from the air and the sea from all four sides." Even by looking at an ordinary school globe one can easily see who is more vulnerable to strikes from the sea and air: the USSR or those who are preparing to attack her. The trouble is that the British general does not want to recognize the fact that now it is impossible to count on attacking other countries with impunity from either the sea or from the air without receiving retaliatory blows, perhaps even more crushing ones. It is well to note that submarines bearing other names and other flags, too, may navigate under the northern ice as well as in other seas and oceans. In our day it is impossible to maintain a monopoly on one or another type of armament. The military leaders of the aggressive Western powers would do well to learn this. . . .[96]

---

[94] L. Zevin and G. Arzumanov, "Arkticheskoe zrenie Amerikanskikh strategov" (Arctic Visions of American Strategists), *Sovetskii Flot,* August 18, 1959.

[95] Prokof'ev, *op. cit.*

[96] A. I. Antonov, "General Gel' gotov demonstrirovat' svoi entuziazm" (General Gale is Ready to Show His Enthusiasm), *Krasnaia Zvezda,* November 21, 1958. A more recent example also may be cited: "Nikita Sergeevich Khrushchev has reminded the zealous admirals of the West that modern weapons systems permit ballistic and homing missiles to be fired from submarines on vital centers . . . of the aggressor. I note in this regard that our missile submarines have learned well how to travel under the Arctic ice and to take

Finally, before leaving the subject at hand, consideration should be given to the amount of credence to be accorded to Soviet claims of having successfully duplicated the underwater launch capability of Polaris missiles. Since modern computer technology readily permits locating the point of origin of a ballistic missile merely from tracking it briefly, and since several minutes, at least, are required between missile firings, the ability to launch missiles from underwater is essential to ensure that the launching vehicle will not be destroyed very shortly after launching the first missile. Initial lack of an underwater launch capability probably goes far towards explaining why Soviet ballistic missile submarines carry only two or three launch tubes as compared to the sixteen in Polaris submarines.[97] In 1957, the Soviet admiral N. Pavlovich noted the U.S. work in developing such an underwater launch capability for Polaris.[98] In March 1962, a younger officer described the firing sequence for the purported submerged launching of a missile.[99] Finally, in early 1963, in reporting on developments in 1962, Admiral Gorshkov stated unequivocally that "the firings of various types of missiles, including the launching of missiles from underwater, were carried out successfully."[100] Subsequently, Soviet parades of military hardware included naval missiles claimed to be capable of underwater launch by Soviet ballistic missile submarines.[101] The most recent comment on the subject by any dependable authority was that of Secretary of Defense Robert McNamara, who denied that the USSR had developed an operational underwater launch capability as of mid-August 1964.[102] However, in view of the early Soviet interest evinced in the capability, the objective military requirement

---

up an exact position for the launching of missiles, which is very important for reliable destruction of land targets." Argunov, Zheltikov, and Larionov, *op. cit.*

[97] *Jane's Fighting Ships 1966–1967,* pp. 433–434.

[98] N. Pavlovich, "Voenno-morskoe iskusstvo i razvitie tekhniku dlia flota" (The Naval Art and the Development of Military Equipment for the Navy), *Sovetskii Flot,* March 6, 1957.

[99] A. Krysov, "Start" (Launch), *Krasnaia Zvezda,* March 3, 1962.

[100] Gorshkov, "Velikye zadachy Sovetskogo voenno-morskogo flota."

[101] "On special mounts are powerful long-range missiles with which ships of the Soviet Navy are armed. They can fire salvos at any minute from a submerged or other position and deliver a nuclear warhead to any point on the largest continent." "Pobedno peet Leninskoe znamia; Voennyi parad i demonstratsiia trudiashchikhsia Moskvy na Krasnoi ploshchadi, rech' Marshala Sovetskogo Soiuza R. Ia. Malinovskogo" (Victoriously Sings the Leninist Banner; Military Parade and Demonstration of the Workers of Moscow in Red Square, Speech of Marshal of the Soviet Union Malinovskii), *Krasnaia Zvezda,* November 10, 1963.

[102] "Each of our Polaris missiles can be launched from beneath the surface. The Soviets have no such operational missile." "Text of McNamara's Statement to Platform Group." In mid-1966, the Institute for Strategic Studies in London opined that "It is now believed that the Soviets have successfully developed submerged firing of the SERB missile, which has been shown in Moscow parades. It is probably being gradually introduced into service...." *The Military Balance 1966–1967,* p. 5.

that exists for the Soviet ballistic missile submarines to have such a capability, especially since missile submarines are claimed to be the main striking arm of the Navy, and in view of the additional elapsed time since Secretary McNamara's statement and the Polaris-type missiles paraded in Moscow, it would be imprudent to do other than credit the USSR with now having such a capability. As the U.S. Navy's Director of ASW Programs, Vice Admiral Charles N. Martell, stated in December 1966 with regard to the USSR's having this capability: "They soon will have it, if they don't have it now."[103]

There is no known reason to question that Khrushchev's construction of the largest conventionally-powered submarine force the world has ever seen was carried out not only to provide the large submarine forces deemed necessary for the defense of each of the USSR's four fleet areas but also to develop a major capability to disrupt Free World shipping despite NATO antisubmarine warfare. As noted previously, Soviet leaders clearly stated during the Khrushchev era that one of the Soviet Navy's primary missions in any future war would be to stop the flow of vital merchant cargoes to Western Nations on the Continent and to England, including irreplaceable material from the United States and oil from the Middle East.[104] Such statements were given considerable credence at the time by Soviet construction of an unprecedentedly large force of long range submarines and the deployment of most of them to the Soviet Northern Fleet where they would have access to the Atlantic shipping lanes.

Soviet military strategists asserted in late 1963 that the Soviet submarine campaign against NATO shipping must start at the very outbreak of the war.[105] This campaign must be made, the strategists argued, to prevent Western Europe from obtaining any logistic support by sea "since the enemy is highly dependent on it for waging war in the ground theaters of military operations."[106] Stalin had no such strategy. Even at the time of his death in 1953, only 30 units out of the total Soviet submarine force of more than 330 were based in the Northern Fleet, from where they would have the geographic possibility of reaching the Atlantic shipping lanes and those 30 constituted merely the same 9 per cent of the total submarine force that the USSR had maintained in the Northern Fleet in 1939 purely for defense.[107] With the postwar acquisitions of much longer

---

[103] "U.S. Admiral on Soviet Missiles."

[104] Sokolovskii, *op. cit.,* 2nd ed., p. 399, Lagovskii, *op. cit.*

[105] Sokolovskii, *op. cit.,* 2nd ed., p. 401.

[106] *Ibid.,* p. 312.

[107] See Table VII, "Distribution of Russian Submarines," in Wilhelm Hadeler, "The Ships of the Soviet Navy," *The Soviet Navy,* p. 158. It shows that in 1939, 15 of the total

coastlines to defend, particularly in the Baltic but also in the Black Sea and in the Far East, and with his concentration on large surface ship fleets, Stalin refrained from building up the very large Northern Fleet submarine force that would have been required to make a bid for success at the same undertaking in which the Germans had twice failed. Khrushchev, once he had decided to give up Stalin's vast project for building big, balanced fleets and had settled for the far less expensive plan for a navy largely of submarines, had little choice but to adopt such a plan if the Soviet Navy were to be able to make at least some contribution to the USSR's strategic deterrent forces. If Stalin intended eventually to employ submarines against NATO shipping, it clearly was to have been only after his ground forces had overrun Western Europe, or at least the area of the Danish Straits. Only if that were accomplished first, so that the Baltic exits were secured against entrance by NATO naval forces, could the great number of submarines considered necessary for the defense of the Baltic be released for a *guerre de course* against merchant shipping in the Atlantic. So, it remained for Khrushchev, apparently largely influenced by Minister of Defense Zhukov,[108] to cast the future of the Soviet Navy with an essentially submarine fleet[109] that was intended to achieve its greatest combat capability against the Free World's vitally important but basically vulnerable merchant shipping. Under Khrushchev, the Northern Fleet submarine force was increased from 30 to 145 units.[110] This was much more rapid than the expansion of the submarine force as a whole since it only increased about 54 per cent, going from 330 to an all-time high of about 510 at the end of 1962.[111]

of 198 Soviet submarines were based in the Arctic. The figure of 30 submarines in the Northern Fleet in 1939 was taken from "Reds Use New Ships in Bid to Shut Baltic," *New York World Telegram,* February 28, 1953, p. 9.

[108] Former Soviet Naval Officer, interview with the author, Newport, Rhode Island, October 30, 1963. Khrushchev was generally considered by Soviet naval officers to have acquired his anti-surface ship views, particularly his disdain for cruisers, from Zhukov. The interviewee added the pungent observation that Khrushchev had to follow his military advisers in such naval matters because he knew no more of them himself than did a pig about orchids!

[109] At the time Zhukov was ousted by Khrushchev in 1957 the latter accused the former of having opposed a strong submarine force as well as the far better publicized charge of having weakened Party control of the armed forces. This first charge was considered in naval circles as having been trumped up by Khrushchev to support his politically-motivated ejection of Zhukov from the Politburo and removal from his post as Minister of Defense. Zhukov was well-known for favoring submarines and opposing surface ships as not required for a continental power such as the USSR whose military goals were limited to the European land mass. Former Soviet Naval Officer. *Ibid.*

[110] This Soviet Northern Fleet submarine strength is for December 1963, less than a year before Khrushchev's overthrow. Lord Kennet, *op. cit.*

[111] Based on all of the standard reference works on the world's navies. Data has been adjusted when necessary to provide for even construction rates rather than the wildly

Not only was a requirement expressed by Soviet military writers for the antishipping campaign to begin simultaneously with the initiation of hostilities but they also stipulated that the campaign should be global in extent.[112] Recalling the 100 or less figure as the number of Northern Fleet submarines capable of operating in the Atlantic, and comparing it with the 220 submarines that the Germans had in action at the height of the Battle of the Atlantic in World War II,[113] it is apparent that the Northern Fleet would have to be greatly augmented to carry out a widespread and successful submarine campaign, even though leaving all of the Mediterranean, Indian Ocean, and Pacific to the Soviet Black Sea and Pacific fleets.

Alternatively, the USSR would have to accept a delay while the Danish and Turkish straits were captured so that the substantial submarine forces of the Baltic and Black Sea Fleet could join in the antishipping campaign.[114] In view of the German experience in World War II of being able to maintain only one-third of their total submarine force in the Atlantic shipping lanes (while the other two-thirds were en route to or from the operating areas or in port for refueling, replenishing stores, and making necessary repairs),[115] it appears reasonably certain that the Northern Fleet submarines, with their much longer transit, could not do as well. Accordingly, the effective level of the Soviet threat to Atlantic shipping in the first few weeks of war probably would not exceed 20 to 25 submarines. In the event that the bulk of the Soviet Northern Fleet submarines were committed at the outset, the USSR would take the risk of giving strategic warning of their intention to initiate hostilities. In the extremely unlikely event that this risk were deemed acceptable, the Soviet Union might opt for such an initial large commitment of Northern Fleet submarines in the anticipation that early capture of the exits to the Baltic could permit reinforcements from the 105 additional submarines in that area to arrive on the Atlantic shipping lanes by the time that the Northern Fleet submarines would reach the time limits of their patrols. Otherwise, an unacceptable lull in the Soviet offensive would occur

---

fluctuating figures that frequently result when a shipbuilding program is not discovered until its third or fourth year and then erroneously considered to have just started.

[112] "Equipping the Navy with atomic submarines with nuclear missile armaments, and also with missile aviation, enables it to successfully solve its complicated mission of combat . . . with the enemy . . . against his oceanic communications in the most distant theaters of military action. . . ." Lomov, *op. cit.*

[113] Donald Macintyre, "The Soviet Submarine Threat," *The Soviet Navy,* p. 169.

[114] Although Soviet submarines may be shifted among the three European fleets by means of the internal waterways during the part of the year that they are not frozen, certainly Soviet naval planners would not expect the canals and locks to remain operable after an initial nuclear exchange.

[115] Macintyre, "The Soviet Submarine Threat." p. 175.

which would be of great advantage to NATO in reorganizing its convoys and its convoy escorts and other antisubmarine defenses.

As mentioned earlier, the listing in *Military Strategy* and numerous press articles of the ASW forces of the NATO navies show the Soviet awareness of the opposition that could be expected to any submarine warfare campaign by the Soviet Navy.[116] Moreover, *Military Strategy* stated that "the enemy will take the most varied measures to safeguard his communication lines: he will create 'giant convoys' requiring fewer protecting forces, and will make extensive use of 'patrolled zones' where transports can proceed without escort. He will use high speed liners (without escort), [armed] merchant ships, minesweepers, and under-water transports, etc."[117]

In view of the apparent Soviet decision that not more than five,[118] and quite likely less than that many, nuclear submarines of all three types (ballistic missile, guided missile, and torpedo attack) are to be produced each year, it is clear that the bulk of the Soviet submarine forces will be forced to endure the disadvantages of diesel propulsion for years to come. The authors of *Military Strategy* asserted that nuclear submarines would be "most important in the destruction of the enemy's maritime communications" because their "flexible use" would enable them to "provide a maximum concentration of forces against communications in a short period." They added the significant caveat that "diesel-electric submarines will obviously still be used against lines of communications. They will be used, as in the last war, to form moving barriers, and to un-dertake coordinated operations or free search."[119]

That this continuing recourse to diesel-powered submarines must be the result of economic limitations rather than other reasons is pointed up by the unfavorable comparison that even a Soviet naval writer has drawn between diesel-powered submarines and those with nuclear propulsion:

> Diesel-electric engines, as is well known, possess serious tactical lim-itations in submarine utilization. The first and second world wars pro-vided many examples in which submarines could not attack the enemy due to the fact that their batteries were exhausted. It is known that such a danger presents no threat to atomic submarines . . . the great speed of nuclear-powered submarines in combination with increased independ-ence of operation (up to three months) increases by many times the dura-tion in the theater of combat operations in comparison with conven-

---

[116] Sokolovskii, *op. cit.*, 2nd ed., p. 401.

[117] *Ibid.*

[118] This was the highest of the estimates available in the open literature. See page 84, footnote 70.

[119] Sokolovskii, *op. cit.*, 2nd ed., p. 401.

tional submarines . . . [Also], it is a known fact that diesel-electric submarines are quite vulnerable to antisubmarine defense ships.[120]

Relatedly, it is worth noting that Soviet plans allegedly provide for the use against convoys of submarine-launched guided missiles armed with nuclear warheads as well as nuclear-tipped torpedoes.[121] Consequently, cost-effectiveness analysts of the Soviet Ministry of Defense may well have decided that the vastly increased destructiveness of nuclear weapons permits a drastic cutback in the number of nuclear-powered submarines required to interdict NATO shipping. Be that as it may, numerous statements by Soviet leaders have claimed that Soviet long-range, shore-based naval aircraft carrying air-to-surface missiles armed with nuclear warheads would be used to supplement the submarine force campaign against merchant shipping.[122] That much consideration has been given to coordinating aircraft and submarine operations so that the greater speed and wide-area search capability of aircraft can be exploited to scout for submarines is attested to by repeated mention in Soviet naval writings.[123] According to Vice Admiral Friedrich Ruge, Federal German Navy (Retired), a noted authority on the Soviet Navy, it appears unlikely that even the postwar *Sverdlov* cruisers would be suitable for commerce raiders.[124] It has been reliably reported that the *Sverdlovs,* along with destroyers and airplanes, would be employed primarily in efforts to destroy NATO ASW barriers of ships, submarines, and aircraft in order to permit Soviet submarines to gain the open ocean and return to their dispersed "maneuvering bases" without the otherwise unacceptably high attrition to which they would be subjected.[125]

However, according to *Military Strategy,* NATO shipping is to be subjected to additional hazards. Mines, perhaps even nuclear ones, and nuclear missiles from the Missile Troops of Strategic Designation and ballistic missile submarines are to be used against ports of departure and destination as well as against narrow straits and canals en route.[126] Additionally, mines and missiles are also to be used against ship construction

---

[120] Zheludev, *op. cit.*

[121] Sokolovskii, *op. cit.*, 2nd ed., p. 312.

[122] "These missions [to destroy merchant and naval ships] can be most effectively executed by submarines and aircraft armed with nuclear missiles and torpedoes." *Ibid.*

[123] Argunov, *op. cit.*, Borzov, *op. cit.*

[124] "They [the *Sverdlov* cruisers] were probably designed for operations in the enclosed seas and off the oceanic coasts, rather than for raiding purposes for which they would be useless anyway owing to their insufficient armament against air attack." F. Ruge, "Soviet Sea Power in the Cold War; A Critical Analysis," *Naval Review 1962–1963,* p. 70.

[125] Former Soviet Naval Officer, Interview with the author, Newport, Rhode Island, October 31, 1963.

[126] Sokolovskii, *op. cit.*, 2nd ed., p. 461.

and repair yards and the naval bases that support the convoy escort ships.[127] This vivid description of all-out attack on NATO merchant shipping, its terminal ports, and other infrastructure, appears frighteningly formidable at first acquaintance—and is undoubtedly intended to be so by the Soviet propagandists. It is only after projecting oneself mentally into the situation of Soviet naval forces and visualizing the paper allocation of those forces to the staggeringly great tasks that would be involved in successfully fulfilling their top priority missions even for minimum defense against Polaris and carrier strikes, that some sense of reassurance returns that the present Soviet threat to shipping has not grown out of all manageable bounds. For the future, as related earlier,[128] the Soviet leaders may have already decided that a submarine force large enough to comprise a major threat to NATO shipping against NATO's large ASW forces would not be cost-effective. This hypothesis is supported by the facts that not only have no more nuclear-powered torpedo attack submarines (i.e., the type most suitable for attacks on merchant shipping) been built beyond the twelve that had been constructed before Khrushchev fell from power in October 1964, but also the number of conventional diesel-powered torpedo attack submarines of medium and long-range cruising radius has decreased since then from 320 to 280, a significant drop of 12 per cent.[129]

Due to the USSR's inability to gain command of the sea for her own use, all of the substantial Soviet trade on the world's shipping lanes would have to cease with the outbreak of war or face the prospect of being hunted down and sunk. However, the USSR clearly would hope to be able to continue its important shipping along Soviet coastal routes. As is also the case in defense against amphibious invasion, the great bulk of Soviet naval forces is constituted so as to be capable of playing a role in the defense of the USSR's coastal lines of sea communications.

Thus, attacks on Soviet coastwise shipping, whether in the open Arctic or Pacific coastal areas or in the enclosed Baltic or Black Sea, could be expected to meet with considerable resistance. Extensive use of defensive mine fields, as used only to a limited extent by the USSR in World War II, could be expected, particularly in the same areas where NATO might be assumed to place submarine, surface-ship, and aircraft mine barriers to prevent Soviet submarines from reaching the major shipping lanes. Such areas logically might include the Turkish and Danish straits, the

[127] *Ibid.*
[128] See page 87.
[129] *Cf.* the numerical changes in the following classes of submarines between the 1964–1965 edition of *Jane's Fighting Ships* and that for 1966–1967: Q, W, R, F, & Z.

Greenland–Iceland–U.K. line, and the exits from the Sea of Japan and the Kurile Islands chain.

Against any threat to merchant shipping from surface warships, the USSR could be expected to provide opposition primarily with missile-carrying aircraft, coastal missile batteries, PT boats carrying missiles or torpedoes, missile-carrying and conventional gun and torpedo-firing destroyers, and even cruisers. In addition to the 14 to 18 cruisers mentioned previously, the Soviet Navy is reported to have available for anti-raider missions 203 destroyers, including 24 fitted with surface-to-surface missiles, and 450 motor torpedo boats, of which 100 are armed with missiles.[130] Of course, many of these forces would be required for other tasks much of the time, such as protecting the coastal flanks of the ground forces from seaborne attack, giving the ground forces missile and gunfire support, or making tactical landings. When used to protect the coastal shipping routes units of these forces could be expected to be employed most frequently as convoy escorts.

As far as NATO submarine attack on the USSR's coastal shipping is concerned, the USSR could be expected to use the 92 destroyer escorts and roughly 300 coastal escorts estimated to be in commission.[131] Soviet naval aviation's ASW capabilities would be utilized as, quite likely, would the ASW capabilities of some of the Soviet submarines.

To counter air attacks on Soviet coastal shipping, the Soviet Union could be expected to employ the fighter planes of Air Defense, coastal surface-to-air missiles (when the attacking aircraft came within range), and the limited antiaircraft capabilities of Soviet warships.

Mines planted in the USSR's coastal shipping lanes and their port terminals would receive the attention of the estimated three hundred minesweepers operational in the four Soviet naval fleets.[132]

All in all, it is quite apparent that the Soviet Navy would be capable of by far its most effective work when engaged in coastal operations such as defending against amphibious invasions or protecting shipping. For in such operations the surface naval forces can be supported by land-based aviation and coastal missile batteries, and use may be made of the numerous PT boats and other coastal craft that can only operate in inshore waters.

Soviet maritime defense is based on three concentric areas extending out from their coasts, with the depth of each area based on the military capabilities of operationally available weapons systems. The "pre-coastal" zone, the one closest offshore and which extends out from the coastline

---

[130] *Jane's Fighting Ships 1966–1967*, pp. 434–442 and 446–447.

[131] *Ibid.*, pp. 443 and 445.

[132] *Ibid.*, pp. 445 and 446.

to about 150 miles, is considered to be the only maritime area in which the USSR can expect, even under favorable circumstances, to exercise command of the sea against the superior power of the NATO naval forces. In this zone can be brought to bear virtually all of the various types of naval missile weapons systems: shore-based coastal sites, air-to-surface launched ones, surface-launched from destroyers and PT boats, and submarine-launched cruise missiles. In addition, conventional torpe-does and mines and ships' guns could all be used in these close offshore areas. It is within the pre-coastal zone that the USSR's vital coastal ship-ping would be convoyed in wartime.

The second and middle of the three maritime defense zones is called the "remote offshore" zone, and embraces the area from the end of the pre-coastal zone at about 150 miles from the coast on out to distances varying from 200 to 300 miles, depending on such factors as the forces and bases in the area, topography, etc. The most distinguishing criteria of this zone is that air cover for surface ship operations cannot be pro-vided on a continuous basis but only on call for periods of limited dura-tion. From this fact it can be seen that the Soviet naval leaders, at least, recognize that the lack of mobile air power that only aircraft carriers could provide begins to be a serious factor within 150 miles from their coasts—an important fact to keep in mind when considering Soviet propaganda claims against NATO strike carriers which can attack from several times further out to sea than 150 miles. The very choice of the name "remote" for the middle defense zone is indicative of the land-limited approach to high-seas naval operations that has prevented the Soviet leaders from developing carrier forces.

The third maritime defense zone—the "open sea"—lies beyond the 200- to 300-mile limit of the "remote offshore" zone. This zone is con-sidered to extend up to the coasts of potential enemies, and is the zone, of course, of most limited Soviet capabilities. In this third zone the main action is assigned to missile and torpedo submarines, with surface ship operations unfeasible for lack of air cover. The boundary between the second and third zones—at 200 to 300 miles offshore—is the locus of planned Soviet efforts to erect barriers of antisubmarine surface ships, submarines, and aircraft to prevent penetration of NATO submarines intent on making conventional torpedo attacks on Soviet coastal ship-ping. This interface between the second and third zones would also be the scene of the first coordinated air-surface ship opposition to any am-phibious invasion forces.[133]

---

[133] This entire concept of zones-of-defense has been kept secret by the USSR beyond the apparent needs of military security for protecting the information relating to the exact ranges involved. The reason for this secretiveness would seem to be obvious: to

In his first book, published in 1953, Raymond Garthoff cited Admiral Alafuzov on a provocative remark concerning a Soviet naval strategic concept involving "zones of operations." Now with the testimony of "Former Soviet Naval Officer" it is clear that the reference was to the three-zone defensive concept outlined above. Dr. Garthoff's comment and quotation ran as follows:

> Soviet naval doctrine differs from their military doctrine in defining its mission in terms of "zones of operations" rather than as missions to destroy certain enemy groupings. Admiral Alafuzov defined this as follows: "The zone of operations of the fleet has been mentioned above. The fulfillment by the fleet of the missions set before it can be considered to be assured in the case when their solution is taking place in its zone of dominion."[134]

Now it can be appreciated that the Soviet naval concept of "zones of operations" is a strategically defensive one, and has as its distinguishing characteristic the very limited distance (150 miles, as noted above) to which the USSR, with its shore-based naval air arm and its lack of aircraft carriers to provide mobile sea-air power, is able to exert its "dominion."

On balance, it can be said that coastal shipping protection is one of the few prospective wartime missions for which the Soviet Navy has substantial capabilities to fulfill, even in face of the probable NATO opposition. Yet, should the submarine forces of NATO be concentrated on Soviet coastal shipping, Soviet antisubmarine warfare, never a strong point with the Soviet Navy, would find itself engaged in a desperate struggle.

The maritime power, or coalition, that is able to exercise command of the sea holds the unique advantage of being able to mount amphibious invasions and support them with such a concentration of firepower that they can effect landings on suitable beaches almost anywhere in the world. As a result of the USSR's total inability to gain command of the sea for her own use, she is not only denied the possibility of transporting the necessary troops and equipment across the Atlantic or Pacific for an invasion of the United States, but she must be prepared to defend herself against such invasions from the United States.

It is in this context of defending against amphibious invasion, com-

---

acknowledge the existence of such zones is to admit that all the Soviet claims that the military-technical revolution has outmoded the surface component of naval power are purely propaganda—and so too, obviously, does their existence admit the falsity of Soviet claims that submarines and aircraft alone provide all of the necessary ingredients for supremacy at sea. Former Soviet Naval Officer, "The USSR's Strategy at Sea," Address at the U.S. Naval War College, Newport, R.I., March 20, 1965.

[134] Garthoff, *Soviet Military Doctrine*, p. 367.

bined with the additional missions of protecting coastal sea communications and of supporting and defending the seaward flank of the ground forces, that the otherwise seemingly oversize submarine, surface ship, and coastal defense forces to be found in each of the four Soviet fleet areas must be considered in order for them to make sense. Particularly in the Baltic, with its direct sea access to the key city of Leningrad and the very vitals of the European industrial areas of the Soviet Union, the concentration of defensive naval forces has always been especially large. For example, a few years ago Swedish Admiral E. Biorklund listed the following Soviet Baltic Fleet naval forces: 9 cruisers, 50 destroyers, "well over 100 submarines," and 150 fast patrol boats.[135] It appears to be a virtual certainty that the main reason such large forces are retained in the Baltic is for defensive use against NATO assault, including those by amphibious invasion forces.

Present distribution of submarines to the enclosed Baltic and Black seas where they can only play strategically defensive roles, at least in the initial stage of any future war until and unless the Danish and Turkish straits were seized, is reported as 105 and 75 respectively.[136] Dividing the current totals of Soviet surface forces by 4 yields the following theoretical average numbers of primarily defensive surface forces that could be made available for each of the fleet areas: 4 to 5 cruisers, 6 missile destroyers, and 51 conventional ones, 23 destroyer escorts, 75 coastal escorts, 75 minesweepers, 88 motor torpedo boats, and 6 guided missile patrol boats.[137] In addition, the Soviet press has made frequent references to nuclear-armed coastal missile launching sites. These could be of optimum potential use against the concentrated naval forces required for the conduct of amphibious invasions.[138] Moreover, the Soviet press has recently printed pictures and articles about the re-established Naval Infantry (Marines) of well-deserved World War II fame.[139] Unquestionably, their primary missions include not only the small-scale, short-distance tactical landings required to support ground operations in coastal areas, but also playing a leading role in the on-the-beach defense against amphibious invasion. Unquestionably, too, in the all-out defensive effort that would be triggered by information of an impending amphibious invasion, not only Soviet naval aviation, but long-range aviation, Army

---

[135] E. Biorklund, "On the Perimeter," *The Soviet Navy,* p. 261.

[136] Lord Kennet, *op. cit.*

[137] *Jane's Fighting Ships 1966–1967,* pp. 432–447.

[138] V. Valin, "Iadernoe oruzhie sovremennykh armii" (Nuclear Weapons of Modern Armies), *Krasnaia Zvezda,* June 13, 1962. Sokolovskii, *op. cit.,* 1st ed., p. 400.

[139] "Boi vedet morskaia pekhota" (The Naval Infantry Carries on Combat), *Krasnaia Zvezda,* July 24, 1964.

tactical aviation, and the fighter planes of Air Defense could all be expected to join in.

It is noteworthy that leading Soviet military writers have, in effect, condemned all strategically defensive operations in nuclear warfare to a theoretical ash bin of inferiority. The authors of *Military Strategy* have stated: "But one must recognize that the present instrumentalities of nuclear attack are undoubtedly superior to the instrumentalities of defense against them."[140] Yet, in the matter of defending the USSR against amphibious invasion, even though it is a strategically defensive mission, it is clear that the USSR's capabilities for conducting such operations are relatively good in comparison to other strategically defensive missions such as countering nuclear strikes from aircraft carriers or, particularly, from Polaris missile submarines. Consequently, of all the bombastic statements that were regularly uttered for public consumption by Marshal Malinovskii while Minister of Defense, it is likely that he privately considered there was actually a stronger element of fact in the one he made to the Twenty-first Party Congress than in most: "Across the ocean it is often said and written that the U.S. Navy is capable of making an assault and effecting an amphibious landing at any point of our coastline. But, as it is said—'Easy to boast but even easier to be discredited.' "[141]

The task of conducting amphibious landings as part of the Navy's mission of supporting the ground forces has been divided into two main types of operations by N. P. V'iunenko, an authoritative Soviet naval writer. First are those involved in seizing ports and naval bases in enemy territory, whether for use by the Soviet Navy and merchant shipping or primarily to deny their use to the enemy. Second are those landings conducted to overcome enemy resistance at "broad water barriers, particularly estuaries, sounds, and channels" so that the ground forces can maintain the high rate of advance deemed by Soviet tactical doctrine to be essential for success on the nuclear battlefield.[142]

Recent Soviet writings have indicated the need for fast specialized landing ships and craft, such as the United States used in World War II, rather than merely using whatever ships, boats, and barges that might happen to be available (as the Soviet Naval Infantry have traditionally been forced to do).[143] The Naval Infantry branch itself is undergoing a

---

[140] Sokolovskii, *op. cit.,* 2nd ed., p. 251.

[141] Malinovskii, "Vneocherednoi XXI s"ezd Kommunisticheskoi Partii Sovetskogo Soiuza, rech' Marshala Sovetskogo Soiuza R. Ia. Malinovskogo."

[142] V'iunenko, *op. cit.,* p. 22.

[143] Svetlov and Shimkevich, *op. cit.,* p. 24. V'iunenko, *op. cit.* V. I. Platonov, "Na

renascence after having been conspicuous for its absence from the Soviet scene for many years.[144] Amphibious tactics stress the use of tactical nuclear weapons, the great importance of achieving surprise, the use of several formations of landing forces dispersed over a wide front, the development of hydrofoil craft for high landing speeds, and the coordinated employment of airborne assault forces.[145] In 1957, an article by Soviet Admiral Iu. Ladinskii indicated that the USSR was stressing further development of amphibious landing vehicles and tactics.[146] Articles in the Soviet press recently have reflected a more active interest in amphibious warfare, including actual conduct of amphibious training exercises.[147] Tass reports and photographs, in September 1964, pictured joint seaborne and airborne landings in Bulgaria by the combined Warsaw Pact forces of Romania, Bulgaria, and the USSR.[148]

Captain O. P. Araldsen, Royal Norwegian Navy, has nicely summed up the situation with regard not only to the Soviet Navy's capabilities for amphibious operations in the Baltic and Black seas and along their oceanic coasts, but also as concerns its capabilities for coastal warfare in general:

> While there is no doubt that NATO today [1958] has supremacy on the open sea, we must point out that the Soviet Union has concentrated to a greater extent than any other nation on warfare in coastal waters. In this field she is probably equal to NATO, or even superior.[149]

---

strazhe Zapoliar'ia" (On Guard of the Sub-Polar Arctic), *Morskoi Sbornik,* April, 1965, p. 17.

[144] Typical of a number of articles and photographs on the newly-revived Soviet "marine", now decked out with berets in the style of the U.S. Special Forces, and ostensibly engaged in amphibious training exercises, is to be found on the front page of *Krasnaia Zvezda* of July 24, 1964. An article the following month seemed to imply that the Naval Infantry were receiving the varied types of training given to U.S. Special Forces. Moreover, the title of the latter article also suggested that Naval Infantry troops were being prepared for limited war duties as well as being trained for traditional general war amphibious operations. V. Artem'ev "Oni gotovilis k raznym roliam" (They Have Prepared for Various Roles), *Krasnaia Zvezda,* August 7, 1964.

[145] Svetlov and Shimkevich, *op. cit.,* pp. 22–27. V'iunenko, *op. cit.,* pp. 21–27. D. A. Tuz, "Rol' morskikh desantnykh operatsii v raketno-iadernoi voine" (The Role of Naval Landing Operations in Nuclear Missile War), *Morskoi Sbornik,* June, 1964, pp. 24–29.

[146] "Naval art [*i.e.,* science] is searching for and investigating more effective means of action by units and forces of the Navy with the aim of increasing the timeliness and organization of loading of troops and landing transport vehicles, successful transit by them of the sea, landings on defended coasts of the enemy, support of their operations on the beach, and their subsequent supply by sea routes until able to exercise operational independence." Ladinskii, *op. cit.,* p. 35.

[147] N. Shalagin and N. Alekseev, "Soldaty shturmuiut bereg" (Soldiers Storm the Shore), *Krasnaia Zvezda,* October 10, 1963. "Boi vedet morskaia pekhota", *op. cit.*

[148] "Ucheniia voisk stran Varshavskogo dogovora" (Exercises of the Troops of the Warsaw Pact), *Krasnaia Zvezda,* September 22, 1964.

[149] O. P. Araldsen, "Norwegian Defense Problems; the Role of the Navy," *United States Naval Institute Proceedings,* October, 1958, p. 44.

The Navy, Present and Future ★

Based on the sum total of the evidence which current research can yield, as meagre as it admittedly is for many aspects of Soviet naval strategy, the following tentative conclusions corresponding to the five series of questions set out in the Preface have been reached:

1. Current Soviet naval strategy is an essentially deterrent and defensive one of dependence largely on missile-equipped submarines and shore-based aircraft supported by numerous and partially missile-armed, light, fast surface craft and coastal missile batteries. The evolution of this strategically defensive stance in naval matters has been heavily influenced by unfavorable geography that has not only required the maintenance of four separate fleets in the Black Sea, Baltic, Arctic, and Pacific, but even has denied to all of them the direct and free access to the oceans of the world that would permit sustained naval operations on the major shipping routes. Despite this situation, no evidence has been uncovered to support (but much to controvert) allegations that the Soviet Russians, like their Tsarist predecessors, are subject to an historic and lemming-like urge to the sea to obtain warm water ports.

Both the Soviet open-source theoretical writings and the actual Soviet naval practice indicate that the USSR already has twice gone full spiral in its publicly avowed naval strategy. This alternation has involved shifts between an "old school" strategy, which requires a balanced high-seas fleet with all types of large and small ships that is capable of contesting for command of the sea, to a "young school" strategy which emphasizes submarines to the exclusion of any large surface ship types and is inherently limited to deterrent and defensive roles. Against the unvarying preference of Soviet naval leaders for following a consistent, long-term, old school strategy, Party and Army leaders have twice joined forces to impose the adoption of a young school strategy—once in the late twenties and early thirties and again after Stalin's death in 1953.

Both decisions appear to have been basically due to the Party's desire to reduce military expenditures and the Army's efforts to get as large a share of the military budget as possible. In practice, however, both periods of young school strategy have shown marked discrepancies between the publicly proclaimed theories and the actual ship construction programs and naval training operations carried out. Large ship types, although theoretically outmoded, have been continued in operation, and naval leaders continue to press for the construction of other big ship types, which they recognize are necessary for balanced naval forces.

In effect, the USSR's naval leaders have consistently tried to obtain the substance even if not the theoretical sanction of an old school strategy. Since Stalin's death, the Navy has managed to gain permission to continue a sizable force of cruisers in operation and even to win a theoretical concession of potentially great future importance: that the Navy does, in fact, have a number of missions to perform that are wholly independent of the Army's ground, air, and missile forces. These developments could conceivably be harbingers of an impending return to the strategic offensive in Soviet naval strategy. However, until the USSR takes the first steps of laying the keels for some of the substantial numbers of big aircraft carriers that would be required to permit sustained Soviet surface naval force operations on the high seas as well as of the smaller antisubmarine carriers needed against Polaris submarines, one is justified in remaining sceptical that the Party and Army leaders have expanded their naval strategic aims beyond deterrence and defense.

Present Soviet naval strategy, it must be concluded, does not support the popular view that the Soviet Union is bent on the build-up of military forces essential to any aim of world domination by force. Rather, that strategy suffers from inherent defects, even for defense, against NATO's carrier strike or Polaris capability. Soviet efforts for the present, as will be discussed subsequently, are apparently concentrated on an antimissile missile system which offers only an unpromising passive defense measure.

2. As to the Soviet Navy's capabilities for carrying out the various missions normal to navies, it is clear that the strongest capabilities exist for executing close-inshore defensive missions and ones which would support the ground forces: defense against amphibious invasions, protection of coastal shipping, tactical landings in the rear of enemy's ground troops, and gunfire support for the seaward flank of the Soviet ground forces. The two major offensive missions for which the Soviet Navy pos-

sesses significant capabilities—those for missile strikes against land targets and for submarine warfare against shipping—do not constitute as much of a threat as Communist and non-Communist journalists alike portray. Rather, there exists considerable doubt that these two missions would be assigned to the Soviet Navy in any third world war, even a protracted one. Any navy which has been designed, constructed, and trained to contest for command of the sea has a single major mission—that of destroying the enemy's naval forces;[1] the Soviet Navy lacks mobile, sea-air power, thus cannot operate far at sea on a sustained basis because of the limited capabilities of its shore-based aircraft. Finally, without the attack carrier striking forces that are essential in the present age to contest for command of the seas outside of narrow coastal waters, any thought of developing the capability for transoceanic invasion of large continental areas (a capability which Soviet strategists hold to be essential to the final successful conclusion of any third world war) becomes the sheerest fantasy. All the transport ships and all the submarines Soviet industry could produce could not carry out a transatlantic invasion of the continental United States in the face of the overwhelming power of the carrier striking forces of NATO.

3. The dominant interest of Party leaders in naval strategy formulation is found to be budgetary—to keep a close control on the funds allocated for naval construction and for the operation of the Navy. Far from being limited to the normal budgetary supervision that governmental bureaus or parliamentary committees exercise, Party involvement extends to the very selection of the strategy to be implemented and even to the types and numbers of ships and weapons systems to be provided. Because of the interlocking Party-government organization in the USSR, in which top Party functionaries also supervise government execution of key functions for which they hold the responsible Party posts, Party control is pervasive and any administrative efforts by government officials to frustrate or transform Party policy directives in the course of administering them are made more difficult.

4. Soviet naval propaganda has been extensively and successfully employed to hide the fact of the USSR's very great and potentially disastrous qualitative naval inferiority vis-à-vis the NATO naval forces. This propaganda has two main aspects. The first has been a concerted and intensive effort to persuade world public opinion that the technological revolution in military affairs has so improved the submarine by arming it

---

[1] "The battle fleet can secure command of the sea either by destroying the enemy fleet in battle or by denying it access to the seas which one wishes to control. The first of these is obviously preferable." Bernard Brodie, *A Guide to Naval Strategy* (Princeton: Princeton University Press, 1944), p. 93.

with nuclear missiles and giving it nearly unlimited submerged endurance through nuclear propulsion that it has replaced the aircraft carrier as the most important ship type and that the latter is obsolescent if not obsolete. Acceptance of this theory begs the fact that the submarine is only able to perform one half of the task of sea power—to deny the use of the sea to the ships of the enemy; it cannot insure the command of the sea necessary to its own use, whether for protection of shipping or for conducting surface antisubmarine operations along with the air and submarine forces required to make antisubmarine operations most effective.

The second aspect of Soviet naval propaganda has been its insistent repetition of the claim that the Soviet Navy is superior to the NATO naval forces in every conceivable way. The failure of Western publicists not only to discredit such claims by refuting them with the readily available facts but to heap on them the ridicule that they deserve all testifies to what purports to be a fundamentally ill-advised willingness to magnify the Soviet naval "threat" out of all proportions in order either to produce more sensational articles or to justify larger naval appropriations to a Congress and a public deemed incapable of understanding a reasoned appeal based on the real facts of Soviet naval weakness and the advantages of keeping the lead in sea power that NATO now enjoys.

The unceasing propaganda claims of the Soviet Navy's superiority bring to mind a statement Khrushchev made in his secret speech on the "Cult of the Individual" at the Twentieth Party Congress in February 1956:

> Before the war our press and all our political-educational work was characterized by its bragging tone: when an enemy violates the holy Soviet soil, then for every blow of the enemy we will answer with three blows and we will battle the enemy on his soil and we will win without much harm to ourselves. But these positive statements were not based in all areas on concrete facts which would actually guarantee the immunity of our borders.[2]

This statement is not only applicable to the Stalinist era of Soviet history but, it would seem, equally to the Khrushchevian and post-Khrushchevian periods. The same tone of braggadocio is constantly employed in Soviet naval propaganda. One comes to wonder if the Party leaders may not have mesmerized themselves by the unceasing repetition of their own propaganda.

5. As concerns the general Western conception of Soviet naval strat-

---

[2] N. S. Khrushchev, "Cult of the Individual," secret speech at the Twentieth Congress of the C.P.S.U. *The Anti-Stalin Campaign and International Communism, A Selection of Documents*. Edited by the Russian Institute of Columbia University. (New York: Columbia University Press, 1956), p. 43.

egy as visibly developing into an offensive, high-seas fleet concept, it would seem the evidence supports the view that Soviet naval strategy will remain defensive for the foreseeable future. However, a caveat should be entered at this point. To merely have shown that Western conceptions of Soviet naval strategy, as well as the Soviet propaganda claims on which those conceptions are at least partially based, are substantially belied by the relevant facts is, of course, not tantamount to having demonstrated that Soviet naval strategy is necessarily irrational. Inadequate as it may be from the orthodox Anglo-American concept that superior capabilities for exercising command over the far reaches of the World Ocean are essential capabilities for a great power, it cannot be logically concluded that therefore Soviet strategy is *ipso facto* an ill-conceived one in the Soviet context.

Rather, the test of the rationality and adequacy of Soviet naval strategy is not how well it corresponds with some modernized version of Mahan's precepts on command of the sea, but must involve a pragmatic weighing of the Soviet naval capabilities deriving from Soviet strategy against the particular Soviet requirements for deterrence and defense and the USSR's potential possibilities for developing into a major naval power. The Soviet potential in this latter regard must be seen in the context of all of the relevant advantages and disadvantages resulting from geography, naval forces in being and their technical modernity, and the size of the gross national product and the amounts budgeted for naval purposes after higher priority demands such as those for ICBM's, ABM systems, and space have been met.

All factors considered, including the relative unlikelihood that the United States would initiate general nuclear war, the great lead that the United States enjoys in aircraft carrier construction and in carrier warfare, the vast outlays that are required for the building, manning, training, and operating of attack carrier striking forces, the USSR's extremely unfavorable position geographically as far as unrestricted access to the open oceans from available bases is concerned, and the greater American economic strength that would permit the United States to outbuild the USSR two or more ships to one in any naval arms race, all combine to greatly diminish the attraction that Soviet Party leaders might otherwise find in the Navy's repeated proposals to develop attack carrier striking forces.

Perhaps the most interesting conclusions of all from a political science point of view are two which relate to the structure of the USSR's governmental organization and the way the top Soviet leaders go about the determination of the Navy's size and composition:

1. Due to the fact that the USSR has a unified ministry of the armed

forces, the dozen or so Army marshals who are all senior to the Commander in Chief of the Navy are able to exclude the Navy from having any substantial influence on the formulation of naval strategy and on the share of the defense budget given the Navy.

2. Although not explicitly stated in recent writings of Admiral Gorshkov and other Soviet naval writers, it is unmistakably clear from these writings that the Party leaders quite arbitrarily decided what types of ships to adapt to nuclear weapons and propulsion and the numbers of each to construct; they then gave them to the Navy as a *fait accompli* with the implied instruction to work out suitable tactics and an overall strategy as best the Navy could. Here one can see the opposite extreme from U.S. Defense Secretary McNamara's methods of tailoring force structures to accomplish the necessary missions. The Soviet Communist Party has completely hobbled the Navy by saddling it with unsuitable, if technologically up-to-date, ship and aircraft weapons systems for carrying out even the defensive missions which objectively confront the Soviet Navy. With such an approach to naval strategy formulation, the Party leaders certainly have no rational basis for considering that the Navy could develop a successful strategy for fighting a war at sea. The Party's otherwise inexplicable action may clearly be attributed to the following factors:

a. The land-oriented outlook of the leaders and of the military theoreticians of both the Party and the Army.
b. The tradition of the Party's omniscience which, in naval strategy formulation at least, holds not only that the subject is the prerogative of the Party, but that the naval leaders could not possibly say anything worth listening to on such matters.
c. The compelling desire to keep military expenditures to a minimum so as to permit larger budgetary allocations to other sectors of the economy.

In reflecting on the Party's arbitrariness in determining the composition and size of Soviet naval forces, as well as its quasi-total disregard for the rational procedure of first formulating an adequate naval strategy and then developing the forces needed to implement it, the tentative conclusion has been reached that the Party leadership not only suffers from a collective lack of understanding of sea power but also entertains a basic conviction that the Soviet Navy will never be required to fight a war. It would seem that this assumption stems in part from the belief that the United States would never start a general nuclear war, and thus the issue of war or peace rests safely in Soviet hands.

The Soviet Navy's ballistic missile submarines may eventually provide the USSR with the same potent mobile deterrent force that Polaris submarines are affording the United States. Such strategic deterrent forces, however, and submarines in general, even though nuclear-powered, lack the mobile sea-air power to replace surface naval forces for exercising command of the sea in whatever areas of the world's oceans such command is needed at any given moment. Even though the Soviet Navy is second in tonnage only to the U.S. Navy, its complete lack of strike carrier forces constitutes a fundamental, qualitative difference that necessitates resorting to the defensive in naval strategy. It is in this area of mobile naval air power that the Soviet Navy is so critically lacking. Even if the USSR were to make herculean efforts to build modern surface naval forces to include strike carriers, unfavorable geography and NATO's great lead in carrier striking forces present such great obstacles that the odds against eventual success would be very heavy. Moreover, the United States with its far greater gross national product and experience in carrier construction and operation could further increase the odds at will by building two or more carriers, and qualitatively superior ones, for each one built for the Soviet Navy.

In no other area does the West have such a commanding superiority over the USSR as in naval power. Even should the present top party and military leaders eventually be persuaded by Admiral Gorshkov or a successor that strike carriers are, in fact, an indispensable military asset for the USSR to develop, the enormous costs in terms of already fully-committed industrial resources very likely would be sufficient to discourage any Soviet attempt to build up strike forces. Instead of trying to offset superior Western naval powers by comparable or greater naval forces of the same type, the USSR has resorted largely to propaganda means. First, they have used propaganda in an effort to persuade world public opinion that submarine forces constitute adequate naval striking power in a nuclear age. Secondly, they have used their propaganda in the hope of discrediting in the eyes of the world public NATO submarine and surface forces, particularly Polaris submarines and strike carriers.

No knowledgeable person would deny that the Soviet's large, conventional submarine forces and the small but growing nuclear submarine forces present great challenges to NATO. The Soviet Navy's major reliance on submarines, the traditional weapon of "have-not" navies, and its lack of carrier striking forces signify that, athough the USSR certainly has a capability for greatly complicating Free World use of the seas, the Soviet Communist protagonist lacks any real potential for actually usurping NATO's supremacy at sea.

As Secretary of the Navy Nitze stated in 1964: "The attack carriers with their manned aircraft are now, and will be for a long time to come, the primary and indispensable ingredient of modern sea-based weapons systems."[3] Research discloses nothing to indicate that the great advances in modern nuclear and missile technology give any support to the view so frequently expressed abroad, even by some British naval writers, that the submarine is destined to replace the carrier as the capital ship of the future.[4] Accordingly, it is difficult to see how submarines could possibly go beyond efforts to deny free use of the seas and actually be able to replace attack carrier striking forces in exercising command of the sea to ensure its use for one's own purposes.

The Soviet Navy's Commander in Chief has made a futile effort to generalize into an accepted tenet of "advanced military thought" the USSR's forced dependence on submarines.[5] Obviously, Admiral Gorshkov is generalizing too broadly from the particular situation of the Soviet Navy as the weaker fleet unable to exercise command of the sea in the broad oceanic areas in which the USSR would have to exert sea supremacy to control the threat from Polaris submarines and strike carriers. Since no Soviet surface naval forces could long be maintained at sea in wartime in face of the overwhelming power of NATO naval forces, it is patently obvious that the USSR is forced to settle for the "half-loaf" of sea power by attempting to deny the free use of the high seas to the NATO naval forces without aspiring to control them for their own shipping, and even more importantly, to be able to use surface warships in an ASW role against Polaris submarines.

On balance, it is concluded that Soviet Party and Army formulators of the USSR's grand strategy entertain no hope whatsoever of exercising any command of the sea outside the range of shore-based naval

---

[3] "Naval officers recall Mr. Nitze's words when the *America* was launched a year ago: 'The attack carriers with their manned aircraft are now, and will be for a long time to come, the primary and indispensable ingredient of modern sea-based weapons systems.' " Cited by Hanson W. Baldwin, "Navy Commissions the *America,* A Huge New Carrier, at Norfolk," *The New York Times,* January 24, 1965, p. 3.

[4] Eventual naval-scene domination by nuclear-powered submarines is predicted by Vice Admiral B. B. Schofield, RN, "Developments in Maritime Forces, 1961–1962," *Brassey's Annual—The Armed Forces Year Book 1962,* p. 19. Similarly, the nuclear-powered torpedo-attack submarine is viewed as the successor to the aircraft carrier as the capital ship of the future in Lieutenant Commander Nowell Hall, "Changes in the World's Navies," *Ibid.,* p. 197.

[5] "It is correctly believed in advanced military thought that the navy best-suited to meet the requirements of modern warfare must be basically a submarine navy. It is in this direction that the Navy of the Soviet Union is now developing." S. G. Gorshkov, "Vernye syny rodiny" (True Sons of the Homeland), *Pravda,* July 31, 1960.

aviation.[6] It is further concluded that the Soviet strategy does not envision any great success in being able to sever NATO's vital Atlantic sea lines of communications.[7]

Rather, considering these two important points, one draws conclusions much closer to those of Captain O. P. Araldsen, Royal Norwegian Navy, who, perhaps because he was trained in the problems of a smaller navy, can understand the nature of the strategically defensive Soviet Navy better than his British and American counterparts, whose experience has been centered on strategically offensive naval operations. Captain Araldsen holds that Russia's primary naval aims are merely "to gain domination of the European coastal waters and as far as possible to hinder seaborne communications of the Western powers." Captain Araldsen goes on to point out that geostrategic factors alone would inhibit a Soviet naval contest with NATO:

> The Soviet bloc's main forces for hindering seaborne communications and for dominating European coastal waters are concentrated in the Baltic and Arctic Ocean, with priority on the Baltic. Neither of these regions is satisfactory as a strategic base of operations for a naval war with NATO. In this respect, the Eastern bloc is in a less fortunate position than Germany was in the two world wars. Furthermore, the strategic position of Norway and Denmark is such that they block an effective Soviet naval and air war against the Western powers.[8]

Despite the Navy's having been assigned some vital missions independent of the ground forces (e.g., to counter carrier and Polaris strikes and to make submarine missile strikes against NATO countries), the basic

---

[6] No less of an authority on military affairs than George Fielding Eliot has penned a highly pertinent paragraph that merits quoting at this point. In answer to the rhetorical question of why the Soviet Navy has no strike carriers, he replies: "Because the Soviet Navy is not designed for the positive purpose of seeking control of the sea, but for the negative purpose of trying to deny the use of the sea to its opponents—especially the United States. Therefore the Soviet Navy does not build *sea-control* weapons systems, but *sea-denial* weapons systems such as submarines and raiding cruisers, supplemented by land-based aircraft and minelaying. The history of warfare teaches us that such attempts at denial are always the expedient adopted by a power which is too weak in capital ships to fight for control of the sea. History also teaches us that such attempts have uniformly ended in failure, though the idea continues to have a seemingly irresistible attraction for the statesmen of countries more habituated to land than to sea warfare, such as Russia or Germany, in World Wars I and II." Eliot, *Victory without War*, p. 108.

[7] As set forth in Chapter VII, time may show that the Soviet strategic theorists in the military section of the Party's Central Committee, the Soviet equivalent of the U.S. Defense Department's "Whiz kids," may well have decided that development of the large nuclear-powered force of torpedo-attack submarines that would be needed for such an effort would not be "cost-effective."

[8] Araldsen, *op. cit.*, p. 42.

thrust of Soviet naval strategy, judging from the nature, composition, and deployment of Soviet naval forces since the fall of Khrushchev and fifty years since the "October Revolution," still appears in practice, although not in publicized theory, to be oriented toward support of the Soviet ground forces. The German writer, Alfred Schulze-Hinrichs, has expressed it well:

> A peculiar concept of naval power has developed in the Soviet Union. This is far removed from a purely maritime concept and, instead, is incorporated in a system of essentially continental, general warfare . . . naval forces, and presumably air forces, would serve primarily as auxiliary arms of the ground forces. In relation to this latter mission, the engagement of naval forces on the high seas would be of subordinate importance.[9]

Until the Soviet Navy builds strong attack carrier striking forces or unless some presently unforeseeable technological breakthrough really does make them too vulnerable for use in both general and limited war, Soviet naval practice will, of necessity, remain strategically defensive.

Nuclear power and its application to submarine propulsion and to ballistic missile warheads have created as difficult and urgent an antisubmarine warfare problem for the NATO powers as they would ever want to face. Yet consider how infinitely more difficult an ASW problem confronts the Soviet Union with up to 41 Polaris submarines operating throughout the oceans of the world at ranges of from 1,500 to 2,500 miles from the geographically remote Soviet and East European naval and air bases at which all their ASW patrol efforts must originate and terminate.

The seemingly insurmountable obstacles even to locating Polaris submarines initially, when considered in connection with Soviet claims of having developed a successful antimissile missile system (ABM), would seem to point to a Soviet decision to postpone consideration of any major antisubmarine warfare programs until after every effort has been made to cope with the Polaris threat by development of an effective antimissile missile-defense system that could be widely deployed when and if the USSR considered the great expense warranted. This would not preclude the construction of a number of helicopter carriers to see if effective ASW tactics can be developed against the fast, deep-running nuclear-powered submarine (as well as for primary use in amphibious landings).

The possibilities for the development of such an ABM system, particularly against missiles with multiple warheads such as will be the follow-on to the A-3 Polaris missile, the Poseidon, seem remote in the extreme.

---

[9] Alfred Schulze-Hinrichs, "The Guiding Principles Behind the Soviet Naval Forces," *Military Review,* December, 1954, p. 97. Translated and abridged from *Marine Rundschau,* No. 3, 1954.

One can easily appreciate both the Soviet Party leaders' interest in the American proposal for a moratorium on deploying ABM systems and the Soviet military leaders' natural fears that the Party leaders might be persuaded by the economics of the situation to omit an objectively necessary defense measure.

It would seem logical, although certainly not necessarily correct, to assume that the Soviet Navy's leadership would not indefinitely and unprotestingly accept the assignment of a mission against Polaris submarines without the aircraft carriers to provide the sustained and mobile air-sea operations that would be essential. Certainly accomplishment of even the anticarrier, let alone an anti-Polaris, mission will remain impossible of fulfillment as long as the Party and Army leaders continue to find it expedient to restrict the Soviet Navy to a neo-young school strategy. That Admiral Gorshkov would be ousted as Navy Commander in Chief the day he openly confronted the Party and Army leaders with the facts that the military-technical revolution has not outmoded carriers, and that all the missile-equipped surface ships, aircraft, and submarines that Soviet industry could build would not provide a substitute for carrier strike forces, seems highly probable.

Despite its propaganda to the effect that the Soviet Navy is the most modern in the world and fully capable of carrying out any mission assigned it, the USSR actually has a painfully accurate appreciation of its naval inferiority as well as its relative weakness in strategic nuclear striking power. Barring unforeseen developments such as a technological breakthrough that basically altered the situation, the Soviet Union has no choice but to avoid a general nuclear war. Instead, given its professed long-term aim of making the world over in its own image, it appears that the Soviet Union has no alternative but to continue to rely on its "peaceful coexistence" strategy of political, psychological, and *economic warfare*. In this struggle, a large merchant marine will be a decided asset. For the short range, the increased foreign exchange that can be saved by carrying her own exports will significantly increase the USSR's ability to purchase industrial and agricultural equipment abroad. Also, as Khrushchev pointed out, merchant ships can carry ideas as well as cargo to the far corners of the world. For the longer range, a large Soviet merchant marine could become a major instrument of economic warfare in the field of international commerce.

Yet, without world-wide surface naval forces to protect them, the multiplying merchant ships of the Soviet merchant marine become just so many hostages to NATO's naval forces—to further discourage the Soviet leaders from undertaking to accomplish their political aims by any use of force that might conceivably escalate to a general nuclear war.

The rapid build-up of the Soviet merchant marine is not the indication of an incipient Soviet drive to become a great offensive sea power, as it is almost invariably portrayed. Neither is the USSR's establishment in 1963 and nearly continuous maintenance since of a naval force in the Mediterranean such an indication.[10] Rather, the latter development should be viewed as intended for the following purposes (in decreasing order of importance):

1. To avoid the continued loss of prestige[11] that has been incurred by the USSR's long failure to even make a pretense of contesting with the United States' Sixth Fleet for naval supremacy in the Mediterranean.

2. To support the USSR's foreign policy objectives in the countries ringing the Mediterranean basin by maintaining a naval "presence," especially by means of port visits to friendly and neutral countries and a show of force at critical times and places in crises between smaller Mediterranean countries. Appearances of Soviet warships in the Aegean and off the coast of Cyprus at moments of greatest tension in the relations between Greece and Turkey over the island is a case in point. The transfer to the Mediterranean from the Black Sea in early June 1967, at the height of the Middle East crisis, of a number of additional warships as a show of force to impress the Arabs with the USSR's support in their vendetta against the Israelis is another example.

3. To add an increment to the USSR's capabilities for deterring nuclear strikes in general and from the American aircraft carriers and Polaris submarines in the Mediterranean in particular.[12] The actual combat value of such a relatively weak naval force would be extremely limited once a war had started and the chance of any of its surface ships or submarines surviving for long would be very small.[13]

4. To collect intelligence on the Sixth Fleet's capabilities for general nuclear and limited warfare. The Commander, U.S. Sixth Fleet, has re-

---

[10] See F. M. Murphy, "The Soviet Navy in the Mediterranean," *U.S. Naval Institute Proceedings,* March, 1967, pp. 38–44. This writer generally concurs with the main conclusions of that article but cannot agree that the Soviet Navy's expansion into the Mediterranean indicates the top Soviet leadership is "now thinking in terms of global strategy for its surface ships."

[11] Particularly in the less developed countries whose evolving political, social, and economic systems are more subject to Soviet influence than are those of the developed states.

[12] "A Soviet naval build-up in the Mediterranean is threatening the United States Sixth Fleet and limiting its capability as a strike force, the Fleet's Commander [Vice] Admiral William I. Martin said today [in a luncheon address to the American Club of Rome] . . . The Fleet now was no longer able to devote itself entirely to mounting strike operations against the Soviet Union, Admiral Martin said." *Reuter,* May 17, 1967.

[13] Except by a wholly unexpected attack, the USSR could not realistically entertain much hope of their missile destroyers or submarines successfully attacking the Sixth Fleet's aircraft carriers let alone the Polaris submarines and, in any event, not before the latter were able to launch their initial retaliatory strike against the Soviet Union.

cently spoken publicly of the "extensive surveillance" conducted by the Russians against the operations of the Sixth Fleet.[14]

5. To afford naval training, a factor that would be unlikely to be of much concern to any elements of the Soviet leadership except the naval and hence scarcely a consideration in the primarily political decision to establish and maintain a Mediterranean naval force.

Although the technological revolution has had a great effect on the Soviet Navy by providing nuclear propulsion for part of its submarines and missiles for some of its land-based aircraft, submarines, cruisers, destroyers, PT boats, and coastal defenses, the greatest influence has been a critically negative one—equipping the naval forces of NATO with the nuclear bomb-carrying carrier aircraft and Polaris submarine missiles that create a "threat" of nuclear devastation against which the Soviet Navy and other Soviet military forces can oppose no effective opposition, either at present or for the foreseeable future. The effect of this Soviet naval weakness should be to greatly lessen the USSR's international standing just as it objectively undermines the USSR's efforts to achieve a military power balance with NATO. Due to clever Soviet propaganda (and its uncritical acceptance in the West) claiming that the technological revolution in military affairs has made the strike carrier obsolete and given the trident to the nuclear-powered missile submarine, the USSR has been able to offset the drop in prestige that would inevitably follow upon a widespread recognition of the true situation. Continuation of Stalin's naval strategy of building up big, balanced fleets with the further addition of strike carriers would have been a *sine qua non* of any real effort of the post-Stalin leaders to implement a long-term military strategy aimed at world domination by military means. The fact that no such naval strategy has been followed[15] by either Khrushchev or subsequent leaders provides convincing evidence that world domination by military means is not an active goal of current Soviet policy. Rather, that policy is more than preoccupied with the imperative needs of developing

---

[14] The Commander, U.S. Sixth Fleet, Vice Admiral Martin, has also recently spoken publicly of the "extensive surveillance" the USSR conducts of Sixth Fleet operations. (*Reuter,* May 17, 1967.) Admiral Martin also admitted the nuisance value of close Soviet surveillance and harassment (thereby giving the Soviet leaders a definite confirmation of the efficacy of such measures and hence encouragement to continue them) when he sent a message to a destroyer of the Soviet squadron: "Your actions for the past five days have interfered with our operations. By positioning your ship in the midst of our formation and shadowing our every move you are denying us the freedom of maneuver on the high seas that has been traditionally recognized by seafaring nations for centuries." (UPI, June 8, 1967.)

[15] Despite reliable reports by U.S. naval leaders as this book goes to press that *helicopter* carriers are under construction in the USSR and vastly less reliable speculation that construction of *strike* carriers will follow. William Beecher, "Soviet Navy Gaining New Role," *The New York Times,* October 22, 1967.

effective defense against the NATO naval threat and contributing to the USSR's national nuclear deterrent and second strike forces.

The Soviet claims to having built up an invincible Navy that fully meets the demands of the nuclear age are unquestionably aimed at covering up Soviet naval weakness, the USSR's "naval gap," so that Soviet prestige will not suffer the diminution that its great naval inferiority objectively merits.

Will the USSR eventually undertake the construction of the major surface forces, including the antisubmarine and strike aircraft carriers that would be required to protect a world-wide merchant fleet, and permit at least some defense against NATO's strike carriers and Polaris submarines? There are no signs heralding the appearance on the Russian scene of another "big Navy" advocate like Stalin, let alone one who would undertake to build a sizable number of strike carriers in an effort to challenge the West for command of the seas. As implied earlier in this chapter, even if the Soviet leaders privately thought well of the idea as a theory, they would hesitate long and search diligently for less expensive alternatives before undertaking such a costly and unpromising long-term program. Actually, they obviously consider their large but far less costly submarine force just such an alternative, even though far from being an adequate one for yielding more than a minimum deterrent effect.

A continued lack of appreciation of sea power's full potential by the dominant Soviet Party and Army leaders can be anticipated. This should hold true even though Khrushchev has been replaced by Brezhnev and Kosygin and they, in turn, yield to others.

Similarly, Soviet naval strategy and naval budgets may be expected to continue to be adversely affected by Army dominance of Soviet grand strategy.

Finally, it can be anticipated that the rigid Party control of the Soviet Navy and the Party monopoly of both naval strategy formulation and shipbuilding programming will continue to be detrimental to the development of not only strategic practice and theory, but also the effectiveness and initiative of Soviet naval operations and personnel.

What are the implications for the United States and the rest of the Free World of all that has been related?

In the first place, it should be realized that, owing to the long-standing predominance of political and Army leaders in the formulation and execution of the USSR's unified military strategy and their general lack of understanding of sea power, the USSR has a basically defective naval strategy for general war purposes. That is, the balanced team that is required to make sea power a winning force in a period when technical advances have literally made the only defense a good offense is wholly lacking in the Soviet Navy. There are no real high-seas surface striking forces and there is no naval air power outside the range of shore bases. Instead, the Soviet Navy is a deterrent-defensive force that fully reflects the Party's post-Stalin decision not to attempt to build offensive, high-seas fleets.

Although Stalin long cherished the dream of building up a big, balanced fleet for deterrence and defense, whether or not with more ambitious long-range aims, this has been beyond the USSR's understanding of sea power, determination, and economic strength to accomplish.

Moreover, with the advent of the nuclear age and the development of long-range, seaborne missiles, Soviet naval strategy no longer constitutes even a sound concept for defense of the USSR's maritime frontiers. Soviet military thought clearly acknowledges the inadequacy of the strategic defense in the nuclear age. Yet, the Soviet leaders, since Stalin, have been either unable, or unwilling, or both, to face up effectively to a naval building program, including strike carriers, that would hold a long-term potential for successfully wresting away the sea supremacy of the NATO naval powers.

Glossary ★

The glossary which follows contains a compilation of terms peculiar to this work. The first use of each term in the text is italicized, indicating that the word is defined in the glossary.

Key: JD—*Dictionary of United States Military Terms for Joint Usage.* Joint Chiefs of Staff Pub. 1. EB—*Encyclopedia Britannica,* 1951 Edition (with some modifications by the author). RH—Author's definition.

Air-to-surface missile (ASM): A missile launched from an airborne carrier to impact on a surface target. (JD)

Attack carrier striking forces: Naval forces, the primary offensive weapon of which is carrier-based aircraft. Ships, other than carriers, act primarily to support and screen against submarine and air threat, and secondarily against surface threat. (JD)

Campaign strategy: The strategy for a given theater of naval operations, or for a particular period of warfare. (EB)

Command and control: An arrangement of personnel, facilities, and the means for information acquisition, processing, and dissemination employed by a commander in planning, directing, and controlling operations. (JD)

Command of the sea: A relative superiority at sea that permits use of the sea oneself while denying its use to hostile powers. (EB)

Convoy: A number of merchant ships or naval auxiliaries, or both, usually escorted by warships and/or aircraft, or a single merchant ship or naval auxiliary under surface escort, assembled and organized for the purpose of passage together. (JD)

Convoy escort: Naval vessels or aircraft in company with a convoy and responsible for its protection. (JD)

Deployment: In a strategic sense, the relocation of forces to desired areas of operation. (JD)

Deterrence: The prevention from action by fear of the consequences. Deterrence is a state of mind brought about by the existence of a credible threat of unacceptable counteraction. (JD)

Economic action: The planned use of economic measures designed to influence the policies or actions of another state, e.g., to impair the war-making potential of a hostile power, or to generate economic stability within a friendly power. (JD)

Economic warfare: Aggressive use of economic means to achieve national objectives. (JD)

Fleet in being: A strategy of the potential offensive in which a fleet is maintained primarily as an implicit threat against a hostile power to persuade it not to attack but to keep its forces committed to a blockade of the fleet in being. (EB)

Fortress fleet: A strategy of passive and nearly immobile defense in which the warships remain at a fixed position, usually in support of coastal artillery guns, defending key coastal cities. (EB)

Grand strategy: The military strategy required to achieve the nation's aims. (EB)

Naval strategy: The theoretical ideas underlying the intended development and employment of naval power to further the foreign policy aims of a state as well as the actual construction, deployment, and use of naval forces that are carried out in practice. (RH)

Old school strategy: A recurrent Soviet naval strategy, presently out of favor with the dominant Party and military leaders although not with the majority of senior naval officers, which calls for the construction of balanced high seas fleets, with all contemporary ship types from submarines to aircraft carriers, designed to contest for command of the sea. (RH)

Psychological warfare: The planned use of propaganda and other psychological actions having the primary purpose of influencing the opinions, emotions, attitudes, and behavior of hostile foreign groups in such a way as to support the achievement of national objectives. (JD)

Second strike: The first counterblow of a war. (Generally associated with nuclear operations.) (JD)

Strategic mission: A mission directed against one or more of a selected series of enemy targets with the purpose of progressive destruction and disintegration of the enemy's war-making capacity and his will to make war. Targets include key manufacturing systems, sources of raw materials, critical material stockpiles, power systems, transportation systems, communications facilities, and other such target systems. (JD)

Strategic vulnerability: The susceptibility of vital elements of national power to being seriously decreased or adversely changed by the application of actions within the capability of another nation to impose. Strategic vulnerability may pertain to political, geographic, economic, scientific, sociological, or military factors. (JD)

Strategic warning: A notification that enemy-initiated hostilities may be imminent. The time element may vary from minutes to hours, to days, or more. (JD)

Submarine striking forces: Submarines having guided or ballistic missile launching and/or guidance capabilities formed to launch offensive nuclear strikes. (JD)

Subroc (submarine rocket): Submerged, submarine-launched, surface-to-surface rocket with nuclear depth charge or homing torpedo payload, primarily antisubmarine. (JD)

Surface striking forces: Forces which are organized primarily to do battle with enemy forces or to conduct shore bombardment. Units comprising such a force are generally incorporated in and operate as part of another force, but with provisions for their formation into a surface striking force should such action appear likely and/or desirable. (JD)

Surface-to-surface missile (SSM): A surface-launched missile designed to operate against a target on the surface. (JD)

Unconventional warfare: Includes the three interrelated fields of guerilla warfare, evasion and escape, and subversion. Unconventional warfare operations are conducted within enemy or enemy-controlled territory by predominantly indigenous personnel, usually supported and directed by an external source. (JD)

Young school strategy: A recurrent Soviet naval strategy, in vogue since Stalin's death, which eschews the offensive by high-seas fleets to gain command of the sea in favor of hindering or denying the enemy's use of the World Ocean through large submarine forces, shore-based naval aviation and surface-to-surface missile batteries, and small surface ships. Adapted for Soviet use from the French *Jeune Ecole* strategy devised by Admiral Aube in the late nineteenth century and which required "mosquito fleet" surface forces and submarines. (RH)

Bibliography ★

Public Documents

U.S. Commissioner Riga. *Report No. 312.* October 19, 1921.

U.S. Congress. House. Committee on Un-American Activities. *Testimony of Captain Nikolai Fedorovich Artamanov.* Washington: Government Printing Office, 1960.

————. Senate. Committee on the Judiciary. *Russia's Burgeoning Maritime Strength.* Washington: Government Printing Office, 1963.

U.S. Embassy Helsingfors. *Military Information Bulletin.* March 15, 1921.

U.S. Military Attache Riga. *Report No. 5553.* October 31, 1926.

————. *Report No. 5862.* September 4, 1927.

————. *Report No. 6510.* April 16, 1928.

U.S. Military Attache Warsaw. *Report No. 1271.* March 1, 1921.

U.S. Naval Attache Berlin. *Report No. 40.* February 27, 1923.

U.S. Naval Attache Copenhagen. *Report No. R-552.* December 17, 1936.

U.S. Naval Attache "L". *Report No. 81–40.* March 18, 1940.

U.S. Navy Department. *German Naval Records.* ONI T-80E, NID PG/49180. Washington: Office of the Chief of Naval Operations, Division of Naval History, 1947.

————. ————. ONI T-93B, NID PG/33738. Washington: Office of the Chief of Naval Operations, Division of Naval History, 1947.

————. Office of Information. *Answers to Questions Concerning the Soviet Navy.* Chief of Information Notice 5720, January 31, 1958.

————. ————. *Estimate of the Soviet Submarine Threat and Portrayal of the Navy's Capabilities to Meet that Threat, Present and Future.* Chief of Information Notice 5720, August 26, 1957.

U.S. State Department. *Foreign Relations of the United States, Diplomatic Papers, The Soviet Union 1933–1939.* Washington: U.S. Government Printing Office, 1952, pp. 457–491, 670–707, and 869–903.

USS *Pittsburgh. Report No. 1440.* August 27, 1923.

USS *Scorpion. Report No. 488.* December 10, 1923.

USSR. Central Committee of the CPSU. *History of the Communist Party of the Soviet Union (Bolsheviks), Short Course.* New York: International Publishers, 1939.

————. ————. *KPSS v resoliutsiakh i resheniakh s"ezdov, konferentsii i plenumov TsK* (The Communist Party of the Soviet Union in Resolutions and Decisions of Congresses, Conferences and Plenary Sessions of the Central Committee). Moscow: Gosizdat, 1954.

————. *Desiati s"ezd RKP(b), Mart 1921 goda, Stenograficheskii otchet* (Tenth Congress of the RKP[b], March 1921, Stenographic Record), 2nd ed. Moscow: Gosizdatpolitlit, 1963.

Memoirs and Personal Interviews

Davies, Joseph E. *Mission to Moscow.* New York: Simon and Schuster, 1941.

Djilas, Milovan. *Conversations with Stalin.* New York: Harcourt, Brace, and World, 1962.

Former Soviet Naval Officer. Interview with the author, Newport, Rhode Island, October 30, 1963.

————. Telephonic interview with the author, Munich to the United States, January 22, 1967.

Hull, Cordell. *The Memoirs of Cordell Hull.* New York: Macmillan, 1948.

Books, General and Reference

The Anti-Stalin Campaign and International Communism; A Selection of Documents. Edited by the Russian Institute of Columbia University. New York: Columbia University Press, 1956.

Baldwin, Hanson W. *The Price of Power.* New York: Harper Brothers, 1947.

Baykov, Alexander. *The Development of the Soviet Economic System.* Cambridge, England: Cambridge University Press, 1948.

Beloff, Max. *Soviet Policy in the Far East 1941–1951.* London: Oxford University Press, 1953.

Brassey's Annual—Yearbook of the Armed Forces, 1940. London: Wm. Clowes and Sons, Ltd., 1940.

Brassey's Annual—The Armed Forces Yearbook 1962. London: Wm. Clowes and Sons, Ltd., 1962.

Brassey's Naval Annual 1938. London: William Clowes Ltd., 1938.

Castex, Raoul. *Theories Strategiques.* Trans. by R. C. Smith, Jr. Newport, Rhode Island: U.S. Naval War College, 1938.

Chamberlin, William H. *The Russian Revolution 1917–1921.* Vol. II. New York: Macmillan Company, 1952.

Cressey, George B. *How Strong is Russia, A Geographic Appraisal.* Syracuse: Syracuse University Press, 1954.

Dallin, David. *The Big Three: The United States, Britain, and Russia.* New Haven: Yale University Press, 1945.

Dinerstein, H. S. *War and the Soviet Union*. Revised edition. New York: F. A. Praeger, 1962.

Eliot, George Fielding. *Victory Without War, 1958–1961*. Annapolis: United States Naval Institute, 1958.

Erickson, John. *The Soviet High Command, A Military-Political History 1918–1941*. London: Macmillan Company Limited, 1962.

Fedotoff-White, D. *The Growth of the Red Army*. Princeton: Princeton University Press, 1944.

Flottes de Combat 1962. Henri le Masson (ed.), Paris: Editions Maritimes et d'outre-Mer, 1962.

Garthoff, R. L. *Soviet Image of Future War*. Washington: Public Affairs Press, 1959.

———. *Soviet Military Doctrine*. Glencoe, Illinois: Free Press, 1953.

———. *Soviet Military Policy*. New York: F. A. Praeger, 1966.

———. *Soviet Strategy in the Nuclear Age*. New York: F. A. Praeger, 1958.

Istoriia velikoi otechestvennoi voiny sovetskogo soiuza, 1941–1945 (History of the Great Patriotic War, 1941–1945). 6 vols. Moscow: Voenizdat, 1960–1965.

Jakobson, Max. *Diplomacy of the Winter War*. Cambridge, Massachusetts: Harvard University Press, 1961.

Jane's All the World's Aircraft, 1966–1967. R. V. P. Blackman (ed.), New York: McGraw-Hill, 1968.

Jane's Fighting Ships, 1966–1967. R. V. P. Blackman (ed.), New York: McGraw-Hill, 1966.

Jane's Fighting Ships, 1963–1964. J. W. R. Taylor (ed.), New York: McGraw-Hill, 1963.

Kennan, G. F. *Soviet Foreign Policy 1917–1941*. Princeton, New Jersey: D. Van Nostrand Company, Inc., 1960.

Lee, Asher. The Soviet Air Force. New York: John Day Company, 1963.

Lenin, V. I. *V. I. Lenin, Voennaia Perepiska* (V. I. Lenin, Military Correspondence), Moscow: Voenizdat, 1966.

Liddell-Hart, B. H. *The Red Army*. New York: Harcourt, Brace and Co., 1956.

The Military Balance 1966–1967. London: The Institute for Strategic Studies, 1966.

Piatiletnyi plan vosstanovleniia i razvitiia narodnogo khoziaistva, 1946–1950gg (Five Year Plan for the Rehabilitation and Development of the Economy, 1946–1950) Edited by N. A. Voznesenskii. Moscow: Gospolitlitizdat, 1946.

Shapiro, Leonard. *The Communist Party of the Soviet Union*. New York: Alfred A. Knopf, Inc., 1964.

Shulman, Marshall. *Stalin's Foreign Policy Reappraised*. New York: Harvard University Press, 1963.

Strokov, A. A. (ed.), Istoriia voennogo iskusstva (History of Military Art). Moscow: Voenizdat, 1966.

Trotsky, Leon. *The Revolution Betrayed*. New York: Doubleday, 1937.

Wolfe, Thomas W. *Soviet Strategy at the Crossroads*. New York: Harvard University Press, 1964. Originally published as Rand Memorandum RM-4085-PR of April 1964.

Books, Naval (in Russian)

Achkasov, V. *Krasnoznamennyi Baltiiskii flot v velikoi otechestvennoi voine* (The Red Banner Baltic Fleet in the Great Fatherland War). Moscow: Voenizat, 1957.

Atomnaia energiia i flot, sbornik statei (Nuclear Energy and the Navy, A Collection of Articles). Moscow: Voenizdat, 1959.

Barbashin, I. P. et al. *Bitva za Leningrad* (Battle for Leningrad). S. P. Platonov (ed.) Moscow: Voenizdat, 1964.

Billevich, B. *Voenno-morskoe delo* (Naval Affairs). Moscow: Voenizdat, 1935.

Chernyshev, V. F. *Nadvodnye korabli v sovremennoi voine* (Surface Warships in Contemporary Warfare). Moscow: 1945.

Glukhov, M. K. *Voenno-vozdushnye sily* (The Air Forces). Moscow: Voenizdat, 1959.

Golikov, G. N. *Pobeda velikoi oktiabr'skoi sotsialisticheskoi revoliutsiu; sbornik statei* (Victory of the Great October Socialist Revolution, A Collection of Articles). Moscow: Gosizdatpolitlit, 1957.

Gordeev, I. *Krasnyi morskoi flot* (The Red Navy). Moscow: Gosvoenizdat, 1925.

Iagling, Boris. *Severnyi flot v velikoi otechestvennoi voine* (The Northern Fleet in the Great Fatherland War). Moscow: Voenizdat, 1949.

Kamalov, Kh. K. *Morskaia pekhota* (The Naval Infantry). Moscow: Voenizdat, 1957.

Kirin, I. D. *Chernomorskii flot v bitve za Kavkaz* (The Black Sea Fleet in the Battle for the Caucasus). Moscow: Voenizdat, 1958.

Kondrat'ev, N. D. *Sovetskii Voenno-morskoi flot* (The Soviet Navy). Moscow: Voenizdat, 1957.

Kononenko, V. M. *Chernomortsy v boiakh za osvobozhdenie Kryma i Odessy* (Black Sea Fleet Sailors in the Battle for the Liberation of the Crimea and Odessa). Moscow: Voenizdat, 1954.

Kornienko, D. I. *Flot nashei rodiny* (Navy of Our Homeland). Moscow: Voenizdat, 1957.

————. *SSSR—Velikaia morskaia derzhava* (The USSR—A Great Sea Power). Moscow: Pravdaizdat, 1950.

————. *Voenno-morskoi flot Sovetskoi sotsialisticheskoi derzhavy* (The Navy of the Soviet Socialist State). Moscow: Voenizdat, 1949.

KPSS i stroitel'stvo Sovetskikh vooruzhennykh sil, 1917–1964 (The Communist Party of the Soviet Union and the Building of the Soviet Armed Forces). Edited by M. H. Kiriaev. Moscow: Voenizdat, 1965.

KPSS o vooruzhennykh silakh Sovetskogo Soiuza: sbornik dokumentov 1917–1958 (The Communist Party of the Soviet Union on the Armed Forces of the Soviet Union: Collection of Documents 1917–1958). Moscow: Voenizdat, 1958.

Kuznetsov, N. G. *Nakanune* (On the Eve). Moscow: Voenizdat, 1966.

Markov, I. I. *Kerchensko-Feodosiiskaia desantnaia operatsiia* (The Kerch-Feodosia Landing Operation. Moscow: Voenizdat, 1956.

Nevskii, N. A. *Voenno-morskoi flot* (The Navy). Moscow: Voenizdat, 1959.

Padalka, G. *Krasnoznamennyi Baltiiskii flot v velikoi otechestvennoi voine*

(The Red Banner Baltic Fleet in the Great Patriotic War). Moscow: Voenizdat, 1949.

Penzin, V. *Chernomorskii flot v oborone Odessy* (The Black Sea Fleet in the Defense of Odessa). Moscow: Voenizdat, 1956.

Piterskii, N. A. *Znai flot* (Know the Navy). Moscow: DOSAAF, 1956.

Pobezhimov, I. F. *Pravovoe regulirovanie stroitel'stva armii i flota* (Legal Regulations on the Construction of the Army and Navy). Moscow: Gosiurizdat, 1960.

Rumiantsev, N. M. *Razgrom vraga v Zapoliar'e 1941–1944gg* (The Annihilation of the Enemy in the Sub-Polar Region, 1941–1944). Moscow: Voenizdat, 1963.

Sergeev, M. A. *Oborona Petropavlovsk-na-Kamchatka* (Defense of Petropavlovsk-on-Kamchatka). Moscow: Voenizdat, 1954.

Sokolovskii, V. D. (ed.). *Voennaia Strategiia.* Moscow: Voenizdat, 1962.
———. ———. Rev. ed. Moscow: Voenizdat, 1963.

Stepanov, A. K. (ed.). *Deistviia voenno-morskogo flota v velikoi otechestvennoi voine* (Operations of the Navy in the Great Patriotic War). Moscow: Voenizdat, 1956.

Svechin, A. *Evoliutsiia voennogo iskusstva* (Evolution of Military Science). Moscow: Voenizdat, 1928.

Tokarev, N. *Voenno-morskoi flot v otechestvennoi voine* (The Navy in the Patriotic War). Moscow: Gosizdatpolitlit, 1943.

V'iunenko, N. P. *Chernomorskii flot v velikoi otechestvennoi voine* (The Black Sea Fleet in the Great Patriotic War). Moscow: Voenizdat, 1957.

Zvonkov, P. *Kirov i moriaki* (Kirov and the Sailors). Moscow: 1940.

Books, Naval (non-Russian)

Armstrong, T. E. *The Northern Sea Route: Soviet Exploitation of the Northeast Passage.* Cambridge, England: Cambridge University Press, 1952.

Bacon, Admiral Sir Reginald and McMurtrie, F. E. *Modern Naval Strategy.* Brooklyn, N.Y.: Chemical Publishing Co., 1941.

Brodie, Bernard. *A Guide to Naval Strategy.* Princeton, New Jersey: Princeton University Press, 1944.

Couhat, J. Labayle. *La Marine Sovietique.* Paris: Ozanne, 1957.

Golovko, Arseni. *With the Red Fleet.* London: Putnam, 1965.

Isakov, Ivan. *The Red Fleet in the Second World War.* London: Hutchinson, 1947.

Kerner, R. J. *Urge to the Sea: the Course of Russian History.* Berkeley and Los Angeles: University of California Press, 1946.

Mitchell, Mairin. *The Maritime History of Russia, 848–1948.* London: Sidgwick, 1949.

Piterskii, N. A. *Die Sowjet-Flotte im Zweiten Weltkrieg.* Trans. from Russian. Commentary by Jürgen Rohwer. Oldenburg and Hamburg: Gerhard Stalling Verlag, 1966.

Potter, E. B. and Nimitz, C. W. (eds.), *Sea Power.* Englewood Cliffs, N.J.: Prentice-Hall, Inc., 1960.

Saunders, M. G. (ed.). *The Soviet Navy.* New York: F. A. Praeger, 1958.

Voyetekhov, Boris. *The Last Days of Sevastopol.* New York: Alfred A. Knopf, 1943.

Woodward, David. *The Russians at Sea.* London: William Kimber, 1965.

Book Chapters and Journal Articles (in Russian)

Achkasov, V. "Sryv planov nemetsko-fashistskogo komandovaniia po unichtozheniiu Krasnoznamennogo Baltiiskogo flota" (Frustration of the Plans of the Fascist-German Command for the Destruction of the Baltic Fleet), *Voenno-istoricheskii Zhurnal,* January, 1964, pp. 36–46.

————. "Operatsiia po proryvu Krasnoznamennogo Baltiiskogo flota iz Tallina v Kronshtadt" (Operations for the Breakthrough of the Red Banner Baltic Fleet from Tallin to Kronshtadt), *Voenno-istoricheskii Zhurnal,* October, 1966, pp. 19–31.

Alafuzov, V. A. "K vykhodu v svet truda *Voennaia Strategiia*" (On the Appearance of the Work *Military Strategy*), *Morskoi Sbornik,* January, 1963, pp. 88–96. Reprinted in *Voennaia Mysl',* No. 8, 1964.

————. "O sushchnosti morskikh operatsii" (On the Fundamentals of Naval Operations), *Morskoi Sbornik,* April-May, 1946, pp. 6–26.

————. "Razvitie povsednevnoi operativnoi deiatel'nosti flota" (Development of the Daily Operational Activity of the Navy), *Morskoi Sbornik,* November-December, 1946, pp. 11–21.

Aleksandrov, V. "Okhrana promyslov i morskikh granits Dal'nego Vostoka kak zadacha voennogo flota" (Defense of the Fisheries and Maritime Frontiers of the Far East as a Mission of the Navy), *Morskoi Sbornik,* August, 1925, pp. 8–12.

Andreev, Iu. A. and Astrakhanskii, I. N. "Amerikanskie piraty na morskikh i okeanskikh putiakh" (American Pirates on the Sea and Oceanic Routes), *Morskoi Sbornik,* January, 1961, pp. 10–16.

Barabanov, P. D. and Lesnikov, N. D. "Novoe polozhenie ob okhrane gosudarstvennykh granits Soiuza SSR" (New Situation on the Defense of the State Borders of the USSR), *Morskoi Sbornik,* February, 1961, pp. 11–19.

Belli, V. "Osnovy vedeniia operatsii na more" (Fundamentals of Conducting Operations at Sea), *Morskoi Sbornik,* July, 1939, pp. 13–24.

Belousov, L. "Konferentsiia o Sovetskoi voennoi doktrine" (Conference on Soviet Military Doctrine), *Voenno-istoricheskii Zhurnal,* October, 1963, pp. 121–126.

Bol'shaia Sovetskaia Entsiklopediia; Ezhegodnik 1957g. (Great Soviet Encyclopaedia, 1957 Yearbook). Article, "Vooruzhennye sily" (The Armed Forces). Moscow: Great Soviet Encyclopaedia Press, 1957.

————. *Ezhegodnik 1963g.* Article, "Vooruzhennye sily" (The Armed Forces). Moscow: Great Soviet Encyclopaedia Press, 1963.

Dmitriev, M. V. "Osobennosti primeneniia aviatsii na more" (Particularities of the Use of Aviation at Sea), *Morskoi Sbornik,* May, 1961, pp. 36–43.

Dombrovskii, A. V. "Kakoi RSFSR nuzhen flot?" (What Navy Does the RSFSR Need?), *Morskoi Sbornik*, January-February, 1922, pp. 79–85.

Efimov, R. "Filippiny—platsdarm agressii SShA v iugovostochnoi azii" (The Philippines—Platform of Aggression for the U.S. in Southeast Asia), *Voennaia Mysl'*, February, 1955, pp. 52–63.

Emel'ianov, L. A. "K voprosu o taktike flota i predmete ee issledovaniia" (On the Question of Tactics for the Fleet and Means for its Development), *Morskoi Sbornik*, April, 1963, pp. 23–28.

Eremenko, A. "Strategicheskoe i politicheskoe znachenie voennykh baz" (Strategic and Political Significance of Military Bases), *Mezhdunarodnaia Zhizn'*, November, 1960, pp. 81–88.

Filonov, S. I. "Vooruzhennaia bor'ba i okeanskie kommunikatsii" (Armed Conflict and Oceanic Communications), *Morskoi Sbornik*, March, 1965, pp. 33–41.

Fokin, V. A. "Priem korablei ot angliiskogo flota i ikh perekhod v Sovetskii Soiuz" (The Acquisition of Warships from the British Navy and their Transfer to the Soviet Union), *Morskoi Sbornik*, April, 1946, pp. 31–45.

Frunze, Mikhail V. "Edinaia voennaia doktrina i Krasnaia Armiia" (Unified Military Doctrine and the Red Army), *Voennaia Nauka i Revoliutsiia*, January, 1921, pp. 4–17.

Gervais, B. "Piat' let raboty Voenno-morskoi Akademii RKKA" (Five Years of Work by the Naval War College of the Red Army), *Morskoi Sbornik*, March, 1927, pp. 3–12.

Glazov, G. "O nekotorykh osobennostiakh vedeniia boevykh deistvii v iadernoi voine" (On Several Features of the Conduct of Combat Operations in Nuclear War), *Kommunist Vooruzhennykh Sil*, No. 3, February, 1964, pp. 41–46.

Golovko, A. G. "Voenno-morskoi flot nashei rodiny" (The Navy of Our Homeland), *Voennye Znaniia*, July, 1959, pp. 1–3.

Gorbovskii, L. "Morskie biudzhety 1922-23g" (Naval Budgets for 1922-23), *Morskoi Sbornik*, September, 1924, pp. 106–125.

Gorshkov, S. G. "Flot Sovetskoi derzhavy" (The Navy of the Soviet Power), *Sovetskii Voin*, July, 1962, pp. 1–2.

———. "Razvitie Sovetskogo Voenno-morskogo iskusstva" (Development of Soviet Naval Art), *Morskoi Sbornik*, February 1967, pp. 9–21.

———. "Voenno-morskoi flot nashei rodiny" (The Navy of Our Homeland), *Kommunist Vooruzhennykh Sil*, No. 13, July, 1963, pp. 18–25.

———. "Zabota partii o flote" (Solicitude of the Party for the Navy), *Morskoi Sbornik*, July, 1963, pp. 9–18.

Grishanov, V. "Den' Voenno-morskogo flota" (Navy Day), *Kommunist Vooruzhennykh Sil*, No. 13, July, 1962, pp. 18–24.

Gruber, Horst. "Moskauer Flottenpolitik," *Osteuropa*, March-April, 1939, pp. 453–444.

Ivanitskii, E. "Morskie desanty" (Naval Landings), *Voennye Znaniia*, February, 1958, pp. 25–26.

Ivanov, B. N. "O predmete issledovaniia taktiki" (On the Principle of Research in Tactics), *Morskoi Sbornik*, June, 1963, pp. 27–30.

"Khronika" (Chronicle), *Morskoi Sbornik*, February, 1919.

Kolesnikov, Iu. V. "O nekotorykh kategoriiakh taktiki flota" (On Several Categories of Naval Tactics), *Morskoi Sbornik,* November, 1963, pp. 9–24.

Konovalov, V. "Iz istorii severnogo flota" (From the History of the Northern Fleet), *Voenno-istoricheskii Zhurnal,* November, 1963, pp. 103–110.

Korotkov, I. "O razvitii Sovetskoi voennoi teorii v poslevoennoi gody" (On the Development of Soviet Military Theory in the Postwar Years), *Voenno-istoricheskii Zhurnal,* April, 1964, pp. 39–50.

Krupskii, M. "Za chistotu marksistko-leninskoi teorii v voenno-morskikh voprosakh" (For the Purging of Marxist-Leninist Theory on Naval Questions), *Morskoi Sbornik,* January, 1932, pp. 18–26.

Kuzmin, A. V. "Operatsii torpednykh katerov severnogo flota po kommuni-katsiiakh protivnika" (Operations of Motor Torpedo Boats of the Northern Fleet Against the Communications of the Enemy), *Morskoi Sbornik,* November-December, 1944, pp. 20–40.

Kuzmin, I. "Bor'ba novogo so starym v razvitii voennogo dela" (Struggle of the New with the Old in the Development of Military Affairs), *Kommunist Vooruzhennykh Sil,* No. 8, April, 1964, pp. 40–45.

Kuznetsov, N. G. "Na strazhe granits Sovetskogo Soiuza" (On Guard at the Borders of the Soviet Union), *Morskoi Sbornik,* February, 1941, pp. 2–5.

———. "Pered voinoi" (Before the War), *Oktiabr'* No. 8, 1965, pp. 161–202, No. 9, 1965, pp. 158–189, No. 11, 1965, pp. 134–171.

———. "Rech' tov. Kuznetsova," *XVIII s"ezd vsesoiuznoi Kommunistiches-koi partii (b), 10–21 marta 1939g; stenograficheskii otchet* (Speech of Comrade Kuznetsov, 18th Congress of the All-Union Communist Party, Bolshevik, March 10–21, 1939; Stenographic Record). Moscow: Gosizdatpolitlit, 1939.

Kvitnitskii, A. A. "Napravlennost' razvitiia sil: sredstv PLO VMS SShA" (Direction of the Development of the ASW Forces of the U.S. Navy). *Morskoi Sbornik,* November, 1966.

Ladinskii, Iu. "O teorii voenno-morskogo iskusstva" (On the Theory of Naval Art), *Voennaia Mysl',* July, 1957, pp. 29–37.

Lisiutin, V. S. "K voprosu o kategoriiakh voenno-morskogo iskusstva v sov-remennykh usloviiakh" (To the Problem of the Categories of Naval Art in Contemporary Conditions), *Morskoi Sbornik,* March, 1961, pp. 14–22.

Ludri, Ivan. "Desiat' let bor'by i stroitel'stva" (Ten Years of Struggle and Construction), *Morskoi Sbornik,* February, 1928, pp. 28–36.

———. "Krasnyi flot v sostave vooruzhennykh sil respubliki" (The Red Navy in the Composition of the Armed Forces of the Republic), *Morskoi Sbornik,* October, 1927, pp. 23–28.

———. "Morskie operatsii" (Naval Operations), *Voennaia Mysl',* February, 1937, pp. 75–86.

Mal'kov, M. K. "Skrytnost'—vazhneishee uslovie uspeshnykh deistvii pod-vodnykh lodok" (Concealment—The Most Important Condition for Successful Operations of Submarines), *Morskoi Sbornik,* April, 1964, pp. 27–33.

Molotkov, B. P. "Ob izmenenii form boevykh deistvii na more v sviazi s razvitie sredstv vooruzhennoi bor'by" (On the Change in the Forms of Combat Activity at Sea Due to the Development of New Weapons), *Morskoi Sbornik,* March, 1963, pp. 24–27.

"Morskaia Khronika" (Maritime Chronicle), *Morskoi Sbornik,* February, 1925.

————. ————. December, 1936.

Muklevich, R. "Desiatiletie Oktiabrskoi Revoliutsii i morskoi flot" (The Tenth Anniversary of the October Revolution and the Navy), *Morskoi Sbornik,* October, 1927, pp. 3–13.

"Nesokrushimyi strazh mira i sotsializma" (Indestructible Guard of Peace and Socialism), *Morskoi Sbornik,* February, 1965, pp. 3–9.

"Neustanno krepit' shefstvo nad voenno-morskim flotom" (Tirelessly Strengthen Patronage of the Navy), *Morskoi Sbornik,* March, 1938, pp. 3–5.

Nosenko, I. "V bor'be sozdanie bol'shogo flota" (In the Struggle for Creation of a Mighty Navy), *Morskoi Sbornik,* August, 1939, pp. 43–48.

"O zadachakh boevoi podgotovka voenno-morskikh sil RKKA na 1932 god" (On the Tasks of Combat Training of Naval Forces of the RKKA in 1932), *Morskoi Sbornik,* January, 1932, pp. 3–4.

Orlov, V. M. "Na strazhe morskikh granits SSSR" (On Guard of the Maritime Borders of the USSR), *Morskoi Sbornik,* March, 1933, pp. 11–21.

————. "Rech' tov. V. M. Orlova na chrezvychainom VIII vsesoiuznom s"ezde sovetov 28-go noiabria 1936g" (Speech of Comrade V. M. Orlov at the Extraordinary VIIIth All-Union Congress of Soviets, November 28, 1936), *Morskoi Sbornik,* December, 1936, pp. 3–8.

Palevich, D. and Posniak, I. "Osobennosti i kharakter mirovoi raketno-iadernoi voiny" (Peculiarities and Character of Global Nuclear Missile War), *Kommunist Vooruzhennykh Sil,* No. 20, October, 1964, pp. 77–82.

P. A. V. "Weyer's *Flotten Taschenbuch* i Sovetskii Flot" (Weyer's *Flotten Taschenbuch* and the Soviet Navy), *Morskiia Zapiski,* No. 1, April, 1955, pp. 68–69.

Pavlovich, N. "V. F. Chernyshev, *Nadvodnye korabli v sovremennoi voine*" (V. F. Chernyshev's *Surface Warships in Contemporary Warfare*), *Morskoi Sbornik,* October, 1945, pp. 115–128.

Petrov, B. F. "Soderzhanie i kharakter sovremennykh boevykh deistvii na more" (The Content and Character of Contemporary Naval Operations), *Morskoi Sbornik,* January, 1965, pp. 7–15.

Petrov, M. "Zametki o taktiki malogo flota" (Notes on the Tactics of a Small Fleet), *Morskoi Sbornik,* September, 1923, pp. 45–61.

Platonov, V. I. "Na strazhe Zapoliar'ia (On Guard over the Sub-Polar Arctic), *Morskoi Sbornik,* April, 1965, pp. 15–25.

"Protiv reaktsionnykh teorii v voprosakh boevogo ispol'zovaniia podvodnykh lodok" (Against Reactionary Theory in Questions of Combat Employment of Submarines), *Morskoi Sbornik,* February, 1932, pp. 53–61.

Pukhov, A. "Partiino-politicheskaia rabota v voenno-morskom flote za 20 let" (Party-Political Work in the Navy for 20 years), *Morskoi Sbornik,* February, 1938, pp. 48–57.

Rall, Iu. "Neskol'ko zamechanii po povodu pervoi poloviny kampanii 1925g" (A Few Comments on the First Half of the Campaign for 1925), *Morskoi Sbornik,* August, 1925, pp. 3–8.

Raskol'nikov, F. "Morskaia Khronika" (Maritime Chronicle), *Morskoi Sbornik,* January-February, 1921, pp. 94–109.

Razumnyi, I. A. "Avianosnye soedineniia flota SShA v voine na Tikhom okeane" (Aircraft Carrier Task Forces of the U.S. Navy in the War in the Pacific), *Morskoi Sbornik,* July, 1946, pp. 61–86.

Rog, V. G. "Vlianie raketno-iadernogo oruzheniia na primenenie aviatsii na more" (The Influence of Nuclear Missile Weapons on the Use of Aviation at Sea), *Morskoi Sbornik,* June, 1963, pp. 31–37.

Rogov, V. P. "Imperialisty SShA delaiut stavku na Polaris" (The Imperialists of the USA Count on Polaris), *Morskoi Sbornik,* May, 1963, pp. 77–85.

Rotmistrov, P. "O sovremennom Sovetskom voennom iskusstve i ego kharakternykh chertakh" (On Contemporary Soviet Military Art and its Characteristic Features), *Voennaia Mysl',* February, 1958, pp. 82–95.

Sbytov, N. A. "Kharakter i zakonomernosti mirovoi raketno-iadernoi voiny" (The Character and Constants of Global Nuclear Missile Warfare), *Morskoi Sbornik,* March, 1964, pp. 9–16.

Selivanov, V. L. "Pervyi vserossiiskii s"ezd voennogo flota (1–8 dekabria 1917)" (First All-Russian Congress of the Navy, 1–8 December 1917), *Morskoi Sbornik,* February 1938, p. 96.

Serebriakov, M. "Agitatory na liniiu!" (Agitators to the Front Lines!), *Krasnyi Baltiets,* June, 1920.

Shner, I. "Avianostsi i ikh rol' v operatsiakh flota" (Aircraft Carriers and their Role in the Operations of a Navy), *Voennaia Mysl',* June, 1946, pp. 77–82.

Shavtsov, D. "O gospodstve na more" (On Command of the Sea), *Voennaia Mysl'* No. 7, 1955, pp. 3–17.

Smirnov, P. A. "Rech' tov. Smirnova" (Speech of Comrade Smirnov), *Morskoi Sbornik,* April, 1938, pp. 8–9.

Sobelov, A. "Na poroge novogo etapa stroitel'stva" (On the Brink of a New Stage of Construction), *Morskoi Sbornik,* January, 1925, pp. 11–23.

————. "Vozrozhdenie morskoi idei" (Rebirth of a Maritime Concept), *Morskoi Sbornik,* August-September, 1922, pp. 39–52.

Stalbo, K. A. "O nekotorykh kategoriiakh voenno-morskogo iskusstva v sovremennykh proiavlenii" (On Several Categories of Naval Art in Contemporary Form), *Morskoi Sbornik,* January, 1961, pp. 17–25.

Svechin, A. "Osnovy sovremennoi Iaponskoi strategii i taktiki" (Fundamentals of Contemporary Japanese Strategy and Tactics), *Voennaia Mysl',* January, 1937, pp. 141–165.

Svetlov, A. G. and Shimkevich, L. A. "Osobennosti vysadki morskikh desantov v sovremennykh usloviiakh" (Characteristics of Amphibious Landings in Contemporary Circumstances), *Morskoi Sbornik,* March, 1964, pp. 22–27.

Svetlovskii, P. I. "K vozrozhdeniiu krasnogo R. K. flota RSFSR" (Towards the Rebirth of the Red R. K. Fleet of the RSFSR), *Morskoi Shornik,* March-April, 1922, pp. 64–72.

Sytov, L. "Vooruzhennie Sily SSSR v poslevoennyi period" (The Armed Forces of the USSR in the Postwar Period), *Kommunist Vooruzhennykh Sil,* No. 3, February, 1964, pp. 67–72.

Tributs, V. "Krasnoznamennyi Baltiiskii Flot v 1942g" (The Red Banner Baltic Fleet in 1942), *Voenno-istoricheskii Zhurnal,* November, 1962, pp. 10–26.

Tukhachevskii, M. P. "Voina kak problema vooruzhennoi bor'by" (War as a Problem of Armed Struggle), *Bol'shaia Sovetskaia Entsiklopediia.* 1928 ed. Vol. XII. pp. 596.

Tuz, D. A. "Rol' morskikh desantnykh operatsii v raketno-iadernoi voine" (The Role of Naval Landing Operations in Nuclear Missile War), *Morskoi Sbornik,* June, 1964, pp. 24–29.

Val, V. "Krasnyi flot dolzhen byt' Leninskim flotom" (The Red Fleet Must be a Leninist Fleet), *Morskoi Sbornik,* June, 1924, pp. 1–5.

V'iunenko, N. P. "Nekotorye voprosy organizatsii i vedeniia morskikh desantnykh operatsii" (Some Questions of Organization and Conduct of Naval Landing Operations), *Voennaia Mysl',* February, 1955, pp. 27–39.

————. "Sovremennye morskie desanty" (Contemporary Naval Landings), *Morskoi Sbornik,* September, 1963, pp. 21–27.

Voroshilov, K. I. "Osnovnaia direktiva" (Basic Directive), *Krasnyi Flot,* February, 1926, pp. 3.

————. "XX let rabotchii-krestianskoi Krasnoi Armii i Voenno-Morskogo Flota" (20 Years of the Workers and Peasants Red Army and Navy), *Voennaia Mysl',* March, 1938, pp. 3–22.

Vorov'ev, V. "Bor'ba za Chernomorskie bazy v 1941–1942 godakh" (Struggle for Black Sea Bases in the Years 1941–1942), *Voennaia Mysl',* July, 1957, pp. 51–69.

Zhilin, P. "Diskussii o edinoi voennoi doktrine" (Discussions on a Unified Military Doctrine), *Voenno-istoricheskii Zhurnal,* May, 1961, pp. 69–78.

Zof, V. "Krasnyi flot za 1924 god" (The Red Navy in 1924), *Morskoi Sbornik,* January, 1925, pp. 13–16.

————. "Mezhdunarodnoe polozhenie i zadachi morskoi oboroni SSSR" (The International Situation and the Tasks of Maritime Defense), *Morskoi Sbornik,* May, 1925, pp. 3–16.

————. "Morskaia Khronika" (Maritime Chronicle), November-December, 1924, pp. 54–57.

Zverev, B. I. "Deiatel'nost M. V. Frunze po ukrepleniiu boevoi moshchi Sovetskogo voenno-morskogo flota" (Activity of M. V. Frunze for Strengthening of the Combat Power of the Navy), *Morskoi Sbornik,* January, 1965, pp. 24–33.

————. "Lenin i nachalo stroitel'stva Sovetskogo Voenno-Morskogo flota" (Lenin and the Start of the Construction of the Soviet Navy), *Morskoi Sbornik,* April, 1963, pp. 12–22.

Pamphlets, Book Chapters, and Journal Articles (non-Russian)

Anders, Dieter. "Baltic Sea, Seventh Meeting at Rostock," *International Affairs,* August, 1964, pp. 91–92.

Araldsen, P. O. "Norwegian Defense Problems; The Role of the Navy," *United States Naval Institute Proceedings,* October, 1958, pp. 38–47.

Armour, R. S. D. "The Soviet Naval Air Arm," *The Soviet Navy.* M. G. Saunders (ed.), New York: F. A. Praeger, 1958, pp. 187–198.

Atkinson, J. D. "The Impact of Soviet Theory on Warfare as a Continuation of Politics," *Military Affairs,* Spring, 1960, pp. 1–6.

Baldwin, Hanson. "Red Flag Over the Seven Seas," *The Atlantic Monthly,* September, 1964, pp. 37–43.

————. "The Soviet Navy," *Foreign Affairs,* July, 1955, pp. 587–604.

————. "Strategic Background 1958," *The Soviet Navy.* M. G. Saunders (ed.), New York: F. A. Praeger, 1958, pp. 105–120.

Barker, E. L. "Soviet Naval Aviation," *United States Naval Institute Proceedings,* January, 1961, pp. 50–59.

Bidlingmaier, Gerhard T. "The Strategic Importance of the Baltic Sea," *United States Naval Institute Proceedings,* September, 1958, pp. 23–31.

Biorkland, E. "On the Perimeter," *The Soviet Navy.* M. G. Saunders (ed.), New York: F. A. Praeger, 1958, pp. 259–265.

Blau, G. E. *The German Campaign in Russia—Planning and Operations (1940–1942).* U.S. Department of the Army Pamphlet No. 20–261a, March, 1955.

Brassey's Annual—The Armed Forces Yearbook 1940. Article, "Foreign Navies, Soviet Union," London: Wm. Clowes and Sons, Ltd., 1940, p. 39.

Breyer, Siegfried. *Die Seeruestung der Sowietunion,* Munich: J. F. Lehmanns, 1964.

————. "Soviet Power in the Baltic," *Military Review,* January, 1962, pp. 41–47.

Brown, Neville. "The Communist Naval Challenge," *Strategic Mobility.* New York: F. A. Praeger, 1964, pp. 131–138.

"Burke Says Russians Seek to Control Sea," *Aviation Week,* December 26, 1955, p. 14.

Carney, Robert B. "Russia—Threat to United States at Sea," *United States News,* June 18, 1954, pp. 56–60.

Carrison, Daniel J. "The Soviet Drive for Sea Power," *United States Naval Institute Proceedings,* October, 1959, pp. 67–71.

Chapman, W. C. "The Soviet Air Forces," *Naval Review 1965.* Annapolis: United States Naval Institute, 1964, pp. 166–199.

Couhat, J. Labayle. "La Strategie Navale Sovietique," *Revue de Defense Nationale,* December, 1962, pp. 1805–1827.

Courtney, Anthony. "The Background of Russian Seapower," *International Affairs,* January, 1954, pp. 13–23.

Crane, Robert D. (ed.). *Soviet Nuclear Strategy.* Washington: Center for Strategic Studies, Georgetown University, 1963.

Daly, R. W. "Russia's Maritime Past," *The Soviet Navy.* M. G. Saunders (ed.). New York. F. A. Praeger, 1958, pp. 23–43.

Eller, E. M. "Implications of Soviet Sea Power," *The Soviet Navy.* M. G. Saunders (ed.). New York: F. A. Praeger, 1958, pp. 299–328.

————. "Soviet Bid for the Sea," *United States Naval Institute Proceedings,* June, 1955, pp. 619–627.

"End of Capital Ships Foreseen in Accord," *United States Naval Institute Proceedings,* November, 1929, p. 1037.

Fedotov-White, D. "Soviet Naval Doctrine," *Journal of the Royal United Service Institution,* August, 1935, pp. 610–616.

————. "Soviet Philosophy of War," *Political Science Quarterly,* September 1936, pp. 343–349.

Galay, N. "The New Reduction in the Soviet Armed Forces," *Bulletin, Institute for the Study of the USSR,* July, 1956, pp. 47–52.

——. "The Numerical Strength of the Soviet Armed Forces," *Bulletin, Institute for the Study of the USSR,* May, 1962, pp. 41–43.

——. "Soviet Naval Forces," *Bulletin, Institute for the Study of the USSR,* August, 1954, pp. 3–8.

Garthoff, R. L. "Sea Power in Soviet Strategy," *United States Naval Institute Proceedings,* February, 1958, pp. 85–94.

——. "Sino-Soviet Military Relations," *Annals of the Academy of Political and Social Science,* September, 1963, pp. 81–93.

——. "Soviet Doctrine on Amphibious Operations; Strategic, Operational, and Tactical," *Marine Corps Gazette,* May, 1958, pp. 55–60.

Garwood, R. C. S. "The Russians as Naval Allies," *The Soviet Navy.* M. G. Saunders (ed.). New York: F. A. Praeger, 1958, pp. 75–83.

Hadeler, Wilhelm. "The Ships of the Soviet Navy," *The Soviet Navy.* M. G. Saunders (ed.). New York: F. A. Praeger, 1958.

Hall, Nowell. "Changes in the World's Navies," *Brassey's Annual—The Armed Forces Yearbook, 1962.* H. G. Thursfield (ed.), London: Wm. Clowes and Sons, Limited, 1962, pp. 189–194.

Hashavia, Arie. "The Soviet Fleet in the Mediterranean," *Military Review,* February, 1967, p. 79–87.

Hellner, M. H. "Sea Power and Soviet Designs for Expansion," *United States Naval Institute Proceedings,* March, 1960, pp. 23–32.

Herrick, Robert W. "The Evolution of Soviet Naval Strategy and the Effect of the Revolution in Military Affairs". *U.S. Naval War College Review,* December, 1964, pp. 1–50.

——. "Soviet Naval Strategy," *The Military-Technical Revolution, Its Impact on Strategy and Foreign Policy.* John Erickson (ed.). New York: F. A. Praeger, 1966, pp. 148–169.

——. "A View of Soviet Naval Strategy," *1967 Naval Review.* Frank Uhlig, Jr. (ed.). Annapolis, Maryland: The United States Naval Institute, 1966, pp. 15–41.

Hessler, William H. "Tug of War in the Baltic," *United States Naval Institute Proceedings,* December, 1959, pp. 1301–1309.

Hilton, Richard. "The Soviet Armed Forces," *Journal of the Royal United Service Institution,* November, 1949, pp. 552–561.

Hittle, J. D. "The Rise of Russian Sea Power," *Marine Corps Gazette,* August, 1955, pp. 20–27, and September, 1955, pp. 12–19.

——. "Why Russian Sea Power?" *Marine Corps Gazette,* November, 1956, pp. 68–75.

Hopker, Wolfgang. "The Black Sea, an Inland 'Red' Sea?" *NATO's Fifteen Nations,* October, 1961, pp. 110–117.

——. "The Polar Sea Fleet of the Soviet Union," *NATO's Fifteen Nations,* September, 1961, pp. 26–29.

Hopwood, H. L. "The Soviets Lack 'True Sea Power' Status," *Army, Navy, Air Force Journal,* September 27, 1958, p. 28.

Horan, H. E. "The Navy of the Soviet Union," *Brassey's Annual—the Armed Forces Yearbook, 1960.* H. G. Thursfield (ed.). New York: The Macmillan Company, 1960, pp. 124–130.

Huan, Claude. "The Soviet Submarine Force," *Naval Review 1964*. Annapolis: United States Naval Institute, 1964, p. 54–81.

Katkov, George and Kowalewski, Jan. "The Russian Navy and the Revolution 1921–1928," *The Soviet Navy*. M. G. Saunders (ed.). New York: F. A. Praeger, 1958, pp. 84–102.

Kennedy, Wm. V. "The Soviet Fleet," *Ordnance,* May-June, 1958, pp. 976–977.

Kerner, R. J. "Russian Naval Aims," *Foreign Affairs,* January, 1946, pp. 290–299.

Kintner, Wm. "The Military as an Element of Soviet State Power," *United States Naval Institute Proceedings,* July, 1955, pp. 770–783.

Knebel, F. "Menace of Russia's Sea Power," *Look,* November 20, 1962, pp. 35–39.

Kuznetsov, N. G. "Before the War," *International Affairs,* May, 1966–March, 1967.

Lee, Asher. "Some Problems of Soviet Strategy," *Brassey's Annual—The Armed Forces Yearbook, 1964*. New York: F. A. Praeger, 1964, pp. 246–255.

Lepotier, R. "L'expansion Oceanique Sovietique," *Revue de Defense Nationale,* August-September, 1964, pp. 1397–1412.

Macintyre, Donald. "The Soviet Submarine Threat," *The Soviet Navy*. M. G. Saunders (ed.). New York: F. A. Praeger, 1958, pp. 168–186.

Morrison, John A. "Russia and Warm Water; A Fallacious Generalization," *United States Naval Institute Proceedings,* November, 1952, pp. 1166–1179.

Murphy, F. M. "The Soviet Navy in the Mediterranean," *U.S. Naval Institute Proceedings,* March, 1967, pp. 38–44.

Nitze, Paul H. "Trends in the Use of the Sea and their Implications on Foreign Policy," *Marine Corps Gazette,* March, 1965, pp. 23–28.

Rairden, P. W. Jr. "The Soviet Sea Power," *United States Naval Institute Proceedings,* January, 1948, pp. 61–67.

Rohwer, Jurgen. "The Russians as Naval Opponents in Two World Wars," *The Soviet Navy*. M. G. Saunders (ed.). New York: F. A. Praeger, 1958, pp. 44–74.

Reynolds, Clark G. "Hitler's Flattop—The End of the Beginning," *United States Naval Institute Proceedings,* January, 1967, pp. 41–49.

Ruge, Friedrich. "German Naval Strategy During World War II," *Naval War College Review,* May, 1953, pp. 1–29.

———. "Soviet Sea Power in the Cold War; a Critical Analysis," *Naval Review 1962–1963*. Annapolis: U. S. Naval Institute, 1962, pp. 62–83.

Saar, C. W. "Offensive Mining as a Soviet Strategy," *United States Naval Institute Proceedings,* August, 1964, pp. 42–51.

Schoenberg, H. "Missile Carrying Submarines, a New Factor of Strategic Planning," *Military Review,* April, 1959, pp. 102–106.

Schofield, B. B. "Developments in Maritime Forces, 1961–1962," *Brassey's Annual—The Armed Forces Yearbook 1962*. London: Wm. Clowes and Sons, Limited, 1962, pp. 19–32.

Schulze-Hinrichs, Alfred. "The Guiding Principles Behind the Soviet Naval Forces," *Military Review,* December, 1954, pp. 95–100.

Shannon, Wm. H. "The Soviet Navy: a Challenge to the Supremacy of the Seas," *Social Studies,* January, 1956, pp. 65–72.

Shaw, J. C. "Naval Strategy," *Encyclopaedia Britannica.* 1951 ed., Vol. XVI. pp. 169.

Shvedkov, Y. "Bases in Pentagon Strategy," *International Affairs,* May, 1964, pp. 57–61.

Smith, C. J. "The Soviet Navy in World War II, 1941–1945," *ONI Review,* (Washington: Office of the Chief of Naval Operations) October 1952—June 1953.

"Soviet Naval Power Cited," *United States Naval Institute Proceedings,* March, 1964, pp. 153.

"Soviet U-Boat Fleet," *United States Naval Institute Proceedings,* December, 1937, pp. 1810–1811.

"Striking Expansion of the Soviet Navy," *United Services and Empire Review,* October, 1954, pp. 6.

Talbot, M. F. "The Battleship, Her Evolution and Her Present Place in the Scheme of Naval War," *United States Naval Institute Proceedings,* May, 1938, pp. 645–653.

Theobald, R. A. "Russian Navy—History and Traditions," *Naval War College Review,* February, 1954, pp. 25–51.

Tuleja, T. V. "The Historic Pattern of Russian Naval Policy," *United States Naval Institute Proceedings,* September, 1951, pp. 959–967.

Uggla, H. C. "Soviet Naval Strategy," *Military Review,* October, 1955, pp. 87–90.

Uhlig, Frank, Jr. "The Threat of the Soviet Navy," *Foreign Affairs,* April, 1952, pp. 290–299.

"USSR," *United States Naval Institute Proceedings,* February, 1937, pp. 281.

"USSR, Progress of Russian Naval Construction," *United States Naval Institute Proceedings,* March, 1939, p. 431.

"USSR, A Survey of Russian Fleets," *United States Naval Institute Proceedings,* May, 1939, pp. 760–761.

"Various Notes," *United States Naval Institute Proceedings,* September, 1938, pp. 1369.

Watt, D. C. "Stalin's First Bid for Sea Power, 1933–1941," *United States Naval Institute Proceedings,* June, 1964, pp. 88–96.

Wilkinson, J. B. "The Soviet Navy," *Ordnance,* March-April, 1949, pp. 340–342.

Wolfe, Thomas W. "Shifts in Soviet Strategic Thought," *Foreign Affairs,* April 1964, pp. 475–486.

————. "U.S. Editor's Analytical Introduction," *Soviet Military Strategy.* Englewood Cliffs, New Jersey: Prentice-Hall, Inc., 1963, pp. 1–78.

Wright, Jerauld. "The Tasks of Nato's Naval Forces," *Department of State Bulletin,* October 31, 1955.

Newspaper Articles (in Russian)

Abchuk, V. "Tsel'—v morskikh glubinakh" (Target—in the Seas Depths), *Krasnaia Zvezda,* September 18, 1964.

Amel'ko, N. N. "Okean trebuet. . ." (The Ocean Demands. . .), *Krasnaia Zvezda*, July 26, 1964.

Antonov, A. I. "General Gel' gotov demonstrirovat' svoi entuziazm (General Gale is Ready to Show His Enthusiasm), *Krasnaia Zvezda*, November 21, 1958.

Argunov, I., Zheltikov, I. and Larionov, V. "Raketnye oruzhiia sovremennykh vooruzhennykh sil" (Missile Weapons of Modern Armed Forces), *Krasnaia Zvezda*, January 10, 1962.

Artem'ev, V. "Oni gotovilis k raznym roliam" (They Have Prepared for Various Roles), *Krasnaia Zvezda*, August 7, 1964.

"Atomnaia lodka stolknulas' s sudnom" (Atomic Submarine Collides with a Merchant Ship), *Krasnaia Zvezda*, January 12, 1965.

Basistyi, N. "Den' Voenno-morskogo flota" (Navy Day), *Trud*, July 27, 1958.

———. "Na strazhe morskikh granits" (Guarding the Maritime Borders), *Izvestiia*, July 29, 1956.

"Batsilly raketno-iadernoi voiny" (Bacillus of Nuclear-missile War), *Krasnaia Zvezda*, November 19, 1961.

Belashchenko, T. "Amerikanskie bazy—forposty agressii i provokatsii" (American Bases—Advance Posts of Aggression and Provocation), *Krasnaia Zvezda*, January 22, 1965.

"Boevaia vakhta Sovetskikh moriakov" (Combat Watch of Soviet Sailors), *Krasnaia Zvezda*, January 9, 1962.

"Boi vedet morskaia pekhota" (The Naval Infantry Carries on Combat), *Krasnaia Zvezda*, July 24, 1964.

"Bol'shie ili malye korabli?" (Large or Small Warships?), *Krasnaia Zvezda*, July 4, 1938.

Borzov, I. I. "Groznaia krepost' nad morem" (Threatening Fortress Over the Sea), *Krasnaia Zvezda*, July 18, 1964.

Bubnov, A. "Voennoe stroitel'stvo na novykh putiakh" (Military Construction on New Paths), *Krasnyi Flot*, January, 1925, pp. 83–91.

Bulatov, A. "Aleutskie ostrova i Aliaska—voennye platsdarma SShA v Arktike" (Aleutian Islands—Military Springboard of the U.S. in the Arctic), *Sovetskii Flot*, November 15, 1957.

Chabenenko, A. "Na strazhe morskikh granits Sovetskoi rodiny" (Guarding the Maritime Borders of the Soviet Homeland), *Ekonomicheskaia Gazeta*, July 30, 1961.

———. "Sovetskii admiral ob atomnoi flote SShA" (Soviet Admiral on the Atomic Navy of the U.S.A.), *Izvestiia*, November 30, 1963.

Chvertkin, I. "Perspektivy voiny na Severnom more" (Prospects of War in the North Sea), *Krasnyi Flot*, September 6, 1939.

"Da zdravstvuet Sovetskii Voenno-Morskoi Flot!" (Hail the Soviet Navy!), *Pravda*, July 28, 1940.

"Delo za vami, Komsomol'skie aktivisty!" (The Job is Yours, Komsomol Activists!), *Sovetskii Flot*, January 31, 1960.

"Den' Voenno-morskogo flota SSSR, materialy dlia dokladov i besed" (The Day of the Navy of the USSR, Materials for Reports and Discussions), *Sovetskii Flot*, July 2, 1958.

Dudkin, V. "Podvodnye lodki v sostave morskikh vooruzhennykh sil" (Submarines in the Composition of the Maritime Armed Forces), *Krasnyi Flot*, August, 1924, pp. 83–88.

Emel'ianov, N. "Kurs na novoe, peredovoe" (Course Toward the New, the Progressive), *Sovetskii Flot,* January 24, 1960.

Evseev, A. "Do kontsa razgromit' vrazheskie teorii v morskoi strategiia" (Eradicate the Last Vestige of Inimical Theory in Naval Strategy), *Krasnyi Flot,* August 28, 1938.

Filipovskii, A. "Voenno-morskoi flot nashei rodiny" (Navy of Our Homeland), *Sovetskaia Belorussiia,* July 24, 1955.

Fokin, V. A. "Boevaia vakhta na moriakh i okeanakh" (Combat Watch on the Seas and Oceans), *Krasnaia Zvezda,* July 28, 1963.

———. "Na strazhe morskikh rubezhei" (On Guard of the Maritime Frontiers), *Sovetskii Flot,* July 14, 1957.

Frinovskii, M. "Voenno-morskoi flot SSSR" (Navy of the USSR), *Krasnyi Flot,* February 22, 1939.

"G.2." "Tov. Zof na Chernomorskom flote" (Comrade Zof on the Black Sea Fleet), *Krasnyi Flot,* June-July, 1923.

Gervais, B. "Flot segodniashnego dnia" (The Navy of the Contemporary Period), *Krasnyi Fot,* February, 1922, pp. 18–30.

Glebov, I. "Razvitie operativnogo iskusstva" (Development of Operational Art), *Krasnaia Zvezda,* April 2, 1964.

Golikov, F. I. "Velikie plody velikoi pobedy" (Great Fruits of a Great Victory), *Kraisnaia Zvezda,* May 9, 1960.

Golovko, A. G. "Pod flagom rodiny" (Under the Flag of the Homeland, *Izvestiia,* July 30, 1961.

———. "Voenno-morskoi flot" (The Navy), *Krasnaia Zvezda,* July 24, 1949.

Gol'tsev, V. "Lednyi pokhod" (Ice Cruise), *Izvestiia,* January 21, 1963.

Gorshkov, S. G. "Flot v bol'shom plavanii" (The Navy on the High Seas), *Krasnaia Zvezda,* March 21, 1964.

———. "Na strazhe mirnogo truda" (Guarding Peaceful Labor), *Pravda,* July 28, 1963.

———. "Na strazhe morskikh granits" (Guarding the Maritime Borders), *Krasnaia Zvezda,* February 20, 1958.

———. "Na straze morskikh rubezhei Sovetskoi derzhavy" (Guarding the Maritime Borders of the Soviet State), *Pravda,* July 29, 1961.

———. "Na strazhe nashei rodiny" (Guarding Our Homeland), *Trud,* February 23, 1961.

———. "Nadezhnyi strazh bezopasnosti Rodiny" (Faithful Guard over the Security of the Homeland), *Sovetskii Flot,* February 23, 1960.

———. "Otvety glavnokomanduiushchego Voenno-morskim flotom SSSR admirala S. G. Gorshkova na voprosy korrespondenta gazety 'Pravda' " (Replies of the Commander-in-Chief of the USSR Admiral S. G. Gorshkov to the Questions of a Correspondent of the Newspaper 'Pravda'), *Pravda,* February 2, 1962.

Gorshkov, S. G. "Sovetskim vooruzhennym silam—45 let" (To the Soviet Armed Forces—45 Years), *Trud,* February 22, 1963.

———. "Velikaia pobeda" (Great Victory), *Sovetskii Flot,* May 9, 1960.

———. "Velikye zadachy Sovetskogo Voenno-morskogo flota" (The Great Missions of the Soviet Navy), *Krasnaia Zvezda,* February 5, 1963.

———. Vernye syny rodiny (True Sons of the Homeland), *Pravda,* July 31, 1960.

Gorshkov, S. G. "Vernye syny rodiny (True Sons of the Homeland), Pravda, July 29, 1962.

———. "Vernyi strazh morskikh granits" (Reliable Guard over the Maritime Borders), Pravda, July 24, 1955.

Grishavon, V. "Na strazhe morskikh rubezhei" (On Guard over the Sea Boundaries), Izvestiia, July 26, 1964.

———. "Povyshat' bditel'nost' i boevuiu gotovnost' " (To Increase Vigilance and Combat Readiness), Krasnaia Zvezda, July 29, 1961.

Grundinin, I. "Ot chego zavisit chislennost' armii" (On What the Size of the Army Depends), Krasnaia Zvezda, February 16, 1960.

Henrikson, N. "Ob'edinenie vsekh sredstv dlia morskoi oborony" (The Unification of All Means for Maritime Defense), Morskoi Sbornik, August, 1925, pp. 111–122.

Isachenkov, N. V. "Novoe oruzhie korablei" (New Weapons of Warships), Krasnaia Zvezda, November 18, 1961.

Isaev, F. "Strategicheskoe iskusstvo Krasnoi Armii v velikoi otechestvennoi voine" (Strategic Art of the Red Army in the Great Patriotic War), Krasnaia Zvezda, February 20, 1946.

Isakov, Ivan. "Problemy voiny na more" (Problems of Warfare at Sea), Izvestiia, June 3, 1962.

Ivanov, L. N. "Bor'ba za gospodstvo na Sredizemnom more" (Struggle in the Mediterranean Sea), Krasnyi Flot, January 14, 1939.

Kasatonov, V. A. "Boevaia vakhta Sovetskikh moriakov" (Combat Watch of Soviet Sailors), Krasnaia Zvezda, July 26, 1964.

———. ———. Pravda, July 29, 1964.

———. "Ot imeni Sovetskikh voinov; chetvertaia sessiia Verkhovnogo Soveta SSSR, rech' admirala tov. V. A. Kasatonova" (In the Name of Soviet Warriors; Fourth Session of the Supreme Soviet of the USSR, Speech of Admiral Comrade V. A. Kasatonov), Krasnaia Zvezda, July 27, 1963.

———. "Tridtsat' slavnikh let" (Thirty Glorious Years), Krasnaia Zvezda, July 27, 1963.

———. "Vysokaia nagrada rodiny" (High Reward of the Homeland), Krasnaia Zvezda, May 13, 1965.

Kholostiakov, G. "Flag nad Novorossiiskom" (Flag over Novorossiisk), Trud, September 16, 1966.

Khrushchev, N. S. "Neobkhodimaia mera, vystuplenie N. S. Khrushcheva" (Necessary Steps, Remarks by N. S. Khrushchev), Izvestiia, June 3, 1962.

———. "Otchet Tsentral'nogo Komiteta KPSS XXII s"ezda Kommunisticheskoi partii Sovetskogo Soiuza, Doklad Pervogo sekretaria TsK tovarishcha N. S. Khrushcheva 17 oktiabria 1961 goda" (Record of the Central Committee KPSS of the 22nd Congress of the Communist Party of the Soviet Union; Report of the Secretary of the Central Committee, Comrade N. S. Khrushchev, October 17, 1961), Krasnaia Zvezda, October 18, 1961.

———. "Razoruzhenie—put' k uprocheniiu mira i obespecheniiu druzhby mezhdu narodami" (Disarmament—Road to Peace and Friendship among People), Izvestiia, January 15, 1960.

———. "Sovremennoe mezhdunarodnoe polozhenie i vneshniaia politika Sovetskogo Soiuza; Doklad tovarishcha N. S. Khrushcheva na sessii Verkhovnogo Sovet SSSR 12 dekabria 1962 goda" (The Contemporary

International Situation and Foreign Policy of the Soviet Union; Report of Comrade N. S. Khrushchev to the Session of the Supreme Soviet of the USSR, December 12, 1962), *Krasnaia Zvezda,* December 13, 1962.

————. "Za novye uspekhi, rech' tovarishcha N. S. Khrushcheva na Vsesoiuznom soveshchanii rabotnikov zheleznodorozhnogo transporta 10 maia 1962 goda" (Toward New Successes, Speech of Comrade N. S. Khrushchev at the All-Union Conference of the Workers of Railroad Transport, May 10, 1962), *Trud,* May 11, 1962.

————. "Zakliuchitel'noe slova tovarishcha N. S. Khrushcheva na zasedanii Verkhovnogo Soveta SSSR 7 maia 1960 goda" (Concluding Remarks of Comrade N. S. Khrushchev to the Supreme Soviet Session of May 7, 1960), *Krasnaia Zvezda,* May 8, 1960.

Kitaev, L. and Bol'shakov, G. "Vizit druzhby" (Visit of Friendship), *Krasnaia Zvezda,* March 23, 1957.

Kruchenykh, A. "Vlianie raket na voenno-morskikh taktik" (The Influence of Missiles on Naval Tactics), *Sovetskii Flot,* November 15, 1957.

Krysov, A. "Start" (Launch), *Krasnaia Zvezda,* March 3, 1962.

Kulakov, N. "Velikii flot velikoi derzhavy" (Mighty Navy of a Great Power), *Leningradskaia Pravda,* July 29, 1961.

Kulinich, D. "Raketa ishchet podvodnuiu lodku" (The Missile Seeks the Submarine), *Krasnaia Zvezda,* February 2, 1962.

Kuznetsov, N. G. "Velikaia pobeda sovetskikh narod i svoikh vooruzhennykh silakh" (The Great Victory of the Soviet People and their Armed Forces), *Sovetskiy Flot,* May 8, 1955.

Lagovskii, A. "Ekonomika i sposoby voorhuzhennoi bor'by" (Economics and Modes of Armed Conflict), *Sovetskii Flot,* February 6, 1960.

————. "Neft' i NATO" (Petroleum and NATO), *Krasnaia Zvezda,* February 26, 1965.

Levchenko, G. I. "Flot—Vernyi pomoshchnik Krasnoi Armii" (The Navy—Faithful Assistant of the Red Army), *Krasnaia Zvezda,* July 28, 1946.

————. "Velikii flot Sovetskoi derzhavy" (Mighty Navy of the Soviet State), *Krasnaia Zvezda,* July 14, 1957.

————. "Voenno-morskie sily Sovetskogo Soiuza' (The Naval Forces of the Soviet Union), *Krasnaia Zvezda,* August 15, 1948.

Likovanie narodov Sovetskogo Soiuza" (Exultation of the Peoples of the Soviet Union), *Pravda,* December 16, 1937.

Lomov, N. "Osnovnye polozheniia Sovetskoi voennoi doktriny; revoliutsiia v voennom dele, ee znachenie i posledstviia" (Fundamental Tenets of Soviet Military Doctrine; the Revolution in Military Affairs, its Significance and Consequences), *Krasnaia Zvezda,* January 10, 1964.

Malinovskii, R. Ia. "Pobedno poet leninskoe znamia; Voennyi parad i demonstratsiia trudiashchikhsia Moskvy na Krasnoi ploshchadi, rech' Marshala Sovetskogo Soiuza R. Ia. Malinovskogo" (Victoriously Sings the Leninist Banner; Military Parade and Demonstration of the Workers of Moscow in Red Square; Speech of Marshal of the Soviet Union R. Ia. Malinovskii), *Krasnaia Zvezda,* November 10, 1963.

————. "Priem v Kremle v chest' sorokaletiia Sovetskoi Armii i Voenno-Morskogo Flota" (Reception in the Kremlin in Honor of the Fortieth Anniversary of the Soviet Army and Navy), *Sovetskii Flot,* February 25, 1958.

———. "Vneocherednoi XXI s"ezd Kommunisticheskoi partii Sovetskogo Soiuza, rech' Marshala Sovetskogo Soiuza R. Ia. Malinovskogo" (The Extraordinary XXIst Congress of the Communist Party of the Soviet Union, Speech of Marshal of the Soviet Union R. Ia. Malinovskii), *Krasnaia Zvezda*, February 4, 1959.

———. "45 let na strazhe sotsialisticheskoi rodiny; Doklad Ministra Oborony SSSR Marshala Sovetskogo Soiuza R. Ia. Malinovskogo" (45 Years of Guarding the Socialist Homeland; Report of the Minister of Defense Marshal of the Soviet Union R. Ia. Malinovskii), *Krasnaia Zvezda*, February 23, 1963.

Mamaev, E. "Misheni v okeane" (Oceanic Targets), *Krasnaia Zvezda*, April 4, 1963.

Maslov, F. "Vnezapno i skrytno (Suddenly and Covertly), *Krasnaia Zvezda*, October 12, 1963.

Mikhailin, V. "Fizika i protivolodochnaia oborona" (Physics and Antisubmarine Defense), *Krasnaia Zvezda*, March 10, 1962.

Moskvitin, Iu. "Okean stavit problemy" (The Ocean Poses Problems), *Krasnaia Zvezda*, May 16, 1965.

"Na strazhe interesov naroda" (On Guard over the Interests of the People), *Pravda*, January 18, 1938.

"Nadezhnyi strazh sovetskikh morskikh rubezhei" (Faithful Guard over the Maritime Borders), *Sovetskii Flot*, July 20, 1960.

"Nastoichivo izuchat' i sokhranit' snariazhenie podlodok" (Persistently Study and Perfectly Maintain Submarine Equipment), *Sovetskii Flot*, October 19, 1957.

Nikolaev, N. "Rol' voenno-morskogo flota v systema vooruzhennykh sil SSSR" (Role of the Navy in the System of the Armed Forces of the USSR), *Sovetskii Flot*, May 29, 1957.

Nikonov, Iu. "Viazvimost' avianostsev v atomnoi voine" (Vulnerability of Aircraft Carriers in Atomic War), *Sovetskii Flot*, August 2, 1958.

Panteleev, Iu. "Bor'ba za gospodstvo na more: iz opyta vtoroi mirovoi voiny" (The Struggle for Command of the Sea: from the Experience of the Second World War), *Krasnaia Zvezda*, January 16, 1947.

"Partiia—Stroitel' flota i vospitatel' ego kadrov" (The Party—Builder of the Navy and Instructor of Its Cadres), *Sovetskii Flot*, July 25, 1958.

Pavlovich, N. "Vlianie razvitiia tekhniki i sposoby vedeniia boevykh deistvii na more" (The Influence of the Development of Weapons and Equipment on the Conduct of Military Operations at Sea), *Sovetskii Flot*, July 26, 1956.

———. "Voenno-morskoi iskusstvo i razvitie boevoi tekhniki flota" (The Naval Art and the Development of Military Equipment for the Navy), *Sovetskii Flot*, March 6, 1957.

Petrov, M. "Bol'she vnimaniia morskoi aviatsii" (More Attention to Naval Aviation), *Krasnyi Flot*, August, 1924, pp. 75–82.

———. "Stroitel'stva flota; bol'she vnimanie morskoi aviatsii" (Construction of the Fleet; More Attention to Naval Aviation), *Krasnyi Flot*, November, 1924, pp. 76–83.

Polianskii, V. " 'Polarisy' raspolzaiutsiia po okeanam" ('Polaris Submarines Are Deployed in the Oceans), *Krasnaia Zvezda*, December, 27, 1964.

Prokof'ev, V. "Glavnaia udarnaia sila v voine na more" (Principal Striking Power in Warfare at Sea), *Krasnaia Zvezda,* January 13, 1962.

"Priem v Kremle v chest' sorokaletiia Sovetskoi Armii i Voenno-morskogo Flota" (Reception in the Kremlin in Honor of the Soviet Armed Forces), *Sovetskii Flot,* February 25, 1958.

"Pust' gromche zvuchit golos propagandista!" (May the Voice of the Propagandists Resound More Loudly!), *Krasnaia Zvezda,* January 21, 1960.

Romanov, V. "Sodeistvie flota primorskomu flangu sukhoputnykh voisk" (Cooperation of the Navy on the Coastal Flank of the Ground Troops), *Sovetskii Flot,* March 4, 1958.

Ruban, S. M. and Antonov, N. "Nad okeanskimi glubinami" (Over the Ocean Depths), *Krasnaia Zvezda,* June 5, 1963.

————. "Tri tochki opory" (Three Points of Leverage), *Krasnaia Zvezda,* April 1, 1961.

Sbytov, N. A. "Revoliutsiia v voennom dele i ee resul'taty" (The Revolution in Military Affairs and Its Consequences), *Krasnaia Zvezda,* February 15, 1963.

Shalagin, N. and Alekseev, N. "Soldaty shturmuiut bereg" (Soldiers Storm the Shore), *Krasnaia Zvezda,* October 10, 1963.

Sharev, Iu. "Kak predskazyvaiut na zapade rol' flota v sovremennoi voine" (How the Role of the Navy in Contemporary War is Envisioned in the West), *Sovetskii Flot,* April 13, 1958.

Shiltov, V. "Raketa startuet iz-pod vody" (The Missile is Launched from Underwater), *Krasnaia Zvezda,* November 1, 1960.

Smirnov, G. "Samolet vzletaet s avianostsa" (The Airplane Takes Off from the Aircraft Carrier), *Krasnaia Zvezda,* February 6, 1964.

————. "Samolety i vertolety protiv podvodnykh lodok" (Airplanes and Helicopters Against Submarines), *Sovetskii Flot,* February 5, 1960.

Smirnov, P. A. "Moguchii morskoi i okeanskii flot" (Mighty Sea and Ocean Navy), *Pravda,* February 3, 1938.

Sobelov, P. "Sovmestnye operatsii flota i sukhoputnykh voisk" (Joint Operations of the Fleet and Ground Troops), *Krasnyi Flot,* October 8, 1939.

Sokolovskii, V. and Cherednichenko, M. "Voennoe iskusstvo na novom etape" (Military Art at a New Stage), *Krasnaia Zvezda,* August 28, 1964.

Starko, V. "Angliia—nash vrag na more" (England—Our Enemy at Sea), *Krasnyi Flot,* January, 1926, pp. 113–115.

Stvolinskii, Iu. Kreiser vycherknut iz spiskov" (A Cruiser is Struck from the Lists), *Leningradskaia Pravda,* March 23, 1960.

Sudets, V. A. "Ostorozhnyi strazh na rodiny" (Vigilant Guard of the Homeland), *Sovetskii Patriot,* February 20, 1963.

"Tikhookeanskii flot" (Pacific Fleet), *Krasnaia Zvezda,* November 12, 1964.

Tolmachev, V. "Voprosy stroitel'stva Voenno-Morskogo Flota v resheniiakh KPSS" (Problems of Construction of the Navy in the Decisions of the Communist Party of the Soviet Union), *Sovetskii Flot,* July 17, 1958.

"Ucheniia voisk stran Varshavskogo dogovora" (Exercises of the Troops of the Warsaw Pact), *Krasnaia Zvezda,* September 22, 1964.

"Udarnaia sila flota" (Striking Power of the Navy), *Sovetskii Flot,* January 31, 1960.

"Ugroza mira" (Threat to the Peace), *Krasnaia Zvezda,* November 19, 1961.

"V ministerstve oborony soiuza SSR" (In the Defense Ministry of the USSR), *Izvestiia*, July 24, 1962.

Valin, V. "Iadernoe oruzhie sovremennykh armii" (Nuclear Weapons of Modern Armies), *Krasnaia Zvezda*, June 13, 1962.

Vasilevskii, A. M. "Vooruzhennye sily Sovetskogo gosudarstva" (The Armed Forces of the Soviet State), *Izvestiia*, February 23, 1956.

Vershinen, K. "Po povodu voinstvennykh zaiavlenii nekotorykh Amerikanskikh, Angliiskikh i Zapadno-germanskikh generalov i gosudarstvennykh deiatelei" (Apropos of the Warlike Declarations of Some American British, and West German Generals and Government Officials), *Krasnaia Zvezda*, September 10, 1957.

Vladimirskii, L. "Moguchii Voenno-Morskoi Flot Sovetskogo gosudarstva" (Mighty Navy of the Soviet Government), *Leningradskaia Pravda*, July 24, 1955.

―――. "Novaia tekhnika na korabliakh" (New Weapons on Ships), *Komsomol'skaia Pravda*, July 23, 1955.

―――. "Reaktivnoe oruzhie v vedenie boevykh deistvii na more" (Jet Weapons in the Conduct of Combat Operation at Sea), *Sovetskii Flot*, September 21, 1956.

"Vsia strana edinodushno odobriaet resheniia Verkhovnogo Soveta SSSR" (The Entire Country Approves of the Decision of the Supreme Soviet), *Sovetskii Flot*, January 17, 1960.

"Vse nashi sily—sluzheniiu rodine" (All Our Strength—At the Service of the Homeland), *Krasnaia Zvezda*, January 21, 1960.

"Zaiavlenie pravitel'stva SSSR po voprosy o razoruzhenii" (Announcement of the Government of the USSR on the Question of Disarmament). *Krasnaia Zvezda*, May 15, 1956.

Zevin, L. and Arzumanov, G. "Arkticheskoe zrenie amerikanskikh strategov" (Arctic Vision of American Strategists), *Sovetskii Flot*, August 18, 1959.

Zheludev, A. "Atomnyi flot" (Atomic Navy), *Krasnaia Zvezda*, January 8, 1963.

Zhukov, G. K. "Obmen rechami na prieme v Budapeshte, rech' G. K. Zhukova" (Exchange of Speeches at the Reception in Budapest, Speech of G. K. Zhukov), *Krasnaia Zvezda*, May 29, 1957.

―――. "XX s"ezd KPSS, rech' tovarishcha Zhukova" (20th Congress of the KPSS, Speech of Comrade Zhukov), *Krasnaia Zvezda*, February 21, 1956.

Zof, V. "Krasnyi Voenno-morskoi flot" (The Red Navy), *Krasnyi Flot*, January, 1922, p. 4.

―――. "Osnovnye zadachi morskogo stroitel'stva" (Basic Tasks of Naval Construction), *Krasnyi Flot*, January, 1925, pp. 93–98.

Zozulia, F. V. "Gordoe imia—moriak" (A Proud Name—Sailor), *Komsomol'skaia Pravda*, July 29, 1961.

Newspaper Articles (non-Russian)

Baldwin, Hanson. "Navy Commissions the *America*, A Huge New Carrier, at Norfolk," *New York Times*, January 24, 1965, p. 3.

―――. "Soviet Submarine Lag," *New York Times*, April 18, 1963, p. 6.

Bingley, Alexander. "A Fresh Look at Defense," *Daily Telegraph,* February 6, 1964.

Duranty, Walter. "Youth Revitalizes the Soviet Fleet," *New York Times,* October 23, 1932, p. E3.

Finney, John W. "Soviet Held Shifting to Atomic Submarines," *New York Times,* December 19, 1957.

Hood, Edwin M. Address to A.F.O.L.-C.I.O. Maritime Trades Department Seminar on Soviet Maritime Development, January 18, 1967. Reprinted in *New York Times,* January 19, 1967.

Jorden, Wm. "Premier Strolls Through City," *New York Times,* September 22, 1959, p. 22.

Kennet, Lord. "Defense and Armaments Committee Report to the Assembly, Western European Union," *Baltimore Sun,* December 3, 1963. Quoted from *United States Naval Institute Proceedings,* March, 1964, p. 153.

Martell, C. B. "U.S. Admiral on Soviet Missiles," *United Press International,* December 21, 1966.

Nelson, Thom. United Press Release, *Washington Post,* April 10, 1958, p. 1.

Orr-Ewing, C. I. Quoted in *Survival,* May-June, 1962, p. 119.

"Reds Use New Ships in Bid to Shut Baltic," *New York World Telegram,* February 28, 1953.

"Text of McNamara's Statement to Platform Group," *New York Times,* August 18, 1964.

Wilson, George C. "U.S. Sub Lore Said to Have 20-Year Lead," *Washington Post,* December 22, 1966.

Unpublished Material

Columbia University. Seminar on International Communism, Minutes of the Second Meeting, October 19, 1966.

Former Soviet Naval Officer. "Soviet Naval Strategy," Address at the U. S. Naval War College, Newport, Rhode Island, October 31, 1963.

———. "The USSR's Strategy at Sea," Address at the U. S. Naval War College, Newport, Rhode Island, March 20, 1965.

Hucul, Walter C. "The Evolution of Russian and Soviet Seapower, 1853–1953." Unpublished Ph.D dissertation, Department of History, University of California, Berkeley, 1954, p. 513.

Ropp, Theodore. "The Development of a Modern Navy: French Naval Policy, 1871–1904." Unpublished Ph.D. dissertation, Department of History, Harvard University, 1937, p. 364.

Smith, C. J. *An Outline of Russian History.* Washington: Office of the Chief of Naval Operations, 1958, Mimeograph.

Index ★

A-3 Polaris missile, 96, 112, 152

ABM defenses. *See* Anti-ballistic missile defenses

Active defense strategy, 13, 14, 16, 17, 35, 61, 62, 74

Aegean Sea, 154

Africa, 104, 110

Airborne forces, 142

Aircraft, naval: prewar, 13, 22, 24, 33, 33n19, 34, 49n17; WWII, 49, 52, 55; lessons of WWII, 54, 54n58; postwar, 54n58, 76, 90–91, 108, 112, 112n16, 113, 119, 119n52, 135, 136, 140, 151n6

Aircraft carriers: construction of impossible prior 1928, 8; early advocates criticized, 10; construction advocated, 10n7, 55, 58, 117; reasons for not building, 26, 32n17, 68–69, 147, 151; unlikely considered in 2nd FYP, 30; non-construction of criticized, 31n12; plans for construction of, 31–32, 31n12, 32, 32n13, 40–41, 61, 63, 64n15; failure obtain U. S. plans for, 32n15, 38; Stalin's apparent opposition to, 32, 34, 35, 36, 64n15, 156, 157; present CinC's views on, 35, 70, 122–123, 123n73; foreign policy considerations re., 42, 43; failure to build prior WWII, 47; postwar propaganda vs., 58, 121n67, 121n68, 122n73, 149; Khrushchev's and Zhukov's opposition to, 67, 68–69; military requirements for, 112n16, 122–123, 122n73, 138, 145, 156; limitations of, 119, 119n58, 119–120; an essential for offensive strategy, 144, 149; submarines no substitute for, 150, 153; possibilities for future construction of, 156, 157. *See also* Surface warships

Air Day show, 1961, 112

Air Defense (PVO), 119, 137, 141

Alafuzov, V. A., Admiral, 58, 88, 90, 97, 99, 103, 104, 105, 106, 116, 116n42, 139

Aleksandrov, A. P., 21

Algeria, 70

Amphibious invasions. *See* Naval missions and requirements for defense against amphibious invasion; Naval weapons systems, tactics, and capabilities for defense against amphibious invasion

Amphibious landings. *See* Naval missions and requirements for con-

187

196 SOVIET NAVAL STRATEGY

Strategy, unified military, 22, 26, 156

Submarine detection system, long-range underwater sound. *See* Antisubmarine warfare

Submarine warfare, 115, 118, 129, 137. *See also* Antisubmarine warfare; Geostrategic factors, Naval mission and requirements for destruction of enemy's naval forces; Naval weapons systems, tactics, and capabilities for destruction of enemy's naval forces; Naval mission and requirements for interdiction of enemy sea communications; Naval weapons systems, tactics, and capabilities for interdiction of enemy sea communications

Submarines, construction of, 7–8, 12, 24, 31, 65, 76–77, 83, 84n70, 85, 123, 124, 134, 136, 151

Submarines, numbers and types of, 24, 24n17, 78, 113, 113n22, 114, 123, 131, 132, 134, 136n129

Submarines, operations of, 50, 114, 125, 126n87. *See also* Antisubmarine warfare.

Submarines, role of, 9–10, 11, 21–22, 24, 72, 77, 78, 84, 87, 108, 113, 114, 114n23, 119, 134, 137, 149, 150, 156

Sukhumi, 52

Supremacy, naval *or* sea. *See* Strategy, command-of-the-sea

Surface warships: construction and numbers of, 4, 24, 31, 79, 137; role and operations of, 10, 22, 25, 34, 50, 51–52, 53–54, 57, 71–74, 71n10, 72n15, 73, 79, 111, 113, 119, 119n53, 137, 144, 153, 156, 157

Sverdlov Class cruisers, 65, 71, 135

Sweden, 151

Syria, 70

Tallin, Estonia, 48

Technology, effects on naval warfare of, 36, 67, 74, 82n67, 89, 90–91, 104, 108, 109, 109n4, 112, 114, 121–122, 128n82, 133n112, 150, 153, 155, 156, 157.

Technology, naval applications of, 9, 10, 63, 70, 72, 73, 76, 77, 90, 120, 120n65, 152, 155

Tevosyan, V., 39, 40

Trotsky, Leon, 4, 9, 19, 20, 25–26, 37–38

Troyanovsky, Alexander A., 37–38

Truman containment policy, 59

Tukhachevskii, M. P., 19, 24, 44

Turkey, 42, 154

Turkish Straits, 56, 111, 133, 136

Ukraine, 51

Underdeveloped countries, 154n11

Unified military doctrine, 22, 26, 156

United Kingdom. *See* England

United States, 34, 36–38, 60, 67, 104, 105, 109, 122, 149, 156; U.S. naval forces, 36–38, 53, 59, 64n15, 84, 87, 95, 96, 101, 103, 115, 117, 141, 154

USS *America,* 150n3

Vershinen, K., 98

Vladimirskii, L., 75–76

Vladivostok, 93

Voroshilov, Klimenti I., Marshal, 4, 7, 19

Voroshilov Naval War College, 9, 20

W-Class submarines, 65, 136n129

War, conventional, 21, 72

War, general nuclear, 126, 141, 148, 152, 153, 154, 156

War, limited, 111, 152, 154

War, psychological, 153

Warm water ports, 143

The text of this book is set in ten-point Times Roman, with two points of leading. The chapter titles are set in Times Roman italic, with the chapter numbers in Caslon.

The book is printed letterpress on sixty-pound white eggshell Mead Moistrite matte paper. The cover is Roxite Blubak A49288; the spine is Roxite Vellum A49246.

Editorial production by Louise Gerretson.

Book and jacket design by Melbourne Smith.

The book was composed, printed, and bound by the George Banta Company, Incorporated, Menasha, Wisconsin.

ROBERT WARING HERRICK was graduated from the United States Naval Academy in 1944. In 1946 he trained as a lighter-than-air pilot and served as such until 1949, when he attended Intelligence Postgraduate School, then Russian Language School. From 1950 to 1953, he served as Soviet Navy Analyst in the Office of Naval Intelligence. Then followed a year at the Russian Institute, Columbia University, where he earned his master's degree in international relations, and completed course requirements for a doctorate. He spent two years, 1954 to 1956, as Assistant Naval Attache at the American Embassy in Moscow, and traveled extensively in Russia at that time, participating in cruises with the Russians aboard a minesweeper of the Northern Fleet and aboard a destroyer of the Pacific Fleet. The next three years were spent in ONI as Soviet Intelligence Desk Officer, followed by two years on the staff of Commander in Chief, U.S. Pacific Fleet. In 1963 he was graduated from the Naval War College and then became Staff Intelligence Officer at the College until his retirement in 1965.

Commander Herrick now serves as Deputy Director, Communist Affairs Analysis Department, Radio Free Europe. In addition to these duties, he devotes himself to research, writing, and teaching Soviet studies on the University of Maryland's Munich Campus.

L. D. TROTSKY

MIKHAIL V. FRUN

M. N. TUKHACHEVSKII

G. LEVCHENKO

G. K. ZHUKOV

N. G. KUZNETSOV

I. S. IUMASHEV

NIKITA S. KHRUSHCHEV

S. G. GORSHKO